AARON SISKIND

MODERN ARTISTS IN AMERICA

First series

Editorial Associates: *Robert Motherwell, Ad Reinhardt*
Photography: *Aaron Siskind*
Documentation: *Bernard Karpel, Librarian, Museum of Modern Art, N.Y.*
Secretary: *Sally Lorin*

Wittenborn Schultz, Inc., 38 East 57th Street, New York 22, N.Y.

Acknowledgments:

The editorial associates and publisher gratefully
acknowledge the assistance of the California Art
Association, 800 Chestnut Street, San Francisco,
California, for their reprint rights to publish
the Western Conference, and to the participating
members of that round table; to the attending artists
of the sessions at Studio 35, and to Joyce Wittenborn.

Published by Wittenborn, Schultz, Inc., 38 East 57th Street, New York 22, N.Y.

Contents

Illustrations are listed in the Index as italicized entries under the name of each artist

A STATEMENT

Today the extent and degree of Modern Art in America is unprecedented. From East to West numerous galleries and museums, colleges and art schools, private and regional demonstrations display their mounting interest in original plastic efforts. One can say that by 1950, Modern Art in the United States has reached a point of sustained achievement worthy of a detached and democratic treatment.

It is true that very recently great attention has been paid to Abstract Art in exhibitions and publications. Yet, on the whole, this solicitude has been characterized by an erratic concern, full of prejudice and confused by misunderstanding. In the light of its actual history, the more radical innovations and variations of Modern American Art rarely obtain recognition based on real accomplishment and in terms of its specific problem: the reality of the work of art.

This biennial is the first of a continuing series which promises to come to grips with that central situation. Through works and documents of its own making the scope and nature of that struggle will be self-revealed. By impartial documentation of the event as it happens, the society in which the artist exists responsibly and the world of imagery and design in which he must exist creatively, stands manifest. This is the program of **Modern Artists in America.**

Bernard Karpel
Robert Motherwell
Ad Reinhardt
New York City, 1951

ARTISTS' SESSIONS AT STUDIO 35 (1950)

EDITED BY ROBERT GOODNOUGH

INTRODUCTION

In the late fall of 1948, three abstract painters, William Baziotes, Robert Motherwell, Mark Rothko, and an abstract sculptor, David Hare, began a small cooperative school in Greenwich Village in New York City; somewhat later, they were joined by another abstract painter, Barnett Newman. In the interests of introducing the students to as wide an experience as possible, other advanced artists, one by one, were invited to speak to the students on Friday evenings. The Friday evenings were open to the general public, and quickly became a physical place for everyone interested in advanced art in the United States to meet; the audiences averaged about 150 persons, all that the loft on Eighth Street that housed the school could hold.

For various reasons, the artists who founded the school, which was called "Subjects of the Artist" (in order to emphasize that abstract art, too, has a subject, and that the "curriculum" consisted of the subjects that interest advanced artists), were unable to continue the school after the end of the year, in May, 1949. In the fall, several teachers in the New York University school of art education, Robert Iglehart, Hale Woodruff and Tony Smith, privately took over the loft and continued the Friday evenings, though not the school; it became known as "Studio 35" after the address, 35 East Eighth Street; the Friday evenings were continued until April, 1950.

Among the artists who lectured to a faithful and somewhat unvarying public during the two seasons, 1948-49 and 1949-50, were Arp, Baziotes, Jimmy Ernst, Ferber, Glarner, Gottlieb, Holtzmann, Kees, de Kooning, Motherwell, Newman, Reinhardt, and Rothko; Joseph Cornell gave several evenings from his fabulous collection of very early films; John Cage, the composer, Nicolas Calas, the poet and art critic, Richard Hulsenbeck, onetime dadaist and now psychoanalyst, Monsieur Levesque, a student of dada, and Harold Rosenberg, the poet and critic, were among the others who addressed the Friday evenings. Many acquaintanceships and friendships grew up among the artists as a result of these meetings, which tended to become repetitious at the end, partly because of the public asking the same questions at each meeting. To sum up the meetings, on the suggestion of Robert Goodnough, a graduate student in the N.Y.U. school of art education, who had been helping his instructors with the meetings of the second season, it was decided to have a closed, three-day session among the advanced artists themselves, with the dialogue taken down stenographically. There was no preliminary discussion of what was to be said; nothing was arranged but the dates, Friday, Saturday and Sunday afternoons, 4 to 7 p.m., April 21-23, 1950.

Among the dozens of advanced artists asked to participate, the following attended one or more sessions: William Baziotes, Janice Biala, Louise Bourgeois, James Brooks, William de Kooning, Jimmy Ernst, Herbert Ferber, Adolph Gottlieb, Peter Grippe, David Hare, Hans Hofmann, Weldon Kees, Ibram Lassaw, Norman Lewis, Richard Lippold, Seymour Lipton, Robert Motherwell, Barnett Newman, Richard Pousette-Dart, Ad Reinhardt, Ralph Rosenborg, Theodoros Stamos, Hedda Sterne, David Smith and Bradley Walker Tomlin.

The moderators were Alfred H. Barr, Jr., the only non-artist participant and one of the most noted modern art scholars, Richard Lippold, the sculptor, and Robert Motherwell, the painter, who had acted as moderator throughout the first season of Friday evenings. Lippold tended to carry the principal burden of moderating the first day, Barr the second, and Motherwell the third; Barr was prevented from being present the first day, and from the first half of the final day.

The meetings were arranged by Robert Goodnough, who has drastically edited the following text (perhaps half) of the original transcript of the proceedings; a few of the artists have made some corrections of what they said; but on the whole, this text retains the spontaneity, the unpreparedness, the rises and falls of intensity and pointedness of the meetings themselves; though a certain pathos and loneliness appears from time to time that was not as evident at the time of the meetings as it is on reading the original text.

Upper Photograph, left to right: LIPTON, LEWIS, ERNST, GRIPPE, GOTTLIEB, HOFFMANN, BARR, MOTHERWELL, LIPPOLD, DE KOONING, LASSAW, BROOKS, REINHARDT, POUSSETTE-DART.

Bottom Photograph, left to right: BROOKS, REINHARDT, POUSSETTE-DART, BOURGEOIS, FERBER, TOMLIN, BIALA, GOODNOUGH, STERNE, HARE, NEWMAN, LIPTON, LEWIS, ERNST.

THE FIRST DAY—APRIL 21, 1950

Moderator Lippold: It might be advisable to list a few things which we will probably not want to discuss. It would seem that the method of work of most of us has been a lonely one. I feel that much is gained from argument. I would like to learn from conversation with my confreres.

Hare: We ought to define terms. Everybody here knows everybody else's work. There is little advantage in talking about schools of painting. I think we ought to discuss a particular problem. I don't see any point in discussing our own work. What a painter thinks he does is very often different from what he does. You can talk about your work but the truth still remains concealed within the work, not within the words. We don't just want to hear everybody talking about his own point of view. I don't see that we can get anywhere unless we state a problem and then discuss that particular problem. Has somebody a suggestion?

Ferber: The public has been mentioned, and it seems to me in a professional group like this we should attempt to identify our relationship to the public, perhaps in two ways. In a personal way, and in a way which relates to our work. By the second I perhaps mean that the public really is asking all the time "What does this work mean?" I think it might be helpful to adopt an attitude towards the public in the sense of an answer to that question. We needn't answer the question. What I am asking is that we should adopt an attitude of either discarding the question or trying to answer it. . . . Another thing I want to suggest we talk about is whether any of us feel that there is any difference in what is happening in America and what has happened heretofore, and in what is happening in Europe. There is some difference which is not a question of geography but of point of view. It is a question of origin or ancestry.

* * *

Gottlieb: It seems to me that we are approaching an academy version of abstract painting. I think that has some bearing on our meeting here, in that I think, despite any individual differences, there is a basis for getting together on mutual respect and the feeling that painters here are not academic, and we should make some distinctions.

Hofmann: What is abstract art in the "good" sense?

Moderator Motherwell: The word "abstract" has a technical meaning. It means "to take from". As a method, it signifies selecting one element from a myriad of elements, for the purpose of emphasis. Whitehead says, "The higher the degree of abstraction, the lower the degree of complexity." I suppose the word was first applied to a certain kind of art that was very highly abstracted (in Whitehead's sense) but consequently with a low degree of complexity. The people who first said abstract must have meant that so much was left out. Picasso represents a higher degree of complexity and a lower degree of abstraction than Mondrian, for example.

* * *

Moderator Lippold: I feel that if we are going to learn something from each other, let's dismiss our problems in relation to the public and concern ourselves with the problems of creativity: how each one begins his piece of work and how he proceeds with it.

Newman: I was going to try to formulate a question out of this discussion. When Gottlieb raises the question of abstraction, I don't think we should just dismiss it. It might be formulated into this question: do we artists really have a community? If so, what makes it a community?

Hare: I see no need for a community. An artist is always lonely. The artist is a man who functions beyond or ahead of his society. In any case seldom within it. I think our problem would seem to be fundamentally psychological. Some feel badly because they are not accepted by the public. We shouldn't be accepted by the public. As soon as we are accepted, we are no longer artists but decorators. Sometimes we think if we could only explain to the public, they would agree with us. They may agree in the course of years. They won't agree now . . . they should not agree now. I think this group activity, this gathering together, is a symptom of fear. Possibly you could connect this with the question of mass production, in the sense that in this country there is a feeling that unless you have a large public you are a failure. The public is concerned with the average. I will always be opposed to this conception. I certainly don't think it is necessary to explain on the assumption that once you explain there will be agreement.

Reinhardt: There are many things that Hare brought up that I would like to discuss. I think we should follow some kind of procedure, isolate some ideas, and find out each artist's opinion. Newman's question is pertinent. Why can't we find out what our community is and what our differences are, and what each artist thinks of them?

Moderator Motherwell: What then exactly constitutes the basis of our community?

Sterne: We need a common vocabulary. Abstract should really mean abstract, and modern should really mean modern. We don't mean the same things with the same words.

Hofmann: Why should we? Everyone should be as different as possible. There is nothing that is common to all of us except our creative urge. It just means one thing to me; to discover myself as well as I can. But everyone of us has the urge to be creative in relation to our time—the time to which we belong may work out to be our thing in common. But to formulate this would not be simple.

Reinhardt: There are a great many differences which we should find out about here. If we are doing the same thing, or have the same problems or have the same fears —what are they?

Poussette-Dart: The museums can, at any moment, bless any one of us. The disaster is that they can cause disparity among us, too.

Reinhardt: Does that have anything to do with the idea that was introduced by Hofmann before, of our art as a way of discovering ourselves?

Hare: I can't see that museums have anything to do with the artist. In general, museums are involved with art as decor, while the artist is involved with art as a way of life.

Moderator Lippold: What we are leading up to is why each person paints or sculpts. Why each person thinks he should paint. Do we do it to be a success, to make money, understand ourselves, or what is the purpose: to describe our own creative nature? Why do we use titles? Where do we pick such titles? Where do we begin?

Ferber: It seems to me that most of the questions revolve around "meaning." The public, the museums and the artists themselves are involved in the question of "meaning." It need not be "meaning" in any simple sense; but when Mr. Lippold asks for a description of the way in which, and the why-for in connection with a piece of sculpture or painting, he is asking about "meaning," I think.

Moderator Lippold: That isn't what I said.

Ferber: Then, I misunderstood you. If we attempt to talk about what in general the work of this group has in common, I think it has been mentioned that it is modern, advanced and non-academic; we can rule out the problem of the museum, because we will be telling the public in our own way what we mean and the museum is no longer a problem. So far as the community of artists goes, it seems to me the question would involve the question of difference—between us and other artists. In that way we may have a feeling of community.

Moderator Lippold: To continue with the suggestion I made before: I would like to suggest that the question of method might be broken down into this: first—is it possible to say why we begin to create a work? Second—how do we begin the work; from an idea, an emotional point of view based on experience, or form? Where does the suggestion come from? Third—when is the work finished? How do we know that? I can't see that my relationship to the museum or to the public is concerned with what I am making. I am interested in how other people work.

Hofmann: A very great Chinese painter once said the most difficult thing in a work of art is to know the moment when to stop.

* * *

Moderator Motherwell: The question then is, "*How do you know when a work is finished?*"

Moderator Lippold: I don't know if I can consider that question without thinking about the first two questions. I would say the work seems finished to me when it concludes successfully the prophecy of its beginning and the problems involved in its working out. It may be that my work, by nature, almost determines its own conclusion; it is not possible to make many changes once the thing is quite far along. The early suggestions of form take place for many of us at the stage of sketching or small model making—if you have to make a model—and when that phase comes to an end, I then begin to work on the piece itself, or a larger piece; so far this seems to be a more or less technical process. I would like to say a little about the beginning of my method. I have never begun a piece from the point of view of "pure form." I have never made a piece without its springing from the memory of some experience—an emotional experience, generally. I almost always, from the beginning, have a title which labels that experience, because I want it to act as a discipline in eliminating any extraneous ideas which might come into the sculpture. As we all know, the first line or brush stroke can lead to millions of possibilities, and for me to keep clear is to keep a title in mind. It is of value to me at the beginning. When an experience has made itself so persistent in my unconscious or conscious mind—or both—that I feel that I want to make something which reflects that experience, I find my eyes constantly observing all things. While that experience is a memory, suitable forms can be suggested by any number of objects in life: a line on someone's face, or a crack on the floor, or an experience at a newsreel theatre. Then the problem

of how to work out the experience which I have had presents itself; I may begin with that idea, and I have to adapt it to my medium. I have to make it clear enough for others to see in its relationships. All of this takes place in the sketch stage—in the models I make from drawings. The drawings become more conclusive as I work. Generally when I work on a piece I make very few changes. I can't talk about conclusions without talking about intent. On rare occasions I have seen a form which suggested some kind of relationship which called back a memory or experience. It is always an interplay between the two, I find. It is never one thing or the other.

Brooks: I think quite often I don't know when a work is "finished," because I often carry it a little too far. There is some peculiar balance which it is necessary to preserve all through a painting which keeps it fluid and moving. It can't be brought to a stop. I think you have to abandon it while it is still alive and moving, and so I can't consider a painting "finished." I can't think of working with a clear intent on a painting, because it often develops as I go. It quite often changes in the middle of a painting. But the "end" is a very difficult thing, something that is determined, not by the form that is "finished," but by the fact that I have worked on it. It satisfies a need of some kind.

Kees: It is usually finished when it defies me to do anything more with it. I start with drawings and when I find that the drawings are incapable of being turned into a painting, then I start to paint.

Baziotes: I consider my painting finished when my eye goes to a particular spot on the canvas. But if I put the picture away about thirty feet on the wall and the movements keep returning to me and the eye seems to be responding to something living, then it is finished.

Gottlieb: I usually ask my wife . . . I think a more interesting question would be, "Why does anyone start a painting instead of finishing it?"

Ferber: I would say that I don't think any piece of sculpture I make is really "finished." Nor do I think it possible to call a piece a realization of any particular idea evolving from a specific emotion or event. There is a stream of consciousness out of which these things pop like waves, and fall back. Therefore works aren't really complete in themselves. I think the day of the "masterpiece" is over. When we look at our own work, in ten or fifteen examples, we really understand what we are doing. The sense of "finishing" a particular work is meaningless.

Moderator Lippold: I would like to ask you if what you describe applies to an individual piece? It is a thing which exists within its own particular shape. How can that come about?

Ferber: For a sculptor to insist that a piece of sculpture rises out of his stream of consciousness is perhaps ridiculous because sculpture is so three-dimensional and hard. But I don't believe there is any great difference between one piece and another in the development and fulfilment of a particular esthetic idea which may permeate several works.

Lassaw: I would consider a work finished when I sense a "togetherness," a participation of all parts as in an organism. This does not mean that I entirely understand what I have created. To me, a work is at first, quite unknown. In time, more and more enters into consciousness. It would be better to consider a work of art as a process that is started by the artist. In that way of thinking a sculpture or painting is never finished, but only begun. If successful, the work starts to live a life of its own, a work of art begins to work.

Ernst: My work consists of two separate stages of development. I consider a painting almost "finished" when I am half finished with it, when I have reached what seems to be the greatest measure of surprise. The rest of the action is disciplinary on my part. When I see that I am beginning to destroy the surprise—the basic element of that surprise—then it is time for me to stop.

Pousette-Dart: For me it is "finished" when it is inevitable within itself. But I don't think I can explain anything about my painting, just as I can't explain anything about a flower or a child. When is anything "beautiful" or finished? I can't discuss things about my paintings. The true thing I am after goes on and on and I never can completely grasp it.

Lipton: I think that we require time and intimacy and aloneness.

Biala: I never know when it is "finished." I only know there comes a time when I have to stop.

Newman: I think the idea of a "finished" picture is a fiction. I think a man spends his whole life-time painting one picture or working on one piece of sculpture. The question of stopping is really a decision of moral considerations. To what extent are you intoxicated by the actual act, so that you are beguiled by it? To what extent are you charmed by its inner life? And to what extent do you then really approach the intention or desire that is really outside of it. The decision is always made when the piece has something in it that you wanted.

Hare: A work is never finished, the energies involved in a particular work are merely transferred at a certain moment to the next work.

Rosenborg: When it stops, why does it stop? While the hands do, the picture moves, having a life (objective, emotional and intellectual) of its own. When I can do no more on it, it is done.

Sterne: Painting is for me a problem of simultaneous understanding and explaining. I try to approach my subject uncluttered by esthetic prejudices. I put it on canvas in order to explain it to myself, yet the result should reveal something plus. As I work the thing takes life and fights back. There comes a moment when I can't continue. Then I stop until next time.

De Kooning: I refrain from "finishing" it. I paint myself out of the picture, and when I have done that, I either throw it away or keep it. I am always in the picture somewhere. The amount of space I use I am always in, I seem to move around in it, and there seems to be a time when I lose sight of what I wanted to do, and then I am out of it. If the picture has a countenance, I keep it. If it hasn't, I throw it away. I am not really very much interested in the question.

Bourgeois: I think a work is "finished" when I have nothing to eliminate. I make constructions that are usually vertical; when I start them they are full of colors and are complicated in form. Every one of the complications goes and the color becomes uniform and finally they become completely white and simple. When there is nothing else to take away, it is "finished." Yet I am

disgusted by simplicity. So I look for a larger form and look for another work—which goes through the same process of elimination.

Grippe: A work of art is never really "finished." There is a feeling of trying to express the labyrinth of one's mind—its feelings and emotions, and to fulfil one's personality. Each work is trying to complete the expression of that personality. Whether it becomes profound, I don't know; but I think an artist is very aware of himself in relation to the rest of the world.

Reinhardt: It has always been a problem for me—about "finishing" paintings. I am very conscious of ways of "finishing" a painting. Among modern artists there is a value placed upon "unfinished" work. Disturbances arise when you have to treat the work as a finished and complete object, so that the only time I think I "finish" a painting is when I have a dead-line. If you are going to present it as an "unfinished" object, how do you "finish" it?

Lewis: I have stopped, I think, when I have arrived at a quality of mytery. I know this doesn't describe it, but it is the best word I can use.

Hofmann: To me a work is finished when all parts involved communicate themselves, so that they don't need me.

Moderator Motherwell: I dislike a picture that is too suave or too skilfully done. But, contrariwise, I also dislike a picture that looks too inept or blundering. I noticed in looking at the Carré exhibition of young French painters who are supposed to be close to this group, that in "finishing" a picture they assume traditional criteria to a much greater degree than we do. They have a real "finish" in that the picture is a real object, a beautifully made object. We are involved in "process" and what is a "finished" object is not so certain.

* * *

Hofmann: Yes, it seems to me all the time there is the question of a heritage. It would seem that the difference between the young French painters and the young American painters is this: French pictures have a cultural heritage. The American painter of today approaches things without basis. The French approach things on the basis of cultural heritage—that one feels in all their work. It is a working towards a refinement and quality rather than working toward new experiences, and painting out these experiences that may finally become tradition. The French have it easier. They have it in the beginning.

De Kooning: I am glad you brought up this point. It seems to me that in Europe every time something new needed to be done in it was because of traditional culture. Ours has been a striving to come to the same point that they had—not to be iconoclasts.

Moderator Lippold: There are those here who feel that the things which they make are simply moments of a continuity and, therefore, in themselves, are not objects for their own sakes, but just moments in the continuity. Is there an irreconcilability in making an object in itself which, at the same time, reflects continuity? This, so far, has been spoken of as incompatible.

Sterne: But that means that you have decided already exactly what *is* "beautiful." "Beauty" can't be pursued directly.

Gottlieb: There is a general assumption that European—specifically French—painters have a heritage which enables them to have the benefits of tradition, and therefore they can produce a certain type of painting. It seems to me that in the last fifty years the whole meaning of painting has been made international. I think Americans share that heritage just as much, and that if they deviate from tradition it is just as difficult for an American as for a Frenchman. It is a mistaken assumption in some quarters that any departure from tradition stems from ignorance. I think that what Motherwell describes is the problem of knowing what tradition is, and being willing to reject it in part. This requires familiarity with his past. I think we have this familiarity, and if we depart from tradition, it is out of knowledge, not innocence.

De Kooning: I agree that tradition is part of the whole world now. The point that was brought up was that the French artists have some "touch" in making an object. They have a particular something that makes them look like a "finished" painting. They have a touch which I am glad not to have.

Baziotes: We are getting mixed up with the French tradition. In talking about the necessity to "finish" a thing, we then said American painters "finish" a thing that looks "unfinished," and the French, they "finish" it. I have seen Matisses that were more "unfinished" and yet more "finished" than any American painter. Matisse was obviously in a terrific emotion at the time, and it was more "unfinished" than "finished."

ALFRED H. BARR, JR.

MOTHERWELL, LIPPOLD

REINHARDT, POUSSETTE-DART

DE KOONING, LASSAW, BROOKS,

THE SECOND DAY, APRIL 22, 1950

Sterne: I think that the titling of paintings is a problem. The titles a painter gives his paintings help to classify him, and this is wrong. A long poetic title or number . . . Whatever you do seems a statement of attitude. The same thing if you give a descriptive title . . . Even refraining from giving any at all creates a misunderstanding.

Reinhardt: If a title does not mean anything and creates a misunderstanding, why put a title on a painting?

Brooks: To me a title is nothing but identification. I have a very hard time finding a title and it is always inadequate. I think when titles are very suggestive, they are a kind of a fraud, because they throw the spectator away from the picture rather than into it. But numbers are inadequate.

Gottlieb: I think the point Miss Sterne raised is inevitable. That is, whenever an artist puts a title on a painting, some interpretation about his attitude will be made. It seems obvious that titles are necessary when everybody uses them—whether verbal or numbers; for purposes of exhibition, identification and the benefit of the critics there must be some way of referring to a picture. It seems to me that the artist, in making up titles for his pictures, must decide what his attitude is.

Moderator Barr: Most people seem to think that titles are a kind of necessity. Does anyone think that titles have real usefulness in supplementing the object?

Rosenborg: The title is always arbitrary because we deal with unseen audiences; the reason for a title is that every Tom, Dick and Harry has to have some link. Once I had a show where I had numbers from one to twenty, and when it came to a question of reviewing, the critics found that number six was better than four, etc. I hope that the onlooker will make up his own title!

Pousette-Dart: I think if we could agree on numbers it would be a tremendous thing. In music they don't have this dilemma. It would force people to just look at the object and try to find their own experience.

Ernst: I would object to doing any such thing as that—such as numbering a picture. I don't particularly care what people classify me as, or whether people understand the title or not. It suggests something to me, or something may pop into my head—so I give it that title.

Smith: I think titles are a positive means of identification. I never objected to any work of art because of its title. The only people who have objected were critics because they did not like the work.

Reinhardt: The question of abandoning titles arose, I am sure, because of esthetic reasons. Even titles like "still life" and "landscape" do not say anything about a painting. If a painting does have a reference or association of some kind, I think the artist is apt to add a title. I think this is why titles are not used by a great many modern painters—because they don't have anything to do with the painting itself.

Moderator Barr: There are some painters who attach a great deal of importance to titles.

Moderator Motherwell: I think Sterne is dealing with a real problem—what is the content of our work? What are we really doing? The question is how to name what as yet has been unnamed.

Moderator Barr: I would like to get some information on this. Would you raise your hands if you name your pictures and sculptures?

(*most raised their hands*).

How many people merely number their pictures?

(*three people raised their hands*).

How many don't title their pictures at all?

(*none raised their hands*).

(*Note: objections to this procedure*).

Hare: It seems to me a minor problem. There are in general two kinds of title, poetic and those which note the content. A number seems to me only a refusal to accept responsibility.

Baziotes: Whereas certain people start with a recollection or an experience and paint that experience, to some of us the act of doing it becomes the experience; so that we are not quite clear why we are engaged on a particular work. And because we are more interested in plastic matters than we are in a matter of words, one can begin a picture and carry it through and stop it and do nothing about the title at all. All pictures are full of association.

Reinhardt: Titles are very important in surrealist work. But the emphasis with us is upon a painting experience, and not on any other experience. The only objection I have to a title is when it is false or tricky, or is something added that the painting itself does not have.

Sterne: I don't think anybody really has a right to know exactly how I feel about my paintings. It seems too intimate to give them a subjective title.

Moderator Barr: Do you think it is possible to enrich the painting by words?

De Kooning: I think that if an artist can always title his pictures, that means he is not always very clear.

Lassaw: In titling a construction, I have used combinations of words or syllables without any meaning. Lately, I have adopted the use of the names of stars or other celestical objects, similar to the way ships are named. Such titles are just names, and are not to imply that the constructions express, symbolize, or represent anything. A work of art "is" like a work of nature.

Ferber: What we all have been saying is that the designation of a painting or a piece of sculpture has become more important as a problem than it has been before. An Assumption or a Crucifixion needed no title. I think that numbering pieces is really begging the question. Because numbering the piece is an admission or a statement or a manifesto that this is pure painting or sculpture—that it stands by itself without relation to any other discipline. We should not cut ourselves off from this great rich world.

Moderator Barr: I don't know how much longer this discussion of titling works will go on. There are a good many interesting implications. It seems to me there are three levels of titles: (1) Simply as a matter of convenience. (2) Questions of titles as explanation or as a kind of fingerpoint and which do not work particularly well. (3) The surrealist title in which the words are a positive part of the work of art, and there is an attraction or conflict set up between the words and the picture. It is the second of those that I would like to hear some conversation about —the question of specific emotion in the work of art. The general public is very much interested in that factor of the work. How did the artist feel when he did the thing?

Was it painful? Was it a matter of love or fear, or what not? Very often he gets no guidance at all from looking at the picture. That's where the factor of titles comes in. At the same time the title may distort the picture a great deal. But to return to the process of painting—how important is (whoever wants to answer) conscious emotion such as pleasure, grief or fear in making your work?

Pousette-Dart: I believe that a true work of art should not only be untitled, but I think it should be unsigned.

Newman: I think it would be very well if we could title pictures by identifying the subject matter so that the audience could be helped. I think the question of titles is purely a social phenomenon. The story is more or less the same when you can identify them. I think the implication has one of two possibilities: (1) We are not smart enough to identify our subject matter, or (2) language is so bankrupt that we can't use it. I think both are wrong. I think the possibility of finding language still exists, and I think we are smart enough. Perhaps we are arriving at a new state of painting where the thing has to be seen for itself.

Moderator Lippold: I think we are getting away from the question—a description of the subject of the picture—especially Mr. Barr's question in relation to an emotional experience we might have felt.

Moderator Barr: I don't want to have the discussion kept on a question of that sort, but I was interested really not in the question of title, but as to whether emotions such as grief or joy or pleasure or fear—how important are they consciously in the production of the works of art. Is the work of art an act of confidence or pleasure?

Bourgeois: I try to analyze the reasons why an artist gets up and takes a brush and a knife—why does he do it? I feel it was either because he was suddenly afraid and wanted to fill a void, afraid of being depressed and ran away from it, or that he wanted to record a state of pleasure or confidence, which is contrary to the feeling of void or fear. My choice is made in my case, but I am not especially interested in talking about my own case.

Brooks: It seems to me that it is impossible generally to clarify the emotions that go into painting. We can't get away from the grief or joy we put into a painting; it is a very complex thing and in some cases a very ambiguous thing. We are in some cases identifying ourselves through our painting and that means everything we are and a great many things we would like to be.

De Kooning: If you are an artist, the problem is to make a picture work whether you are happy or not.

Moderator Barr: Could you raise your hands to this question: "How many people name their works of art after they are completed?"

(thirteen raised hands to this question)

"How many people name their works when they are half-way through?"

(six raised their hands to this.)

"How many people have their work named before they start on it?"

(one person responded).

(Note: Mr. Barr said the above was just a rough count of hands.)

Moderator Lippold: It has seemed to me that the whole business of title or what to make is a phenomenon peculiar to our times. The job was a great deal easier, in any any period but our own. The idea of what to paint was already pre-determined. I am talking of such cultures as the oriental and our middle ages—in which a sculptor was asked to carve a king or queen. It wasn't his job to complain because he did not want to make a king or queen. And there are people like that now, too. I believe that in our own time the discipline that is enforced upon our work has to come from ourselves. The title for me exists at the beginning and all through the piece, and it keeps me clearly on the road, I believe, to the conclusion of the work. The only thing I am interested in resolving is that intent with which I begin, because I feel in our time there is very little else with which to begin. To grope through a series of accidents is not the function of the artist. The job of the artist is only the job of a craftsman.

Baziotes: Mr. Lippold's position, as I understand it, is that the beginning of a work now has something about it that would not have seemed quite logical to artists of the past. We apparently begin in a different way. Is that what you mean, Mr. Lippold?

Moderator Lippold: Yes.

Baziotes: I think the reason we begin in a different way is that this particular time has gotten to a point where the artist feels like a gambler. He does something on the canvas and takes a chance in the hope that something important will be revealed.

* * *

Reinhardt: I would like to ask a question about the exact involvement of a work of art. What kind of love or grief is there in it? I don't understand, in a painting, the love of anything except the love of painting itself. If there is agony, other than the agony of painting, I don't know exactly what kind of agony that would be. I am sure external agony does not enter very importantly into the agony of our painting.

Moderator Barr: I would like a show of hands on this question: Is there anyone here who works for himself alone—that is, purely for his own satisfaction—for himself as the sole judge?

(scattered showing of hands)

De Kooning: I feel it isn't so much the act of being obliged to someone or to society, but rather one of conviction. I think, whatever happens, every man works for himself, and he does it on the basis of convincing himself. I force my attitude upon this world, and I have this right—particularly in this country—and I think it is wonderful, and if it does not come off, it is alright, too. I don't see any reason why we should go and look into past history and find a place or try to take a similar position.

Biala: I don't think a work of art is finished until it has found its audience.

Moderator Motherwell: Is the artist his own audience?

Reinhardt: How many artists here consider themselves craftsmen or professionals? What is our relationship to the social world?

Brooks: When we paint pictures, we assume other people feel the way we do.

Biala: Nothing exists by itself. It only exists in relation to something else: when it can find one other person in the world.

Pousette-Dart: Is prayer a creative act? I should say that it depends upon the prayer itself, but there is no other person necessarily involved. A painter can paint for the satisfaction of his soul, but he can mean it for everyone.

De Kooning: There was that cave of paintings which were found in France just lately. Were they works of art before we discovered them? This is the question.

Newman: I would like to go back to Mr. Lippold's question—are we involved in self-expression or in the world? It seems to Lippold you cannot be involved in the world if you are a craftsman; but if you are involved in the world, you cannot be an artist. We are in the process of making the world, to a certain extent, in our own image. This removes us from the craft level.

De Kooning: This difficulty of titling or not titling a picture—we ought to have more faith in the world. If you really express the world, those things eventually will turn out more or less good. I know what Newman means: it is some kind of feeling that you want to give yourself a place in the world.

Newman: About specifying—if you specify your emotions —whether they are agony or fear, etc.—I believe it is bad manners to actually say one is feeling bad.

De Kooning: I think there are different experiences or emotions. I feel certain parts you ought to leave up to the world.

Newman: I think we start from a subjective attitude, which, in the process of our endeavour, becomes related to the world.

Ferber: I want to add to what Newman has said, which is that it is impossible to escape an attitude towards the world. I would like to bring into this discussion, if possible the artist, not as being, but as man, and not as a mere practitioner or craftsman, because if we have any integrity at all, it is as men and women.

Pousette-Dart: Why does the modern artist feel the need to sign his work?

Baziotes: When we make a work of art we must get our praise after it is finished.

Pousette-Dart: In certain cultures none of the works were signed.

Baziotes: If you were commissioned to do a picture of the Madonna in the middle ages that was praise to begin with.

Gottlieb: I think the answer is that the work that really has something to say constitutes its own signature.

De Kooning: There is no such thing as being anonymous.

Hare: A man's work is his signature. In this sense art has never been anonymous.

Rosenborg: It is a beautiful question. In our society, with manufacturers, businessmen, etc., it is necessary to sign something for the purposes of identity. But still the thing is, how could one maintain an identity without signing. Who wants to title a work? To sign a work?

* * *

Lewis: But how are you going to get that to the public?

Moderator Barr: You are interested in the problem of how to get your painting to the public?

Lewis: During the period of impressionism you had the artists showing their work in cafes and other places where they ate. At one time they were exhibiting in the open air shows in the Village. Then there was the Federal Art Project. People no longer have this intimacy with the artists, so that the public does not know actually what is going on, what is being done by the painter. I remember

organizing for a union on the water-front. People then didn't know the function of a union, or what was good about it, but gradually they were made aware of it. They saw a need for it. The same is true of our relationship with the people; in making them aware of what we are doing. Certainly you are going to run into ignorance.

Hare: Sometimes a young artist becomes too quickly known. He already is a member of the reaction. He can't help it. It is not always such a good thing to find yourself an accepted part of the culture.

Reinhardt: Exactly what is our involvement, our relation to the outside world? I think everybody should be asked to say something about this.

Moderator Barr: Apparently many people don't want to answer the question.

De Kooning: I think somebody who professes something never is a professor. I think we are craftsmen, but we really don't know exactly what we are ourselves, but we have no position in the world—absolutely no position except that we just insist upon being around.

Ernst: I am rather happy with my position in society. In other words, I would much rather be unattached to any part of society than to be commissioned to carve a picture of Mr. Truman, because I am not interested in that. I think what we are overlooking here—and I have believed this for a long time—is the fact that we cannot draw our reaction altogether from the present, nor can we create out of past experience alone.

Tomlin: It seems to me before we examine our position in relation to the world we should examine our position in relation to each other. I understood that to be the point of this discussion and that is why we came together. I am sure there are a number of people who are interested in the matter of self-expression alone and there are others who are not.

Newman: I would like to emphasize Mr. Motherwell's remarks: we have two problems. (1) The problem of existing as men. (2) The problem of growth in our work.

Moderator Barr: There seems to be some feeling that this is a practical body rather than a deliberative. Do you want to discuss whether you want to do something practical or go ahead in the search of what we call truth?

ERNST, GRIPPE, GOTTLIEB, HOFMANN

THE THIRD DAY.

Moderator Motherwell: The questions we all have written down fall into three categories, though they overlap. On one is a series of questions that are historical, which Grippe, Ernst, Hare, Reinhardt, Barr and Gottlieb ask; the largest number of questions are strictly esthetic questions, about the process of creation and about the quality of creative works—the questions of Ferber, Hare, Baziotes, Lippold, Smith, Sterne, Hoffman, Biala, Lassaw and Bourgeois. Five people, Pousette-Dart, Lipton, Tomlin, Newman and Brooks, have asked an identical question: a question of community—what is it that binds us together (if there is something that binds us together)? Would you like me to read all the questions, either anonymously or signed?
All: Read them signed.

(Note: The following are written questions by the artists, read aloud by Moderator Motherwell)

Ernst: To what extent are the artists in this group making use of some of the methods and theories that were developed by the various earlier movements and groups of modern art? Are the artists in this group searching for a personal vocabulary, and if so, what is their method of familiarizing their public with this language? Is not a pure painting a self-portrait?

*

Reinhardt: What is your work (of art)? Do you consider the production of it a professional activity? Do you belong to Artists Equity? Why or why not?

*

Gottlieb: Is there any difference in direction between advanced American and French painting or sculpture? If there is a difference, what is its nature, and what does it mean?

*

Hare: Do you work from a previously formed conception, or does your work become its own inspiration as it progresses? What do you feel about the unavoidable changes which are forced upon a work during its birth?
Which do you feel is of fundamental value to you—the success with which you are able to say it, or the importance to you of what you have to say? Do you paint your subject, or is painting your subject (subject in the sense of content, not in the sense of realism versus abstraction)? Of what value do you feel your work is to society? If any, what changes would you wish it to effect, and why?

*

Barr: What is the most acceptable name for your direction or movement? (it has been called abstract-expressionist, abstract-symbolist, intra-subjectivist, etc.)?
I now jump the second to the third category, and ask if there is any unity here?

*

Lipton: Is there anything that binds this group together historically?

*

Pousette-Dart? Can we find some binding factor or practical common denominator between us—a common purpose upon which we can all *work* as well as talk—perhaps each to paint or sculp upon an agreed subject, theme, idea or problem and exhibit these works together (myself preferring neither signature nor titles)?

*

Tomlin: Assuming that painters in this group hold similar views in relation to the picture plane, are there other plastic convictions held in common sufficient to establish a body of objective criteria? Does painting which excludes automatic technical processes, but which involves a concern with the subconscious, necessarily fall into the classification of subjective?

*

Newman: What ties us together as a community of artists?

*

Brooks: What are the qualities, or is the quality in their work that establishes a community of the artists of which this roundtable is a section?

*

Rosenborg: What can we do about making a group such as this more permanent? In coming together on an artistic and social basis?

Now we come to the group of questions that seem to me to tend to be strictly esthetic:

Smith: Is painting leading sculpture or have they separated?

*

Lassaw: Conceding that an all-embracing definition or explanation of art has not yet been generally accepted by artists, it would be of great interest and enlightening both to the public and fellow artists alike if each member of this round-table answers in his own way the question: "What is art?"

*

Biala: Like many of us, I was raised on the notion of "painterliness"—that what is most moving in painting is just its painterly quality. But what I think of the art that I love—for example, the art of Spain, with its passion and noblesse—I wonder if painterliness is not meant to serve something beyond itself, and it is then that I question a great deal in modern art. Consequently, is modern painting impoverishing itself, and is this inevitable?

*

Hofmann: What do you think quality is?

*

Sterne: Is art a problem of *how* or *what*?

*

Lippold: Is it possible to make a work while under the influence of an immediate experience—i.e., fear, disgust, love, etc.?

*

Baziotes: What do you feel is more important in the art movement today—intuition or reason?

*

Ferber: Can purity in the arts be compared to the medieval notion of discussing how many angels can stand on the head of a pin. A notion of refined disembodied essence which is no longer consonant with modern ideas which embrace the whole man and his human engagements.

*

Bourgeois: The Genesis of a Work of Art; or in what circumstance is a work of art born:

1. *Definition* of the term "genesis"—process of creation. Is it the process of being born or the process of giving birth?
2. What *causes* the work of art to be born? What is the primary impulse? What makes the artist work? Is it to escape from depression (filling a void)? Is it to record confidence or pleasure? Is it to understand and solve a formal problem and re-order the world?
3. What conditions the birth and growth of the work of art?
   (a) Before the act of creation:
      Sociological aspect (surroundings and milieu).
      Taine ato theory of the milieu.
      Personal aspect.
   (b) During the process of creation:
      Experience undergone while the work is being done.
      Resistance of the medium.
      Properties of the medium.

*

Moderator Motherwell: I would suggest, to expedite matters, that we vote on which category of these three groups we wish to begin with. Most people here are involved in the esthetic question and would prefer to give it preference, no doubt. Would it seem agreeable to vote?

Reinhardt: There are really only two categories—historical and community are really the same thing. The question of community is, in practice, the historical problem, and would take less time than the esthetic question.

Moderator Motherwell: The questions that are dealing with the creative process tend to revolve around the question of how a work originates: what it is really referring to, and in that sense what its actual content is and how clearly it is known at the inception. And the other series dealing with creative process tend to revolve around the question of quality—what quality is. However, it also involves some social problems—why we are together? Shall we begin with the questions that have to do with origin? It seemed to me quite clear the first day that there were two differences mentioned which overlap. One is a notion that a work in its beginning has its conclusion implied. The conclusion follows the original line of thought and the process is to cut out anything that is irrelevant to that line of thought. The other notion is a notion of improvising—that one begins like a blind swimmer and what one finds en route often alters the original intent. The people who work like that are involved in the problem of inspiration. That's enough to annoy somebody, perhaps.

Ferber: I wasn't making any point about inspiration.

Pousette-Dart: Would you say a work was an experience of discovery—that you are turning up new stones?

Moderator Motherwell: Sterne said that any other position involves an *a priori* notion of what beauty is.

Pousette-Dart: You have to know if you are . . .

Moderator Lippold (interrupting): We have moved forward only when a specific problem presented itself and we have groped around for a conclusion. I attempted to explain that my method seems to be to have a problem with which to begin and then proceed with it. I would like to take some questions which have been suggested which have to do with the genesis of a work.

Ferber: What about this problem of how a piece is begun?

Moderator Lippold: I think Miss Stern's question has to do with origin. I would ask regarding origin: is it a question of wanting to say a specific thing, or of how one says it? And where do the two meet? Do we begin with the necessity to convey a message, or do we become intrigued with the way in which it is to be said?

Ferber: Could the process which I suggested as one process be compared to the way in which one handles a kaleidoscope? One's relationship to the world in which we live might be a kind of base from which one starts. If you turn the kaleidoscope you stop at an image which takes form in a satisfactory way; and the painting becomes the realization of that image—which is only a moment in the whole process—then you turn the kaleidoscope and make another image.

Moderator Motherwell: Are the elements in the kaleidoscope essentially "hownesses" or "whatnesses?"

Sterne: I think that for the artist himself the problem is not "beauty," ever. It is one of accuracy, validity and life.

Moderator Barr: Would you say preoccupation with the idea of beauty is a bad thing?

Sterne: No, but it does not lead anywhere, because "beauty" is a matter of conception.

Newman: A concern with "beauty" is a concern with what is "known."

Pousette-Dart: "Beauty" is unattainable, yet it is what gives art its significance, it *is* the *unknown.*

Newman: The artist's intention is what gives a specific thing form.

Pousette-Dart: I have the feeling that in the art world "beauty" has become a discredited word. I have heard people say you can't use the word "God." When a word becomes trite it is not the word that has become trite but the people who use it.

Sterne: I am not here to define anything; but to give life to what I have the urge to give life to. We live by the particular, not by the general.

Moderator Motherwell: It is not necessary for Sterne to define "beauty" for what she is saying. "Beauty" is not for her the primary source of inspiration. She thinks that "beauty" is discovered en route.

Reinhardt: Is there anyone here who considers himself a producer of beautiful objects?

Gottlieb: I agree with Sterne that we are always concerned with the particular, not the general. Any general discussion of esthetics is a discussion of philosophy; any conclusion can apply to any work of art. Why not have people tell us why they do what they do. Why does Brooks use swirling shapes? Why Newman a straight line? What is it that makes each person use those particular forms that they use?

Smith: I agree with Miss Sterne. The question of "beauty" does not inspire the creator, but is a result of recognition.

Lipton: I feel that Sterne's view is valid. The work of art is an end result. The other concern (formulated by Lippold) is an *a priori* kind of view. I see Sterne's concept of art in its relation to "beauty"; why she is concerned with "beauty" and yet leaves it out of the discussion.

* * *

Brooks: I suggest that the artists begin with a discussion of their own particular points of view.

Moderator Motherwell: (to Brooks) I am extremely interested in something you do, which is painting behind the canvas.

Brooks: My work is improvisation to start with. My purpose is to get as much unknown on the canvas as I can. Then I can start digesting or changing. The first thing is to get a great many unfamiliar things on the surface. The working through on another side is an unfamiliar attack. There are shapes suggested that start improvising themselves, which I then start developing. Sometimes there is a terrible confusion, and a retreat into tradition. If then, for example, I rely on cubism, my painting loses its newness to me. If I can manage to keep a balance with improvisation, my work can get more meaning; it reaches a certain fulness

Gottlieb: Isn't it possible that a straight line could develop on your canvas? I am inclined to think that it does not appear because it is excluded. Swirling shapes are not just the result of unconscious process.

Brooks: It is not as deliberate as you think. I have a preference for it, but that is as far as I can go.

Tomlin: Can one interchange the words "automatic" and "improvise?"

Brooks: No, I don't consider them synonymous.

Tomlin: Do you feel that the "automatic" enters into your work at all?

Brooks: I am not able to define what the mixture is.

De Kooning: I consider all painting free. As far as I am concerned, geometric shapes are not necessarily clear. When things are circumspect or physically clear, it is purely an optical phenomenon. It is a form of uncertainty; it is like accounting for something. It is like drawing something that then is bookkeeping. Bookkeeping is the most unclear thing.

Reinhardt: An emphasis on geometry is an emphasis on the "known," on order and knowledge.

Ferber: Why is geometry more clear than the use of swirling shapes?

Reinhardt: Let's straighten out our terminology, if we can. Vagueness is a "romantic" value, and clarity and "geometricity" are "classic" values.

De Kooning: I meant geometry in art. Geometry was against art—the beauty of the rectangle, I mean.

Moderator Lippold: This means that a rectangle is unclear?

De Kooning: Yes.

Moderator Motherwell: Lippold resents the implication that a geometric form is not "clear."

De Kooning: The end of a painting in this kind of geometric painting would be almost the graph for a possible painting—like a blueprint.

Tomlin: Would you say that automatic structure is in the process of becoming, and that "geometry" has already been shown and terminated?

De Kooning: Yes.

Moderator Motherwell: It seems to me that what de Kooning is saying is plain. He feels resentful that one mode of expression should be called more clear, precise, rational, finished, than another.

Baziotes: I think when a man first discovers that two and two is four, there is "beauty" in that; and we can see why. But if people stand and look at the moon and one says, "I think it's just beautiful tonight," and the other says, "The moon makes me feel awful," we are both "clear." A geometric shape—we know why we like it; and an unreasonable shape, it has a certain mystery that we recognise as real; but it is difficult to put these things in an objective way.

Newman: The question of clarity is one of intention.

Sterne: I think it has to do with Western thinking. A Chinese thinks very well, but does not use logic. The use of geometrical forms comes from logical thinking.

Reinhardt (to Sterne): Your work to some extent looks generally planned and preconceived. I would like some discussion on it.

Sterne: Preconceived only partly. Because as I go, the painting begins to function by rules of its own, often preventing me from achieving my original vision.

Kees: In regard to this issue of clarity, it might be interesting if we could find anyone who could say that he doesn't care very much about clarity as an element in his painting.

Smith: I am not involved with clarity, but a straight line is a form which is the most abstract thing you can find. It is a support, not an element.

Hofmann: I believe that in an art every expression is relative, not absolutely defined as long as it is not the expression of a relationship. Anything can be changed. We speak here only about means, but the application of the means is the point. You can change one thing into another with the help of the relations of the things. One shape in relation to other shapes makes the "expression"; not one shape or another, but the relationship between the two makes the "meaning." As long as a means is only used for itself, it cannot lead to anything. Construction consists of the use of one thing in relation to another, which then relates to a third, and higher, value.

Moderator Motherwell (to Hofmann): Would you say that a fair statement of your position is that the "meaning" of a work of art consists of the relations among the elements, and not the elements themselves?

Hofmann: Yes, that I would definitely say. You make a thin line and a thick line. It is the same as with geometrical shapes. It is all relationship. Without all of these relationships it is not possible to express higher art.

Ferber: The means are important, but what we were concerned with is an expression of a relationship to the world. Truth and validity cannot be determined by the shape of the elements of the picture.

De Kooning: About this idea of geometric shapes again: I think a straight line does not exist. There is no such thing as a straight line in painting.

Reinhardt: We are losing Ferber's point. I would like to get back to the question of whether there is another criterion of truth and validity, apart from the internal relationships in a work of art.

Moderator Motherwell: It would be very difficult to formulate a position in which there were no external relations. I cannot imagine any structure being defined as though it only has internal meaning.

Reinhardt: I want to know the outside truth. I think I know the internal one.

* * *

Moderator Motherwell: Reinhardt was emphasizing very strongly that the quality of a work depends upon the relations within it. Between Ferber and Reinhardt the question is being raised as to whether these internal relations also relate externally to the world, or better, as to what this external relation is.

Tomlin: May I take this back to structure? In what was said about the parts in relation to Brooks' work, the entire structure was embraced. We were talking about shape, without relation to one possibility of structure. I would like to say that I feel that geometric shapes can be used to achieve a fluid and organic structure.

Hofmann: There is a fluidity in the elements which can be used in a practical way, which is often used by Klee. It is related to handwriting—it often characterises a complete personality. It can be used in a graphic sense and in a plastic sense. It leads a point to a relation with another point. It is a relationship of all points considered in a plastic relation. It offers a number of possibilities.

Reinhardt (to Hofmann: Do you consider the inter-relationships of the elements in a work of art to be self-contained?

Hofmann: It is related to all of this world—to what you want to express. You want to express something very definitely and you do it with your means. When you understand your means, you can.

Moderator Motherwell: I find that I ask of the painting process one of two separate experiences. I call one the "mode of discovery and invention," the other the "mode of joy and variation." The former represents my deepest painting problem, the bitterest struggle I have ever undertaken: to reject everything I do not feel and believe. The other experience is when I want to paint for the sheer joy of painting. These moments are few. The strain of dealing with the unknown, the absolute, is gone. When I need joy, I find it only in making free variations on what I have already discovered, what I know to be mine. We modern artists have no generally accepted subject matter, no inherited iconography. But to re-invent painting, its subject matter and its means, is a task so difficult that one must reduce it to a very simple concept in order to paint for the sheer joy of painting, as simple as the Madonna was to many generations of painters in the past. An existing subject matter for me—even though I had to invent it to begin with—variations gives me moments of joy . . . The other mode is a voyaging into the night, one knows not where, on an unknown vessel, an absolute struggle with the elements of the real.

Reinhardt: Let's talk about that struggle.

Moderator Motherwell: When one looks at a Renaissance painter, it is evident that he can modify existing subject matter in a manner that shows his uniqueness and fineness without having to re-invent painting altogether. But I think that painters like Mondrian tend to move as rapidly as they can toward a simple iconography on which they can make variations. Because the strain is so great to re-invent reality in painting.

Reinhardt: What about the reality of the everyday world and the reality of painting? They are not the same realities. What is this creative thing that you have struggled to get and where did it come from? What reference or value does it have, outside of the painting itself?

Moderator Lippold: I should like to find where I think I am. It is the general impression that it is a great problem as to what to paint, and with what to begin. Unfortunately, it is never a problem for me. I have material for the next ten to fifteen years in my sketch books . . . We have talked about formal relationships. This is not a new thing with the abstractionists. It would seem to me that people of Mondrian's school have been interested in exploring formal relationship internally. Other schools have been concerned with the relationship of art to propaganda.

Others seem to explore the areas of a dream world. If we are aware of the things which happen to us in our immediate past, those things come into our consciousness and into our work. We cannot pretend to sit down with no idea as to what has happened before, and to create something entirely new which has never happened before. I feel that all I am doing is synthesizing something which has happened in the past. My materials are not new; my relationships are not new.

Moderator Motherwell: We have some questions which have not been read—they are by people who came in late:

Stamos: Is automatic painting conscious or not? In the early 1900's Ernest Fenellosa wrote an essay with an introduction by Pound on the Chinese character as a medium in poetry. Are the artists today familiar with it, or are such characters or writing unconscious? There is an amazing connection between the two. Are certain artists working closer with the tradition of the Hudson River School in the sense of the organic esthetics? If they are, what are the binding factors of both?

*

Lewis: Is art a form of self-analysis?

*

Moderator Motherwell: Are you saying that art is not a form of analysis, and that we should not be here analyzing what is going on? Or that art is a way of analyzing the world?

*

Lewis: Yes, psychoanalysis.

*   *   *

De Kooning: If we talk in terms of what kinds of shapes or lines we are using, we don't mean that and we talk like outsiders. When Motherwell says he paints stripes, he doesn't mean that he is painting stripes. That is still thinking in terms of what kind of shapes we are painting. We ought to get rid of that. If a man is influenced on the basis that Modrian is clear, I would like to ask Mondrian if he was so clear. Obviously, he wasn't clear, because he kept on painting. Mondrian is not geometric, he does not paint straight lines. A picture to me is not geometric—it has a face . . . It is some form of impressionism . . . We ought to have some level as a profession. Some part of painting has to become professional.

Newman: De Kooning has moved from his original position that straight lines do not exist in nature. Geometry *can* be organic. Straight lines do exist in nature. When I draw a straight line, it does exist. It exists optically. When De Kooning says it doesn't exist optically, he means it doesn't exist in nature. On that basis, neither do curved lines exist in nature. But the edge of the U.N. building is a straight line. If it can be made, it does exist in nature. A straight line is an organic thing that can contain feeling.

De Kooning: What is called Mondrian's optical illusion is not an optical illusion. A Mondrian keeps changing in front of us.

Gottlieb: It is my impression that the most general idea which has kept cropping up is a statement of the nature of a work of art as being an arrangement of shapes or forms of color which, because of the order or ordering of materials, expresses the artist's sense of reality or corresponds with some outer reality. I don't agree—that some

20

expression of reality can be expressed in a painting purely in terms of line, color and form, that those are the essential elements in painting and anything else is irrelevant and can contribute nothing to the painting.

Ferber: It seems that Gottlieb is making the point that non-objective art is a relationship that is internally satisfactory.

Gottlieb: That's not satisfactory.

Moderator Motherwell: It is not the real issue. All of the people here move as abstractly or back to the world of nature as freely as they like to, and would fight at any time for that freedom.

Newman: We are raising the question of subject matter and what its nature is.

* * *

De Kooning: I wonder about the subject matter of the Crucifixion scene—was the Crucifixion the subject matter or not? What is the subject matter? Is an interior subject matter?

Hofmann: I think the question goes all the time back to subject matter. Every subject matter depends on how to use meaning. You can use it in a lyrical or dramatic manner. It depends on the personality of the artist. Everyone is clear about himself, as to where he belongs, and in which way he can give esthetic enjoyment. Painting is esthetic enjoyment. I want to be a "poet." As an artist I must conform to my nature. My nature has a lyrical as well as a dramatic disposition. Not one day is the same. One day I feel wonderful to work and I feel an expression which shows in the work. Only with a very clear mind and on a clear day I can paint without interruptions and without food because my disposition is like that. My work should reflect my moods and the great enjoyment which I had when I did the work.

Reinhardt: We could discuss the question of the rational or intuitional. That might bring in subject matter or content. We have forms in common. We have cut out a great deal. We have eliminated the naturalistic, and among other things, the super-realistic and the immediately political.

Rosenborg: We are also trying to cut out by still putting in everything.

Reinhardt: You're putting in everything about yourself, but not everything outside yourself.

Rosenborg: The object is not to put yourself in the middle and say, "That's me."

Ernst: I know I can't paint when my mother-in-law is in the house.

* * *

Moderator Motherwell: Thus we go on with the practical questions:

    Reinhardt: What is your work (of art)? Do you consider the production of it a professional activity? Do you belong to Artists' Equity? Why, or why not?

*

    Barr: What is the most acceptable name for our direction or movement? (It has been called Abstract-Expressionist, Abstract-Symbolist, Intra-subjectivist, etc.)

*

Smith: I don't think we do have unity on the name.

Rosenborg: We should have a name through the years.

Smith: Names are usually given to groups by people who don't understand them or don't like them.

Moderator Barr: We should have a name for which we can blame the artists—for once in history!

Moderator Motherwell: Even if there is any way of giving ourselves a name, we will all still be called abstract artists . . . Do you regard painting as a profession?

Reinhardt: All of us exhibit in large exhibitions alongside of artists who consider themselves "professional" or commercial artists and business men, such as the members of Artists' Equity.

Moderator Motherwell: Do you regard it as a profession to earn your living as a painter?

Reinhardt: You could be unemployed and still be a "professional" or a member of Artists' Equity.

Moderator Motherwell: If you define "profession" in terms of what you do most often, of what is your major activity, then everybody here is a "professional" painter.

Reinhardt: Then should or shouldn't we belong to Equity?

Ernst: I joined because I was tired of being asked why don't I belong.

Newman: The thing that binds us together is that we consider painting to be a profession in an "ideal society." We assume the right of insisting that we are creating our own paradise. We should be able to act in a professional way on our own terms. We go out into normal society and insist on acting on our own terms.

Smith: I exist in the best society possible because I exist in this time. I have to take it as the ideal society. It is ideal as far as I am concerned. I can not go back, I cannot admit that there is any history in my life outside of the times in which I live. Nothing can be more idealistic for work than right now—and there never will be an ideal society.

Moderator Motherwell (to Newman): You mean that we are not acting in relation to the goals that most people in our society accept?

Newman: Yes.

Smith: This is the time in which I live and have to function. Therefore, it has to be ideal. How can I consider an ideal society as ideal in one that I can't possibly live?

Moderator Motherwell: What distinguishes these people is that they are trying to act ideally in a non-ideal society.

Pousette-Dart: It is an ideal society, but only the artist realizes it.

De Kooning: You can't call yourself "professional" unless you have a license, such as an architect has. There are differences, we can make money without a license, but to call ourselves "professionals," we can't do that; you must be a "professional" to someone else—not to yourself.

Smith: It is just an attitude of mind.

Reinhardt: Does not one have to remove oneself from the business world in order to create "fine" art or to exist as a "fine artist"?

Moderator Motherwell: Can we say that every one here accepts the fact that in most societies people have a "career" of one kind or another? To choose painting as career and, at the same time, to insist on the integrity of one's own expression, is really to make an idiotic choice of a career.

Ernst: Can we say that no one here is an amateur?

Rosenborg: I wouldn't advise anyone in the outside world to be an artist, but if I had to do it all over again I would do it.

Brooks: "Professional" conveys, to the outside world, that people spend a great deal of time in what they are doing.

Newman: "Professional" for me means "serious."

Moderator Motherwell: In relation to the question of a name, here are three names: Abstract-Expressionist; Abstract Symbolist; Abstract-Objectionist.

Brooks: A more accurate name would be "direct" art. It doesn't sound very good, but in terms of meaning, abstraction is involved in it.

Tomlin: Brooks also remarked that the word "concrete" is meaningful; it must be pointed out that people have argued very strongly for that word. "No-objective" is a vile translation.

Newman: I would offer "Self-evident" because the image is concrete.

De Kooning: It is disastrous to name ourselves.

BIALA, NEWMAN, HARE,

BAZIOTES

TOMLIN

LEWIS, ERNST, GRIPPE, ROSENBORG

THE INTRASUBJECTIVES

OPENING WEDNESDAY, SEPTEMBER 14; THRU OCTOBER 3, 1949

SAMUEL M. KOOTZ GALLERY • 600 MADISON AVENUE • NEW YORK 22

catalogue

WILLIAM BAZIOTES
sleepwalker

WILLEM DE KOONING
the attic

ARSHILE GORKY
hugging

ADOLPH GOTTLIEB
pictograph

MORRIS GRAVES
joyous young pine

HANS HOFMANN
the red table

ROBERT MOTHERWELL
the voyage

JACKSON POLLOCK
untitled

AD REINHARDT
number II

MARK ROTHKO
untitled

MARK TOBEY
geography of fantasy

BRADLEY WALKER TOMLIN
death cry

Grateful acknowledgement is made to the following for loans to this exhibit:
Egan Gallery, Julien Levy Gallery, Betty Parsons Gallery and Willard Gallery.

The colored sketches for this catalogue are by Baziotes, Gottlieb and Hofmann.

L to R: GOLDWATER, BATESON, TOBEY, RITCHIE, MILHAUD, FRANKENSTEIN, BOAS, DUCHAMP, BURKE

THE WESTERN
ROUND TABLE ON MODERN ART (1949)

Edited by Douglas MacAgy

This abstract contains approximately 18 per cent of the total number of words in the original.

PREFACE

The following abstract of proceedings of the Western Round Table on Modern Art aims at a balanced treatment of topics covered and a fair representation of individual contributions to each topic. For the convenience of writers who may wish to comment on the symposium, material in this abstract is grouped by topic. All direct quotations in the present digest have been checked in transcript and approved by each contributor, but the indirect quotations, omissions and re-arrangement are the sole responsibility of the editor.

INTRODUCTION

The Western Round Table on Modern Art met in San Francisco April 8, 9 and 10, 1949. Three sessions were scheduled for the first two days; an unscheduled fourth session was added the third day at the request of some participants. Conference time totalled nine hours. The second session was open by invitation to the public and to members of the San Francisco Art Association; the three other sessions were closed.

All sessions were transcribed by two court reporters and also recorded on wire. The typed transcript was then corrected and approved by each contributor.

A special exhibition of modern art was assembled for the event and shown concurrently at the San Francisco Museum of Art, where the meetings were held.

Sets of photographic reproductions of works in this exhibition were made in advance and sent to members of the symposium for preparatory reference. During the discussion, points were illustrated from time to time by examples in the exhibition. At the outset, however, it was decided that lengthy devotion to analysis of specific works of art would emphasize individual preference and idiosyncrasy at the expense of ideas with possibilities of wider and deeper implication.

A list of works in the exhibition is appended to this abstract.

The Round Table and its Exhibition were sponsored and financed by the San Francisco Art Association, a non-profit corporation, with the assistance of the Art Commission of the City and County of San Francisco.

A list of the boards, commissions, committees and officials involved in this sponsorship is appended.

The Round Table and its Exhibition were organized by Douglas MacAgy, then Director of the California School of Fine Arts.

The object of the Round Table was to bring a representation of the best informed opinion of the time to bear on questions about art today. A set of neat conclusions, as the outcome of the conference, was neither expected nor desired. Rather, it was hoped that progress would be made in the exposure of hidden assumptions, in the uprooting of obsolete ideas, and in the framing of new questions.

Two quotations may emphasize this intention. Alfred North Whitehead pointed out, in discussing the basic assumptions by which we live, that " . . . assumptions may appear so obvious that people do not know what they are assuming because no other way of putting things has ever occurred to them." Pursuing this statement, Suzanne Langer wrote that "a philosophy is characterized more by the formulation of its problems than by its solution of them. Its answers establish an edifice of facts; but its questions make the frame in which its picture of facts is plotted."

Judgment of what was said at the Round Table is invited in terms of these general purposes.

Describing the meetings later, one of the participants put it this way: "There in that room, were a bunch of guys trying to think. We were most of us prima donnas, and from time to time we stopped thinking to try to pull off an epigram. But still—a bunch of guys trying to think. Still more difficult, we were trying to think aloud and trying to communicate with each other—trying to get things clear which have never been gotten clear."

PARTICIPANTS:

GEORGE BOAS (Moderator): Philosopher; Professor of History of Philosophy, Johns Hopkins University; Trustee, Baltimore Museum of Art.

GREGORY BATESON: Cultural anthropologist, Lecturer, Langley Porter Clinic of the University of California Medical School; authority on Bali and New Guinea.

KENNETH BURKE: Literary critic, philosopher, novelist; Professor, Bennington College, Vermont.

MARCEL DUCHAMP: Artist.

ALFRED FRANKENSTEIN: Critic; Music and Art Editor, San Francisco Chronicle.

ROBERT GOLDWATER: Critic and art historian; Editor, Magazine of Art; Associate Professor of Art, Queens College.

DARIOUS MILHAUD: Composer and conductor; Professor of Composition, Mills College.

ANDREW C. RITCHIE: Art historian and critic; Director, Department of Painting and Sculpture, Museum of Modern Art.

ARNOLD SCHOENBERG: Composer.

(Note: Mr. Schoenberg, prevented by ill health at the last minute from personal attendance, contributed a statement by means of a wire recording and typescript).

MARK TOBEY: Artist.

FRANK LLOYD WRIGHT: Architect.

THE PROCEEDINGS

(Note: Quotation marks are used for all statements made directly by members of the symposium. Sections cut from a given statement are indicated by a row of dots. Chronological gaps are shown by a separate line of asterisks. Editorial paraphrases and indirect quotations appear outside quotation marks. Editorial observations are enclosed by parentheses.)

WESTERN CONFERENCE—THE PROCEEDINGS

(Early in the discussion Mr. Duchamp made a sharp distinction between "taste" and what he termed the "aesthetic echo." He claimed that, at any given time, the former could be experienced by many and the latter by few. Frequent reference was made to these assertions as the talk progressed.)

Duchamp: " . . . Taste gives a sensuous feeling, not an aesthetic emotion . . . Taste presupposes a domineering onlooker who dictates what he likes and dislikes, and translates it into 'beautiful' and 'ugly' . . .

"Quite differently, the 'victim' of an 'aesthetic echo' is in a position comparable to a man in love or a believer who dismisses automatically his demanding ego and helplessly submits to a pleasurable and mysterious constraint . . . "

* * * *

"My personal conclusion is that, generally speaking, very few people are capable of an aesthetic emotion—or, an 'aesthetic echo.' While many people have taste, only a few are equipped with aesthetic receptivity."

THE CULTURAL SETTING

Intelligibility and Communication:

Bateson: "My job is not so much with modern or contemporary painting, but with art products of cultures that haven't got themselves into quite such a confused state—in New Guinea, Dutch East Indies and such places. And if you go there, you find that the people who make and who look at the works of art, live, for them, in a world which is totally intelligible. They would know that a sky is blue; they know why water is wet. They do not live in a culture of which most of what happens is mysterious, or is concealed in the Encyclopaedia Britannica, or in more obscure places even. They feel they know the world they live in, and the art objects which they see are produced out of that homogeneous world . . .

"In Mr. Duchamp's 'aesthetic echo' terminology, the 'aesthetic echo' is a thing which can be shared by a very large number of people in that group.

"But we live in a culture which is changing very rapidly, and the 'aesthetic echo' that is carried in modern art, as far as I can see, tends to be the aesthesia—if that be the word—of a changing world. Very often it is the aesthesia of nostalgia for an unchanging world, or the aesthetics of trying to resist the change—feeling anxious about the change . . . A very much more complicated story than the sort of thing that I professionally deal with."

Burke: "Does not the problem center in the specialized nature of our modern culture? As regards possibilities of communication, a specialized culture has one notable embarrassment, which we might illustrate by comparing, say, a bridge-builder with a poet or painter.

"The bridge-builder must understand the particulars of his craft, while laymen who use his bridge need know nothing of this specialized lore . . . You get a sufficient act of communication in scientific and technological production by merely carrying out the appropriate specialized operations.

"The artist too is a specialist, in his fashion . . . But insofar as the public does not understand his special language, his *act* of communication is ineffective. Does he not, as a specialist, thus face an extra problem of communication which technological specialists are spared? "So I take it that our culture, with its high degree of specialization, will always be shifting between the norms of universal appeal on one side, and the requirements of specialization on the other. Occasionally you can expect a happy accident where the work meets both tests at once, but these moments will be comparatively rare . . . "

Goldwater: "What Mr. Burke has just said seems to me to bring up one problem. He has referred to special kinds of communication . . . I think that might be carried further . . . There is a general assumption on the part of the public that though there are specialists in the various fields, it is possible not only to understand, but also to have that 'aesthetic echo' towards all kinds of art—particularly all kinds of contemporary art.

"Couldn't it be said that this assumption is mistaken? That precisely as there are specialists in creation, there are also special tastes in appreciation? And that we need feel no concern, and the public need feel no bewilderment or shame, if there are certain kinds of contemporary works towards which they feel attracted, and other kinds towards which they do not? This by no means would rule out the varieties of contemporary art as a group."

* * * *

Burke: "There is always communication . . . The communication is there the minute the painting is done." *Tobey:* "But the artist, when he is painting, is not thinking of communication . . . " *Wright:* "Not if he is a true artist."

* * * *

Tobey: " . . . I think the artist is concerned with his art, not with himself. He may later on have to be concerned with himself . . . but he is only concerned with himself when his position is attached in relation to this thing which is sacred to him . . . "

* * * *

Goldwater: "Isn't this the result of the apparent identification of self-expression with communication? . . . What is held against the modern artist is his so-called unintelligibility. If you talk to the modern artist about that, you find he feels he is being true to himself, and will allow nothing to disturb the integral expression of his own personality as he conceives it—be it dealers, be it patrons, be it the concept of society in general.

"The problem I would like to propose here is whether that division between communication on the one hand, which presupposes a public to whom the artist is talking, and integrity on the other, which presupposes that the artist is concerned only with himself, is not something wider than a purely aesthetic problem. Is it not a basic problem, not only for the artist in contemporary society, but for the individual—as individual—whether artist or not?"

* * * *

Burke: "My general notion as to what is going on in the world hinges about the shift from a theological vocabulary of motives to secular terms. As our culture has become increasingly secularized, and the theological or religious terms for human motivation have fallen into relative disuse, creative vitality in the symbolizing of motives is more likely to be found in secular expressions.

"And basically, the reason that I watch modern art with such avidity and earnestness is: Here is an area where the

27

motives of our world are being enunciated profoundly. For motives are being enunciated not merely intellectualistically, but with their emotional and ethical ingredients. Hence, the full range should be present here. That's why we should take modern expression so seriously —because it is concerned with the basic motives of life, with the things over which men will lurk, and mull, and linger, and for which they will seek new statements."

The Heritage:

Tobey: "When I was a young man, I never heard of Byzantine art . . . Now, above the horizon has come the beauty of Byzantine art—not only that, but the art the colored people have, and the art of the Coptics, and all of the Orient and everything has flooded the world.

"Now it seems to me that we are in a universalizing period . . . If we are to have world peace, we should have an understanding of all the idioms of beauty because the members of humanity who have created these idioms of beauty are going to be a part of us. And I would say that we are in a period when we are discovering and becoming acquainted with these idioms for the first time . . . "

* * * *

Burke: "I have one little notion to offer on that. It refers to a possible way of introducing the matter of the museum. Could we think of our times as a kind of second-level civilization? I mean, could this civilization flourish under conditions that might have been fatal to another culture?

"Consider technology, for instance. It allows for certain kinds of rationalization. And these kinds of rationalization in turn allow for compensatory or antithetical cults of irrationalism. A similar percentage of irrationalism in other societies might have pulled them apart. We have so much coordination, so much regularization, in technology and its routines, that we can tolerate a high degree of aesthetic latitude without a corresponding degree of risk . . .

"There is an Alexandrian, cosmopolite motive here . . . There are opportunities indigenous to such a situation, too, in this culture of libraries, collections, exhibits, surveys, compendia, encyclopaedias, outlines, botanical gardens, zoos, schools, museums. And you really have a 'second-level' of living here, with a perspective that may culminate in world-mindedness. We transcend time and space—that is, our peculiar time and space . . . "

* * * *

"I would propose to tie that in with another aspect of our 'museum culture.' Once you have the museum, you have the possibility of other tests. For instance . . . here you can consider a kind of art representing such distresses and disturbances as a person might not want to have on his walls—to live with every day. The museum can thus, for our times, exhibit turbulent kinds of art that were, in earlier ages, usually confined to churches. And all such motivation could be expressed, as vital aspects of the human psyche."

Wright: "I guess we are all living a kind of museum life today."

Burke: "Well, out of this you may derive a paradoxical possibility: a balance of imbalances. You can take a group of artists, each in his peculiar way extreme, and you can get your poise as a result of the lot—out of their 'mutual cancellation.' Put them all together, and you might thus have a kind of New Liberalism /for in this respect I think there is an essential 'liberalism of museums'./ The balance may come from the total exhibit, rather than from balance in the single artists."

Wright: "What is the museum now but a kind of morgue? Is it anything else?"

Burke: "Well, to live a dying life—the Christian culture, for instance, was built on this injunction, to 'live a dying life' /as enjoined in *The Imitation of Christ*/. And I think the secularization of that principle is a very important motive in the modern world, underlying even the motives of science.

"You can detect it in the whole cult of abstraction, as you see if you consider the dialectics of Plato. For abstraction, as a transcending of the sensory, is a way of dying and yet living."

* * * *

Goldwater: "One of the characteristics of 19th and 20th century civilization has been its sense of historicity; and the critic, as well as the contemporary artist, cannot avoid that sense of history . . . "

* * * *

" . . . The reaction against the qualities and values of the art of our western culture, at least since the Renaissance, takes the form, in a great many (modern) works, of an overtone of ironic restatement of the qualities of some previous art . . . When we look at this Magritte, which is called—already ironically in its title—*The Portrait,* what we have in our minds is the whole 17th and 18th century still-life tradition of Chardin . . . and that adds a great deal to the depth of reference and the emotional quality— the emotional tensions—which such a picture carries."

* * * *

Ritchie: " . . . More and more, we are coming to believe that art museums are not simply storehouses of the art of the past. They must exhibit both past and present art together, if one is to illuminate the other . . . "

Moderator Boas: "Well, isn't that, Mr. Bateson a peculiarity of modern occidental culture?"

Bateson: "I am not sure that it is. It is some sort of piling up and of exhibition of the spiritual heritage of the culture; you will find it everywhere, or almost everywhere. Bali is as near to a place with no history—with no interest in its own history—as can conceivably be imagined. They feel that time is circular and not progressive, and that the past was undoubtedly like the present . . . . In general, they reconstruct the past in terms of the present, if they pay attention to the past at all. But in Bali you still have collections of the past, magpie habits of various kinds, and I think it's important."

Moderator Boas: "I mean, are these used as Mr. Ritchie was saying they use our modern museums?"

Bateson: "Well, they are used as affirmations, which is not quite the same thing. We live in a culture which is changing, where the things and the collections are used almost as methods of exploration, rather than as affirmations."

———

28

The Beautiful:

Wright: " . . . I think that what passes for a work of art in a true culture—in a civilization that we might call worthy of the name—would be something that would give an impression to whoever beheld it of what he or she would call 'the beautiful.' And I think the test of that work of art, so far as the person was concerned, would be the extent to which he could respond to it with the feeling it was a thing of beauty . . . "

* * * *

Ritchie: "I think Mr. Wright is perhaps begging the question. At least, he is putting it in a very circular way: a work of art must be beautiful, and only the beautiful is a work of art. We are right back where we started from and we must define what is beautiful and what is a work of art."

Wright: "Then we arrive at the conclusion that the only man who can define it is the man for himself, and not for anybody else."

* * * *

Duchamp: "We aren't dealing with any absolutes, are we, in this life? We are dealing only with that which is in motion, not which is an absolute and fixed . . . "

Moderator Boas: "Well, of course, even though these things change from age to age, Mr. Wright may be quite right in saying, in each age, the artist is seeking the beautiful."

Bateson: "There are many cultures that classify together the two extreme ends of the sacred-secular scale. The word 'sacer' in Latin, from which we get our word 'sacred,' is a word for the extremely beautiful and desirable end of the magical scale. In contrast, there is a middle range of that, which is secular, which is everyday, which is normal. And at the other extreme, you come again to the 'sacer,' the sacred, which is the supernatural and horrible.

"Now it seems to me that art is very much concerned with both ends of that scale."

* * * *

"In conversation last night, Mr. Wright, we agreed that love and hate are very closely mixed emotions—or, especially, love and anger, perhaps. Now that means the artist is not, in fact, out to destroy love; he has got to accept the facts of hate as well as the facts of love."

* * * *

Wright: " . . . I think the expression of hate, as tragedy, could be beautiful, as Hamlet was."

Principle:

Wright: "I think every artist, great or worthy of the name, has his feet on what he considers principle, and from that his work, his utterance, his realization of his feeling proceeds . . . "

* * * *

Ritchie: "Mr. Wright, whose principle?—the artist's own independently arrived at principle?"

Wright: "Principle is. Man doesn't make it, he perceives it. Principle is not designed. Principle *is*. God to me is the heart of cosmic principle."

* * * *

Goldwater: "One important thing to keep in mind is that the problem of 'eternal principle,' doesn't exist for the modern artist . . . The modern artist begins with a notion that principles—as eternal—are not something to be accepted; rather he must make his own discoveries, or re-discoveries. And that is why we have such a continuous succession of styles, and why we place so much importance on individuality and the newness of a particular communication . . . "

Bateson: "Would you say that the modern artist is in search of principles, rather than engaged in reiterating the principles of former cultures?"

* * * *

Moderator Boas: " . . . Mr. Wright has maintained that there is a distinction between real artists and fake artists. The real artists express in their works of art, eternal unchanging principles . . . "

* * * *

Duchamp: "There are several kinds of basic principle: first, the basic principles that change with every generation, like the concept of the 'beautiful' . . . But I don't believe in the existence of eternal laws governing art metaphysically."

* * * *

Bateson: "I think the 'eternal principles' have got to come out on the mat and be faced. Now, obviously, if you take two societies—even the English and the French, or the English and the American—you are going to get pretty different evaluations of good and bad. But let's say that there are different ways of listing the things, but that the notions of good and bad are more or less the same, somehow. Now, unfortunately, that isn't true either, because the principles on which principles are built vary enormously from culture to culture; and that begins to be serious."

Wright: "Mr. Bateson, that is where I think you make an initial mistake. It is only the use or abuse that varies."

Bateson: "Could you consider the difference between the occident and China on the one hand, and Japan on the other?"

Wright: "You are talking about ethnic eccentricities, not about a difference of principle."

Bateson: "No, I don't think so. We deal very much in dualisms of one sort or another, and we think that you can choose one end of a dualistic contrast. You can choose democracy in preference to communism, or you can choose good in preference to evil, day in preference to night, and so on. But among the Chinese, you find an assumption that the opposing ends of a polarity are functions of each other. The good is a necessary development out of evil . . . . as you feel that love and hate are related."

Wright: "And yet, a man who is nearest, who has come nearest, to expressing in philosophy the truth and the principles which animate organic architecture did so five hundred years before Jesus. His name was Laotze."

Bateson: "There is a case for saying that we are changing— that the principle on which we have built our principles is changing much more closely towards the Chinese position. You find it among the psychiatrists, can recognize it in Jung, and so on."

Wright: "Because Laotze was the man (the prophet) who first declared that the reality of the building did not consist of four walls and a roof, but in the space within— to be lived in—and that's our organic architecture today. That's the basic principle on which we perform our miracles, and miracles they are . . . All the buildings that really have had quality unconsciously derived their essence and their validity from that unknown-to-them Principle . . . "

Science and Art:

Wright: "May I say here that a scientist *cannot* see this innate thing. That's what sets the scientist apart from the creative artist. Now these twain some day shall meet, but not for centuries . . . The scientist . . . is the enemy at the present time of all the artist would represent . . . The scientist doesn't mean to be that enemy. He thinks he is benefactor . . . Religion by way of science has virtually disappeared so far as real vitality is concerned . . . Artists have all been 'had' by science and education . . . We have tried to substitute sanitation for civilization. Our redemption does not lie in the hands of scientists, because they can only give us tools in a tool-box; the scientist gives us magnificent tools, but he can't tell us what to do with them or how to do what we most need."

Moderator Boas: "What do you say for your craft, Mr. Bateson, after that?"

Bateson: "I would say, first of all, that I think Mr. Wright is referring to a scientific epoch which was wholly materialistic. It was concerned with causal sequences in straight lines—A sets off B, B sets off C. In such a system, I could manipulate you and you will manipulate some body else . . . That scientific epoch is, I think, very rapidly coming to an end.

Mr. Duchamp's position, for example, is one which recognizes the phenomena of circular causal systems— most of the circle being inaccessible to us. In such a system, there is not the opportunity of manipulation because we are *inside* the system."

Wright: "That is altogether too dramatic a figure . . . You miss the new romance as a scientist would—as he would himself have to miss it . . . But he would become a much greater scientist if he *would* get inside and see from the inside outward, rather than from the outside inward. And right there is the difference, I think, very nearly expressed between what I would call the creative Artist and the Scientist. The creative Artist is, by nature, inside the thing and his vision outward. The Scientist is outside looking in, trying to take the thing apart to see what makes it click. And he would fail to put it together again, were he to try."

Bateson: "No, the scientist is not outside . . . The scientist is part of the thing which he studies, as much as the artist. And it is that move—the discovery that the observer is a significant part of the thing observed—that marks the change of epoch."

Degeneracy and Primitivism:

Wright: " . . . I thought we would come together here, perhaps, and do something for the public in their confusion concerning this thing we call 'modern art'—to clear the thing up a little bit and explain why this portrait of a time, of this generation of a civilization, where this particular art of painting is concerned, is also degenerate . . . "

* * * *

Bateson: "As I see the age in which I live, I think it's a very difficult and very confused age. And I think there

are several patches in it which are laboring and sweating and striving to get towards a clarity—often in very confused ways, but still laboring and sweating and I think these pictures are a part of that sweating and striving. I don't believe they are on the way down. I believe, on the whole, they are on the way up."

Frankentein: "I don't suppose anyone in Rome knew they were in a decline . . . "

Tobey: "I presume there were some, but they were called Christians!"

* * * *

Moderator Boas: "I ask the privilege of the gentlemen to participate a bit in this discussion as a historian of ideas . . . "I suppose I'm the only person present who knows anything about the history of man's appraisal of his own civilization. I started a four-volume work some years ago which is now at the end of its second volume, and we have only got up to the 13th century. You find that, beginning with Homor and running straight down to 'Joachim of Florus' a constant succession of people who say every single age they are living in is not only bad, but the worst of all ages; and they give precisely the same reasons for it.

"In Homer, you find old Nestor says to the heroes: 'You people don't know what men were like in my day. Heroes were real men' . . . "

Wright: "Where are these civilizations now?"

Moderator Boas: "I think they are still alive. I don't believe that civilizations die, as Toynbee does . . . We have a lot that is Egyptian in our present civilization; a lot that is ancient Greek; a lot of Rome—Louisiana is still living under Roman Law."

* * * *

Milhaud: "I want to hear about what that artist called 'degenerate art,' because we heard that term not so many years ago from another artist called Adolph Hitler."

* * * *

Wright: " . . . we instinctively hark back to the primitive. We find it in Negro sculpture, in those things Picasso presents to us, which could hang on the wall in any of the primitive African performances. I like to think we find either Picasso despairing, or in absolute collapse, spiritually speaking . . . "

* * * *

Duchamp: "Why do you call it 'degeneracy? You seek in the primitive what might be good to take."

Milhaud: "And healthy."

Wright: "Would you say homosexuality was degenerate?"

Duchamp: "No, it is not degenerate."

Wright: "You would say that this movement which we call modern art and painting has been greatly, or is greatly, in debt to homosexualism?"

Duchamp: "I admit it, but not in your terms . . . I believe that the homosexual public has shown more interest or curiosity for modern art than the heterosexual : so it happened, but it does not involve modern art itself."

Wright: "But no man in his confusion, in his inability to conduct his life and himself on a plane more or less of manhood as we understand it—maybe it's a mistake— feels the need of this refreshment, and goes to the darkie, goes to the primitive, wherever he can find it, and feeling strengthened by it begins to copy it, begins to imitate it . . .

this thing that belonged like a property of childhood to the early days of the race . . . "

Milhaud: "I don't understand the word 'copied.'"

Bateson: "I was going to challenge exactly the same point. I have seen in Bali an Indian dancer, a Hindu from India, who went to Bali to learn Balinese dancing . . . He had one of the top Balinese dancers as a teacher. And you see the Balinese trying to copy the Indian. The two things cannot copy each other. The bodies aren't put together the same way. The notions of beauty and human relations are deeply and implicitly different in the two creatures. And the same applies to us: the possibility of copying when you go to a primitive society is not there."

* * * *

Wright: "Isn't this true: that primitive man—. . . that earlier periods in the art life of the savage races were more childlike?"

Duchamp: "No."

Moderator Boas: "No."

Bateson: "No, no, no; they think we are children."

* * * *

Frankenstein: "I wonder if you are not referring to what I often call the 'evolutionary fallacy.' That is to say, first of all, the idea that the evolution of society proceeds in a straight line; secondly, that that which comes at the end—at our end of the line—is somehow greater in quality, more significant, than that which comes at the lower end of the line.

"It seems to me that the whole line of thought involved there is completely fallacious, and furthermore overlooks an obvious fact . . . that that which we frequently call 'primitive' culture is infinitely more sophisticated in terms of different experiences than we ordinarily admit it is."

Moderator Boas: "Isn't the very term 'primitive' a relic of the evolutionistic period?"

Bateson: "I find it a very useful term to separate these cultures which have not got script from those cultures which have got script . . .

"It means, and it's relevant to this problem about progress that you are raising, that the addition of script to a human community—the fact that they can record, they can time-bind, they can send messages of various kinds—is a shift in the order of complexity . . .

"Now this is what we are all fighting about. Those of us who are on the side of the 20th century and see a lot of these things as striving toward new degrees of awareness, new principles of awareness that come up from the guts— I am not saying they are intellectual strivings, they are deep strivings—have a case, I think, for saying that that is a shift in order of complexities."

* * * *

Moderator Boas: " . . . Now, if I can express my own opinion flatly, I don't think the present age is any worse than any other age . . . I am very, very deeply moved by modern painting, much more so than by most classical paintings; and by modern music much more than classical; and by modern architecture much more so than by architecture of the Beaux-Arts . . . I think it's a perfectly swell age. I see nothing degenerate, and I don't care what the sexual life of its inmates is, or anything of the sort."

Ritchie: " . . . the greatest pleasure I have received from modern art is basically its extraordinary freshness. Looking back, we have spoken of the feeling for history, which is certainly a part of us; but I think the most exciting thing in our day is the tremendous break with all past periods of civilization in an attempt to search for new forms . . . "

———

ART AND ARTIST

Art in a Changing Culture:

Bateson: "Looking at these pictures (exhibition of modern art selected for the symposium), I see a culture in a state of change—changing its very deep premises. If you take the Villon . . . What he has done is to say something like this: 'Cartesian coordinates, perspective—hm' and then he has put this free-flowing line on top of them, to say: 'Yes but—, as against those rigid coordinates, the point can still go for a walk.'

"All right, he has stated a protest against the rigidities of 19th century science which come into the culture via the rectangularity of every room we sit in, and so on. All those coercions are essentially *static* coercions, and the Villon, the Matta, the Surrealist Ernst, the Duchamp 'Nude,' this Mondrian which flickers—all are making statements about process, movement and dynamics. I think there is an extraordinary uniformity actually in what these people are trying to put down. And it is a strife with a large number of fronts, fighting all sorts of battles in different directions, but with a common theme that we are not going to be coerced in certain forms.

"Now . . . if you consider a thing like the famous picture of Ophelia—is it Burne-Jones?—with green weeds and flowers on her nose. That picture, or the artist when he makes the picture, says essentially: 'If you have tears to shed, prepare to shed them now!'—To quote Mark Anthony, and Mark Anthony was a sentimental fake too And the position of the modern artist, as I see it as an anthropologist, is a shift in our notions of human relations in which we refuse to accept that sort of coercion and are reverting to something much closer to Greek tragedy. Greek tragedy does not say: 'If you have tears to shed, prepare to shed them'; it says: 'It's thus, and it's thus, and maybe the gods not only laugh at it, maybe they cry at it—that's your affair.' All they are concerned to say is 'That's how it goes.'

"Or take T. S. Eliot's *The Wasteland*, which is neither funny nor tragic. It is a grim, diagnostic statement, and you can laugh at it, or you can cry at it, but there it is. And its sincerity is the sincerity of diagnosis of an age of which *The Wasteland* is a description. It is an expression of that age swallowed into the deep interior. 'Crime without passion'—yes, sir (Mr. Wright had so characterized 'modern art'); but the corruption of passion is the thing with which we are striving; and we have to fight that battle, I think. That is what I think modern artists feel."

Art as Magic:

Bateson: "I would like to use the word 'magic' in a sense which is not orthodox in anthropology, but which has been suggested by R. G. Collinwood. I would say that an action, an ritual, a work of art . . . contains magic insofar as it lays down in the actor or participant—usually unconsciously—some essential value premise. Maybe a premise of mockery, conceivably. I am not saying it is a *plus* premise. It might be plus or minus. It may be a hatred or a love or a capacity for hatred or love . . . but the distinction which I would like to make is between those acts and objects which have that effect . . . versus those which are essentially entertainment . . . The business of catering to spectatorship is entertainment . . . You see a movie; the movie is done; you have been through something and you haven't got any more emotion than you had before. There has been no change—no force in you laid down or liberated by the thing you have seen . . .
"Perhaps an important point we ought to think about, is to think about the question of whether these pictures are laying down something of that order."

* * * *

Burke: "There's an element that I think is relevant to this matter. I refer to Diderot's remarks on the 'positions of pantomime,' his view of all human society as pantomime.
"I would relate this idea to the Klee pictures, recalling how at one period Klee worked with masks, and then went from masks to a subtler kind of mask—for his objects themselves are masks, the images that the painter uses are 'positions of pantomime.' Here is where the magic of these images enters. That is, they bear on an underlying hierarchic structure. And such hierarchic structure is the formative factor in the world today, as we go from nature to real estate, and next would go from real estate to what we would call nature—but what is really nature as approached through real estate. Or similarly, we go from nudity, to clothing, to nudism. /For, as a matter of fact, the nude in painting is far from being merely an unclothed creature. In his 'philosophy of clothes,' *Sartor Resartus*, Carlyle depicts all sensory appearances as kinds of 'clothing,' and accordingly the nude would be but a highly generalized 'uniform.'/
"Now, 'mystery' arises when there is communication between different kinds of beings. Thus, there is 'mystery' in the raltion between the sexes, or between youth and age, or between persons of markedly different social status . . . And it seems to me that the basic motives infusing the images of a work are 'enigmas' of this sort, as these images, or the objects corresponding to them, are 'masks' standing for the complexities of our social structure . . .
"It seems to me that such motives are gradually disclosing themselves in our society where, because of its strongly democratic tradition, we have tended to think in individualistic terms—looking upon the work of art primarily as the artist's means of self-expression."
"But I see a different emphasis emerging here. 'Very well, the artist is expressing himself, but he must use some kind of language'—and such a language will be a language of 'enigmas,' of objects as 'masks,' as 'positions of pantomime,' as a pageantry, while the mystery of the whole pageant goes by."

* * * *

Bateson: "To extend, in fact, the word 'magic' to cover not only affirmations about the artist's insides, or the spectator's insides, but also affirmations about the world in which we live."
Burke: "Yes, and the objects of our sensory experience, as imaged in art, are infused with a 'divine' essence. When Thales said, 'the world is full of gods,' he was not just talking outmoded polytheistic nonsense. He was making a fundamentally correct statement about objects and images. The world *is* full of gods—it's full of different 'spiritual' entities in the sense that each of the forms with which the artist deals has a spirit, and it is the spirit of hierarchy. There are kingly objects, judicial objects, policeman objects, salvation objects—there are hell objects—and in this respect, they are 'enigmatic.'"
Bateson: "Could I put on record the name of Wallace Stevens, the poet who has made works of art, poems, dealing specifically with this problem."

Magic and Non-Coercive Art:

Bateson: "I landed myself in a contradiction yesterday . . . When we were taling about magic . . . I praised the magical, which is, in a sense, the preachment. And, on the other hand, I said that the great virtue of modern art is that it does not do that—it does not take the spectator by the buttonhole and say that you shall feel such and such. There is some slide in the levels of abstraction in those two statements, and I don't know how to resolve it."
Burke: "Might we try a somewhat roundabout approach, and see if that will help? I approach these matters first from the literary point of view, but I would look for the corresponding elements in the motives of painting . . . "
"I have in mind the distinction, in literary theory, between rhetoric and poetic . . . Poetic deals with the work in itself, its kind, its properties, the internal relations among its parts, etc. Rhetoric deals with the work's persuasiveness, its appeal, and eventually involves ethical considerations . . .
"But note what happens along about the beginning of the 19th century, as regards theories of art and literature. Here the study of aesthetics came to the fore. It had many good results. It gave new vitality to the analysis of artistic excellence. But it also had one unfortunate result. Aesthetics was conseived largely in terms of a flat antithesis to the practical. Hence, if the practical realm included the useful and the moral, then the aesthetic became, by the dialectics of the case, useless and nonmoral.
"But another important development was involved—and I believe that here, Mr. Bateson, is where your position would figure. Precisely as the concern with the rhetorical aspects of expression was dropped from the formal study of literature and art, it was informally welcomed elsewhere. The new sciences—such as sociology, social psychology, anthropology, and, now recently, semantics—took in these same fields of inquiry which art theory /aesthetics/ had thrown out. Thus, for instance, with your word 'magic.' Anthropology reaffirmed, in terms of 'magic,' the motive of persuasion that fell into neglect with the neglect of the rhetorical /as the aesthetic stress upon expression had slighted the elements of appeal, communication, and the like./ . . . "
Bateson: "I think I have squashed my own contradiction, with some help from you. Would it be fair to say the Klee

exhibit is even a valid or very intense affirmation of some sort of the proposition: 'Thou shalt not coerce me. I have the right to my own retinal view, and you have the right to your own retinal objective receptiveness,' so that the Klee paintings are on the magical side, inasmuch as he makes that particular affirmation? . . . There is not only no coercion, there is an insistence on non-coercion, which is a step towards the positive."

The Work of Art

Duchamp: "We don't emphasize enough that the work of art is independent of the artist. The work of art lives by itself, and the artist who happened to make it is like an irresponsible medium. No artist can say at any time: 'I am a genius. I am going to paint a masterpiece.'"

Bateson: "Now, Mr. Duchamp, what you are saying is that the artist is the picture's way of getting itself painted. That is a very serious and reasonable thing to say, but it implies that, in some sense, the work of art exists before it is there on canvas."

Duchamp: "Yes, it has to be pulled out."

* * * *

Frankenstein: " . . . I should like to ask Mr. Milhaud if he feels that the creation of works of art in his own case is the result of a mysterious and completely incomprehensible suggestion?"

Milhaud: "Not completely, but there is enough of it. When you start a work, sometimes you feel it is not ready to be started. Why? Because the work is still far away from you. One day, it comes, Why? Because it is ripe."

Bateson: "We have just the same experience with a new scientific theory."

Milhaud: "And even sometimes, as Mr. Duchamp said—and I agree completely—the work guides you. Often a creator, in another work, contradicts himself completely. And thanks be to God! Otherwise, he remains under one label. But he is led, not only by his thought, but by—call it what you like, inspiration, if you are not afraid of such a word. There is the work that guides you too of course, but if you don't have a responsive technique, then it begins to be pretty bad."

Ritchie: "Then, in other words, Mr. Milhaud, the work might run away with itself?"

Milhaud: "Certainly it might. And so much the better, because if it runs away, probably it should not have been started in the first place."

Duchamp: "It is a kind of race between the artist and the work of art."

* * * *

Schoenberg: " . . . In the creation of a work of art, nothing should interfere with the idea. A work of art must elaborate on its own idea and must follow the conditions which this idea establishes."

"This does not mean that an artist must have principles which he obeys and which he carries out under all circumstances. Such principles would probably, in general, be external; and their application would certainly deprive a work of art of its natural condition."

* * * *

Goldwater: " . . . One of the things that psychological science in the 20th century has pointed out most clearly to us is that the well-springs of art are at least nine-tenths

subconscious and so it is perfectly correct that the critic shall see certain things in a work which the artist, in his one-sided passion of creation . . . had no inkling were there.

"And it is a peculiarity of the American artist . . . that he likes to hold on to his work of art after it has been created, instead of allowing it to go its own way—and allowing the public . . . to find in it the total richness and complication of meanings and suggestions and allusions, whether or not the artist originally knew and intended them to be there . . . "

The Artist's Concern with the Public:

Wright: "Does it matter what the reaction of the public is concerning a work of art?"

Milhaud: "Absolutely not."

Wright: "I don't think it really matters."

* * * *

Wright: "I think that he is talking much to himself, and especially if he is trying to talk to 'the public,' he is off his beat . . . "

* * * *

"An artist is not a missionary."

* * * *

Schoenberg: "There is, perhaps, only one principle to which every artist should pay obedience. That is, never bow to the taste of the mediocre—to the taste of minor people who prefer what an artist should never do. This does not mean there does not exist a popular art which has its own viewpoints and its own code of honor, even . . . There is nothing wrong in such creation, but it is wrong for a serious composor to write or include in his works such parts which he feels would please the audience . . . "

* * * *

Tobey: " . . . I would say that the modern artist . . . is trying to maintain his relationship to . . . his inspiration . . . Now, the economic conditions and the low standards . . . come in and try to destroy that contact unconsciously, as do many, many people, including his friends, his relatives, and everybody else. If they can destroy that, they will. They do not know they are destroying it, so he fights to maintain that; and if he doesn't, he is lost, it seems to me . . . "

The Artist and Communication

Burke: " . . . Can't (the artist) create for a communication? Certainly he is not talking to himself, is he? He is using a communicative structure of terms."

* * * *

Tobey: "I think that the artist is not concerned with communication while he is in action; but after he is through, he likes to feel there is a communication from his work. In other words, he is pleased if someone is moved or gets something from it. How can he not be?"

Frankenstein: "May I ask also, if the artist, having completed the work of art, finds in it a degree, or sense of communication, to himself? That is to say, does he find in it especial qualities which he did not know were there during the moment, or at the time of, creation?"

Tobey: "I think that is very special. I think you are right . . . because who can say what we can get out of meditating on a work of art, or who can say how long it will take to digest a work of art? If the thing isn't a work of art, I think it is digested very quickly; but I think that a painting which is a work of art is digested very slowly and must have been lived with a long time."

The Artist as Self-Critic

Burke? "There is the critical function, there is an artistic function. We may treat them as distinct—yet what of an artist who revises his work? What is he doing? Is he not *criticizing* himself? . . . "

* * * *

Duchamp: "You forget that the work of the artist is based on emotion and that the work of the critic is based on an intellectual translation."

* * * *

Burke: " . . . I was trying to show that the distinction between the two processes isn't as sharp as it sometimes appears to be when seen through differences of profession. The important thing is to recognize that a critical function is an integral part of the creative act . . . "

* * * *

" . . . take Mead's notion of the 'generalized other.' When you criticize yourself, you are 'taking the attitude of the other.' You are making allowance for what Freud might call the 'super-ego.' You are thus taking into account a social character. It is not merely yourself. You are 'answering' somebody.
"There is also an internal process: the artist's interaction with his own work in the course of creating it. The drawing of one line becomes a partial determinant for the next line . . . Now, that is not a purely self-critical process, but it is related to the correcting of the work, and there is a likeness between the two processes . . . "
Duchamp: "It's not criticism then."

* * * *

Burke: "I would go back to the Socratic idea of the internal dialogue. Once a complex world has been built up, no one is just talking to himself. Each individual contains several roles of personalities which have been built out of his situation. And he learns how to develop a thought by a process that could be reduced to alternating statements and rejoinders . . . Mead . . . illustrates his point by such examples as this: if you are going to pick up a glass, you anticipate its weight, its resistance to your hand, etc. Thus, there is a kind of criticism implicit in your very act of grasping the glass. The object's 'attitude' will be one of resistance to your way of seizing it. Hence, you grip in accordance with the attitude you anticipate.
"Now, if we apply such a dialectical explanation to account for the producing of a work of art, we find that an artist is not merely expressing himself; he is considering the 'attitude of the other,' he is anticipating objections. There is thus a critical function interwoven with the creative function . . .
"Such a perspective would help bring these two processes together—though I admit that, like everything else in our modern world, they become separated into compartments, through professional specialization . . . "

THE CRITIC
Cultural Circumstances

Goldwater: " . . . One of the characteristics of 19th and 20th century western civilization has been its sense of historicity; and the critic, as well as the contemporary artist, cannot avoid that sense of history . . . I don't know whether it would be going too far to say that, perhaps the critic only comes into existence at the time when this sense of historicity pervades a culture as a whole . . . because he, himself, comes in as a preacher of that sense of the historic."

Frankenstein: " . . . A very important function of criticism is to close the gap, as far as any kind of verbal exercise can, between the creative artist and the public. I believe, personally, that that gap . . . has always existed . . . "
"That means that criticsim is not addressed to the artist, but to the general public . . . "

* * * *

Goldwater: "One of the prime functions of the critic is simply to serve as a method whereby the observer is arrested by a work of art for a longer time than, were he unaided, that work of art could hold his attention . . . "

* * * *

Bateson: " . . . If the critic is to bridge that gap, and to do it by *talking* about the work of art, I have a kind of suspicion that there is a danger of his killing the work of art . . . The emotional kick, the aesthetic experience that comes out of an act, is relatively intense; but it is reduced perhaps to its square root when we *talk* about acting, and to its fourth root, when we talk about talking about acting . . . We say: 'Tout comprendre, c'est tout pardonner' . . . But, perhaps, to understand is merely to feel a little less intensely.
"Now, then, if that is so, there is a case for saying that the critic is a very, very dangerous person—as dangerous as the scientist, and I am one of these. I smell in the critic a fox rather like myself. For me, as a scientist, this is one of the central problems which we have to deal with, the problem of how we are going to discuss such things as human emotion without destroying the life of the emotion. This seems to be a technical scientific problem which is unsolved, but conceivably soluble. And it faces the critic as much as it faces me."

* * * *

Goldwater: " . . . I don't quite see how a critic pointing out the various elements of a work of art . . . can minimize the liking or disliking that the observer will have, once the exploratory lecture is finished . . . "

* * * *

"I think Mr. Bateson . . . would agree that, though it is perhaps true that the critical analysis of a given work of art will weaken the hearing of Mr. Duchamp's 'aesthetic echo' of that particular work at that particular time, an understanding is thereby gained by . . . the layman, to whom the critic is talking, which is useful in opening up avenues . . . that permit the hearing of the 'aesthetic echo' . . . in another work of art at another time . . . "
Bateson: "I feel the matter is more delicate and more complicated . . . I would like to say that, after all, the mind—let's say the mind rather than the material object—

the mind has itself various parts and functions; and the part which we consciously understand, with which we think, in fact, is pretty different from this unconscious part of which we have agreed that the work of art is largely created, and out of which the 'aesthetic echo' springs. And we know that it is exceedingly difficult, in general, to make the thing work backwards . . . The normal dynamics operate when the pressures come from below upward; and it is exceedingly difficult to work it the other way around—to sink what one has learned consciously into unconscious levels . . . "

* * * *

Ritchie: " . . . It seems to me (the critic's) chief role is to present his enthusiasm, and by exciting his public, he may finally bring that public more quickly to the work . . . "

* * * *

Goldwater: " . . . All that the critic is doing is increasing depth and the acuity in the range of public perception."
Ritchie: "I would like to take exception to that . . . What we are doing in the long run is attempting to interest the public finally in the work of art. But with our criticism I don't think we necessarily increase the perception of that public . . . But if we can excite someone to go and look at the work of art, that is our function, and that is all of our function."

* * * *

Wright: "I would like to see (art) . . . put up to the people that really should be allowed to react to these things quite naturally of themselves, and not because they are told, or taught, or somehow fashioned by critics into the shape of appreciation."

Judgement:

Frankenstein: "Criticism can change just as art changes; and it seems to me that, in an older time, criticism was an effort to judge a work of art according to certain external principles, certain basic canons, certain eternal laws. I think that modern art and modern life have taught us that, actually, there are no such things as eternal principles of art . . .
"Criticism has, in the past, attempted to set works of art against principles derived from the experience of previous eras. They never fit, and so criticism has been wrong.
"Contemporary criticism, it seems to me, takes its base on a different level . . . or attitude—the attitude of attempting to discover what the principles of each given work are, and to assay that work on a basis of its own given principles . . . That leaves the critic on fairly slippery ground . . . In other words, the only final court of appeal which modern criticism has to work toward . . . is the general agreement of informed and intelligent people . . .
"If one is completely out of joint with one's time, it is perhaps better not to attempt to interpret one's time. Such interpretation is, after all, the only real function which criticism can serve."

* * * *

Goldwater: "Now, Mr. Frankenstein outlined what seemed to be the function of the critic as an explanatory one, quite apart from any evaluation . . . I think that there were in Mr. Frankenstein's words (omitted from this abstract) however, as you heard them, discrepancies which are all to his credit. You will notice that he referred to the con-

tinuing creative vitality of the world, and he indicated, when he said that, a belief in that vitality. He implied a belief in certain values of contemporary art which undoubtedly influence him in his explanations . . . "

* * * *

Frankenstein: " . . . There is something dreadfully pontifical about a cleavage—good or bad; a simple separating of the sheep from the goats; a simple casting into limbo or exalting into heaven. The contemporary critic is more than likely to express his judgements in a rather roundabout way. You may say that it's a hedge, if you want to, but it is there, I think no less positive—perhaps even more positive—than the clearcut, out-and-out value-judgement would be. And certainly, as Mr. Ritchie suggested, the communication of enthusiasm . . . expresses a value-judgement."
Goldwater: " . . . I would carry that further and say that the enthusiasm must be based on a certain point of view which the critic is generally aware of . . . A complete eclecticism seems to me to be an impossibility. These critics who pretend to complete eclecticism are actually saying that there are things which they do not like but that they would rather not come out and say so."

* * * *

Milhaud: "I am not at all against injustice. I rather like it. I think it is better to really stand for something, even if it is completely a pose . . . "

* * * *

Frankenstein: " . . . An extremely sharp distinction should be made, at least in the critic's own mind, between a confident adverse opinion, and non-comprehension . . . Very frequently . . . non-comprehension will express itself in terms of adverse opinion . . .

* * *

"We lash out in this way when things have been presented for our admiration and we have failed to understand them . . . It is a kind of violent, pathological aberration of the critical sense that is exceedingly easy to spot, and which invariably means that the person involved has not perceived anything at all, but has merely perceived the affront to his own lack of understanding and has let his own egotism and his own limitations stand in the way of letting the work of art do anything for him or to him . . . "

Critic and Artist:
Moderator Boas: "Mr. Wright, what, after all, can an artist learn from a critic?"
Wright: "He can learn the futility of criticism and to avoid the critic by all means in his power."

* * * *

" . . .(the critic) is of no benefit whatever to the artist unless he happens to be some way in the employ of, or subsidized by, the picture dealer with whom he makes and breaks the reputations of almost every painter. Fortunately, he hasn't got around to the architects, but the painters—and the painters, by way of the critic, come under the heel of what is called 'the public.' "

* * * *

Duchamp: "I have no feeling against the critic . . . Criticism against modern art is the natural consequence of the freedom given the artist to express his individualistic view. Moreover, I consider the barometer of opposition a healthy indication of the depth of individual expression. The more hostile the criticism, the more encouraged the artist should be."

* * * *

Goldwater: "Would the artists present admit that . . . however their perception about the works of others has been increased by criticism, that such criticism has, in some way, been useful to them in future creations?"
Milhaud: "I don't think so, because . . . nobody—even the artist himself—knows exactly what is going to come about, and he won't take any element from the past . . . I think complete moral solitude in his field is necessary and healthy."
Duchamp: "I only want to add, in some cases it may have an influence and a bad effect."
Milhaud: "I know, my dear Duchamp, but there is another thing and that is that you also have two kinds of creative artists. There are some who are affected by the critic and some who are not."
Duchamp: "Exactly, it can't really be dismissed so simply as that."
Milhaud: "And I don't know what the point of view is of the one who is affected. I have had criticism for over thirty years and it has never influenced me . . . Sometimes you are astonished to find extremely violent reviews of a work from practically all critics. And then, then years after, everybody says: 'What he is writing now is just nonsense; but that was a beautiful thing we had ten years ago' . . . Why should we bother?"

* * * *

Burke: "I would like to try, if possible, to see whether the critic can make peace with the artist. Could we find a common ground in one respect, one notable respect, by considering the distinctive attribute of man, *qua* man?
"Man is a symbol-using animal . . . We might discern the rudiments of symbolism in domestic animals. A dog's bark might be called a kind of speech. But whereas the dog can bark, it can't bark-about-barking. It can't talk-about-talk. It can't advance to this second level of expression . . . It is at this second level that you come upon the peculiarly human motives.
"We are all, as human beings, on this second level, using systems of symbols. Some systems of symbols are used by scientists, some by philosophers, some by artists, some by critics, etc. Each of these symbolic structures is an organized vocabulary which a man learns to manipulate for purposes of expression, discovery and communication . . . These symbols give us the dignity of ethical standards, they shape our notions of beauty and purpose. Our natural appetites, in their rudimentary simplicity, would be easily satisfied. The great goads to social activity—'ambition' generally—are provided by the vast symbolic structure that has been built above the natural appetites.
"In our situation . . . we may try to plumb the resources of symbols, for guiding conduct, or expressing and communicating our experiences . . . And besides merely exploiting the pragmatic and aesthetic resources of symbols, we must try to peer beyond all symbolism, towards a level of immediate experience that transcends any purely symbolic, or linguistic, structure.
"In this search, there is no fundamental antithesis between the artist and the critic . . . There are many ways of lining up reality, with varying degrees of accuracy and relevance. And the job for us all, I believe, is to scrutinize the work of everyone who is sincerely and earnestly seeking to use symbols . . ."

THE COLLECTOR

Scarcity:

Ritchie: " . . . Not nearly enough people collect pictures and sculpture. Every museum man is aware of the unhealthy concentration of collecting in museums, almost to the exclusion of private collecting . . .
"I know that there are supposedly many economic reasons why more pictures and sculptures are not bought by private individuals. In America, at least, I don't think these economic arguments hold water . . .
"There has been a general tendency in the past few years for museums to attack this problem from another direction . . . The thought has come about that perhaps the private collector needs first to collect, not, shall we say, the higher forms of art, but the more lowly ones; that is to say—furniture and furnishings in the home . . . That explains, I think, the springing up of industrial departments in museums. It is the old pedagogic principle to start first with the familiar . . . If one could encourage a greater understanding of the aesthetic value of these objects, then one might go on from there to painting and sculpture . . . "

———

Market Value:

Duchamp: "The great public, today, is guilty of having introduced as a criterion the quantitative evaluation of the work of art—the market value. People today often buy paintings as an investment. It seems to me that a hundred years ago, fewer painters, fewer collectors, fewer critics and fewer dealers made a little world outside the great public and gave preference to qualitative evaluation —with little or no speculation."

* * * *

Goldwater: "I would just like to add to what Mr. Duchamp said, this opinion: that though I agree with him that there is commercial collecting, and that there is perhaps some dealer influence in taste, it is possible to say that the dealer and such commercial collecting has had only a short-range influence on certain reputations and the personal lives of individual artists. But I doubt very much whether such commercial influences have, as has sometimes been suggested, actually put over on the public or society in general any broad style or direction of contemporary art."

———

The Ideal Collector:

Goldwater: "I wonder if Mr. Duchamp would offer the opinion, which I know he has about collecting, relating the experience of the 'aesthetic echo' to the collector?"
Duchamp: "The collector—the real collector, the one I oppose to the commercial collectors who have made modern art a field comparable to a Wall Street affair . . . . is, in my opinion, an artist—*au carré*. He selects paintings and puts them on his wall; in other words, 'he paints himself a collection.' "

———

THE MUSEUM

Responsibility:

Ritchie: "I am quite convinced that art museums, in general, are doing a more comprehensive job than symphony orchestras or literary publishers in presenting the art of today. For this reason, art museums have taken the brunt of the attack by the conservative element of the public where modern art is concerned. Perhaps if this same public were made more fully aware of comparable experiments in the field of music and literature, the experimental or advanced visual art of today would not so readily be branded queer and unintelligible.

"Certainly, also, if advances in the social and natural sciences were more generally understood, their intellectual and emotional reflections in today's art would be taken for granted. As it is, our critics are quite willing to accept the actuality and the necessity of forward seeking sciences — whether they understand the advances or not—while denying, at the same time, the right of artists to explore new worlds of emotional expression.

"To be sure, there are neo-humanist romantics, who long for a comfortable return to a Hellenic or Renaissance world, glorifying the dignity of man. Their wish to deny all the consequences of the industrial revolution is pathetic; and, in this turbulent post-war period, perhaps understandable. But in the face of all the changes our century has witnessed, it is profoundly unrealistic to set the clock back.

"The overwhelming materialism of our day should be resisted to the best of every man's ability. To be blind to the fact, however, that modern artists, of all people, are the very ones who are putting up the strongest fight against a dominant materialism, is either to be naively innocent of the modern artist's temperament or to wilfully misunderstand his best intentions . . . "

Moderator Boas: "As trustee of a museum, Mr. Ritchie . . . I should like to ask a question myself. It costs us . . . over a hundred thousand dollars every year to show exhibitions to the people of Baltimore. Now, what in the world are we doing it for? . . . I ought to be able to tell you, I realize, but I am asking you to tell me."

Ritchie: "Well, I suppose those of us who are deeply concerned have, whether rightly or wrongly, a missionary sense—that we must bring culture or bring works of art to the public's attention . . . To be sure, there are elements or activities in the museum that appeal only to the few, but any museum that attempts to be a success—that is, a museum that is attempting to get public moneys—must appeal to a wider and wider audience . . . "

Appropriateness:

Wright: " . . . so far as the museum is concerned, it seems to me largely a morgue . . . "

    *   *   *   *

Goldwater: "Haven't you recently designed one?"

Wright: "I am supposed to be designing a mortuary here, but the man didn't want an architect, he wanted a grave-digger."

Goldwater: "I am thinking of a museum."

Ritchie: (to Mr. Wright): "I understand you are building a modern morgue?"

Wright: "No, I am not. I am building, in no sense, a morgue; because I believe the direction of this art which you are calling 'modern art,' and which—as you see exemplified here—is taking an upward trend by way of what is being called, for lack of a better name, the 'non-objective art.' It is a bad name. But I believe that line, form and color are a language in themselves. I think they can best express beauty independently of the physiognomy of any object in nature by way of these very qualities. You can by means of them create amazing refreshment for the human soul and the human mind.

"Now this museum that I have made is . . . in the spirit of this very thing that I have just described and the only home which that veracious thing can have today. The 'non-objective' can't go into the 'static' of these old buildings and live. It can't go into—what do you call this thing—this layer cake we call modern building . . . it must have a new background, a quality, an atmosphere, to go with its art.

"I am creating that new background, and I am creating it for what I believe to be the higher and better life which art is bound to have."

Cultural Function:

Goldwater: "On the one hand, what we are trying to do is to preserve what can be summed up in the word 'aristocratic.' That is to say: the right and the privilege of every artist to express himself completely in his own terms. That is something which the past has had. What we are adding to that is the right and privilege of every person in the public to have access to that art, and, at the same time, to allow that art to exist for itself. We feel defensive when a large audience first tries to approach an unfamiliar form, because we know the audience may be disturbed by this right of the artist to preserve his individuality, to express the world in the way in which he sees it. Unfortunate incidents, have taught us that the audience may even try to destroy the artist's freedom. Therefore, the duty of the middle man, to whom Mr. Wright has referred, be he the museum director or critic, is precisely to preserve and eventually to combine these two rights and privileges."

VILLON   *ABSTRACTION*   *Arensberg Collection*

APPENDIX

LIST OF WORKS EXHIBITED

Artist	Title	Collection
BAZIOTES	THE DWARF	Museum of Modern Art
BRAUNER	PSYCHOLOGICAL SPACE	Mr. and Mrs. Gordon Onslow-Ford
CALDER	THE FOREST IS THE BEST PLACE	California Palace of the Legion of Honor
DE CHIRICO	DELIGHTS OF THE POET	Museum of Modern Art
DALI	AGNOSTIC SYMBOL	Louise and Walter Arensberg
DELVAUX	THE MIRROR	Mr. and Mrs. Gordon Onslow-Ford
DUCHAMP	NUDE DESCENDING THE STAIRCASE	Louise and Walter Arensberg
ERNST	THE TOTTERING WOMAN	Mr. and Mrs. Gordon Onslow-Ford
GRAVES	BIRD AND THE SEA	lent anonymously
HARE	THE DEAD ELEPHANT	San Francisco Museum of Art
HOWARD	FIRST WAR-WINTER	San Francisco Museum of Art
KANDINSKY	IMPROVISATION	Louise and Walter Arensberg
KLEE	DORF CARNIVAL	Louise and Walter Arensberg
DE KOONING	PAINTING, 1948	Museum of Modern Art
LAM	BEAGLE AND GREEN BIRD	Mr. Wright Ludington
LEGER	CONTRAST OF FORMS	Louise and Walter Arensberg
MAGRITTE	THE SIX ELEMENTS	Louise and Walter Arensberg
MAGRITTE	THE PORTRAIT	Mr. and Mrs. Gordon Onslow-Ford
MATISSE	PORTRAIT OF MLLE. LANDSBERG	Louise and Walter Arensberg
MATISSE	WOMAN WITH A HAT	Mr. and Mrs. Walter A. Haas
MATTA	(untitled)	Mr. and Mrs. Gordon Onslow-Ford
MATTA	DISPLACED CONTINENT	Mr. Wright Ludington
MIRO	THE HERMITAGE	Louise and Walter Arensberg
MIRO	PERSON THROWING A STONE AT A BIRD	Museum of Modern Art
MONDRIAN	ABSTRACTION, 1919	Louise and Walter Arensberg
MONDRIAN	COMPOSITION, 1925	Museum of Modern Art
MONDRIAN	ABSTRACTION, 1936	Louise and Walter Arensberg
MOORE	RECLINING FIGURE	Mrs. and Mrs. Gordon Onslow-Ford
PAALEN	TROPICAL NIGHT	Mr. and Mrs. Gordon Onslow-Ford
PICASSO	SEATED FIGURE OF A WOMAN	Louise and Walter Arensberg
PICASSO	GIRL BEFORE A MIRROR	Museum of Modern Art
POLLOCK	GUARDIANS OF THE SECRET	San Francisco Museum of Art
ROTHKO	SLOW SWIRL AT THE EDGE OF THE SEA	San Francisco Museum of Art
SHEELER	CACTUS	Louise and Walter Arensberg
STAMOS	SOUNDS IN THE ROCK	Museum of Modern Art
STILL	(untitled)	lent by the artist
SUTHERLAND	PALM PALISADE	Mr. Wright Ludington
TANGUY	SLOWLY TOWARD THE NORTH	Museum of Modern Art
TOBEY	ELECTRIC NIGHT	lent by the artist
TOBEY	MOCKERS--2	lent by the artist
VILLON	ABSTRACTION, 1932	Louise and Walter Arensberg

A special exhibition of modern art was assembled for the event and shown concurrently at the San Francisco Museum of Art, where the meetings were held.

MAGRITTE   *THE PORTRAIT*   Onslow-Ford Collection

MONET

Illustrations on p. 37–39 relate to comments made in the progress of the conference.

LIPCHITZ

INTRODUCTION TO THE ILLUSTRATIONS

The collecting of these illustrations was begun by us in 1949, at the start of the 57th Street exhibition season; and they are in the main restricted to 1949–50. Despite our plans for an annual covering of each exhibiting season, it turned out not to be possible—for technical, as well as more personal reasons—to publish a modern annual within the year. The completed records were somewhat enlarged towards a biennial—a more practical method for us of reporting the modern aspect of art in America.

Since then the scene continues to change, with the modern aspect better, if haphazardly reported. Thus though this volume bears the mark of its date in a few respects, it is of value for its orderly documentation and completeness. And since what is continually needed is a systematic and sympathetic treatment of our chosen area, avant-garde art in America, we intend to document similarly the seasons of 1950–51 and 1951–52 in the second series of Modern Artists in America, *in which other artists will appear in turn. Had it been our intention to reproduce only those artists by whose work we are especially moved, they would have been fewer, and the proportions different; had our intention been wholly critical and analytical, concentrated on the problems of modern art in America, rather than documentary, the emphasis likewise would have shifted—even so, there is perhaps too much of the non-figurative. Still, this is where "the pressure of reality," in Wallace Stevens' phrase, has led the majority of our most imaginative and fertile artists: "It is not that there is a new imagination but that there is a new reality." To this might be added his preceding remarks: "It is one of the peculiarities of the imagination that it is always at the end of an era. What happens is that it is always attaching itself to a new reality, and adhering to it." It is this new reality, as it appears, that we want to document.*

Selection of contemporary works of art, whether for exhibition or reproduction, is neither easy nor simple. And though it may be thankless, if not worse, in this instance, it has seemed to be an essential step—regardless of personal vanities or professional pique. Plainly an honest attempt to picture the modern aspect of painting and sculpture on 57th Street can gain from the stress of limitation and elimination, since two or three national magazines report all exhibitions. We are concerned with the modern aspect. It is odd that this effort to bring some order into the situation should come not from critics or scholars, but from practising artists; still, this may have its good side.

Robert Motherwell
Ad Reinhardt
New York City, Fall, 1951

MIRO *MAN WITH A PIPE* (*1934*) *Dec. 1949* *Matisse Gallery*

41

MONDRIAN *TREE (1912) Nov. 1949 Janis Gallery*

THE SEA (1913)

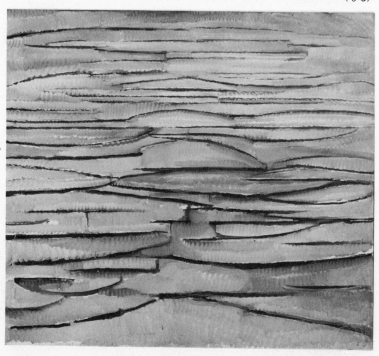

COMPOSITION (1914)

COMPOSITION (1919)

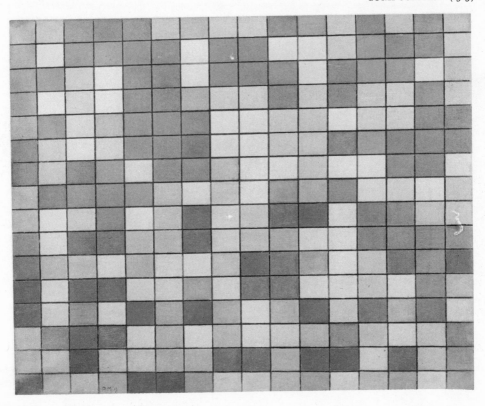

43

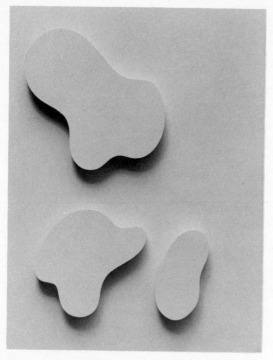

ARP *RELIEF* (*1932*) *Oct. 1949 Janis Gallery*

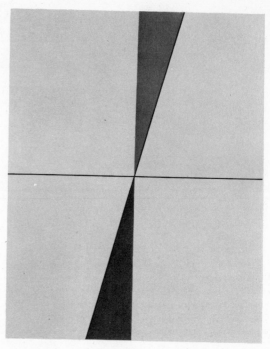

TAEUBER-ARP *POINTE SUR POINTE* (*1931*)

PICABIA *EDTAONISL* (*1913*) *Feb. 1950 Fried Gallery*

KANDINSKY *PAYSAGE* (*1913*) *Dec. 1949 Janis Gallery*

MOHOLY-NAGY *SPHERES (1923) Fried Gallery*

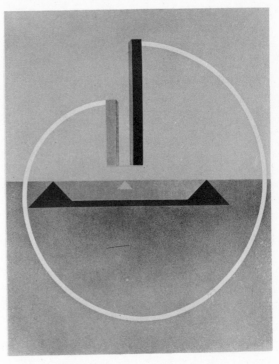

LISSITZKY *PRAUN 98 Oct. 1949 Fried Gallery*

MASSON *LA CAMARQUE (1949) Nov. 1949 Buchholz Gallery*

TORRES-GARCIA *PINTURA CONSTRUCTIVA (1943)*
March 1950 Janis Gallery

45

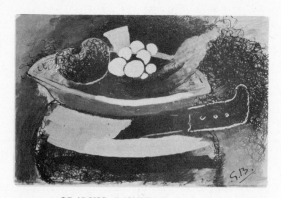

BRAQUE *GRAPHIC PAINTING*

Nov. 1949   Hugo Gallery

GLEIZES *LA FEMME A LA CUISINE* (*1911*)

Oct. 1949   Passedoit Gallery

GRIS *L'HOMME AU CAFE* (*1914*)

Jan. 1950   Buchholz Gallery

LE FAUCONNIER *THE HUNTSMAN* (*1911*)

Neumann Gallery

MATISSE *STILL LIFE* (1947) *Matisse Gallery*

PICASSO *NATURE MORTE* (1944) *Jan. 1950* *Carré Gallery*

47

VAN GOGH, *SELF-PORTRAIT*   *Metrop. Museum of Art*

ROUAULT   *LA PETITE PAGE* (1937)   *Oct. 1949   Perls Gallery*

KLEE   THE CROOKED MOUTH AND THE LIGHT
GREEN EYES OF MRS. B.   (1925)

Museum of Modern Art 1950

JEAN DUBUFFET *Jan. 1950* *Matisse Gallery*

MUNCH *SUMMER NIGHT* (1895) *June 1950* *Museum of Modern Art*

49

NICOLAS DESTAËL

MAURICE ESTÈVE

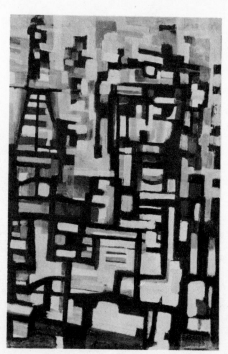

ANDRÉ LANSKOY

JEAN BAZAINE

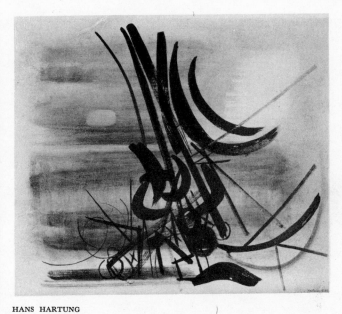

HANS HARTUNG

CHARLES LAPIQUE

BERNARD BUFFET   *Dec. 1949   Kleemann Gallery*

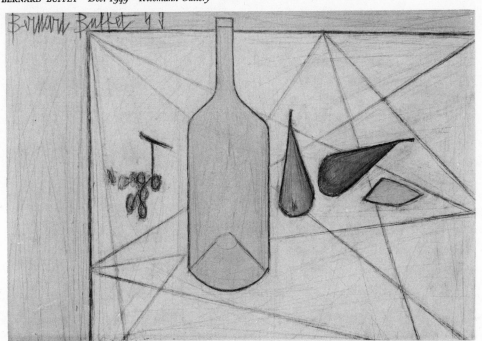

ARSHILE GORKY   *MEMORIAL SHOW*   *March 1950*   *Kootz Gallery*

HANS HOFMANN *Nov. 1949 Kootz Gallery*

ROBERT MOTHERWELL *Oct. 1949 Kootz Gallery*

53

ROLLIN CRAMPTON   *Woodstock Art Conference Show   1950*

AD REINHARDT   *Oct. 1949   Parsons Gallery*

WELDON KEES   *Nov. 1949   Peridot Gallery*

MARK TOBEY   *Nov. 1949   Willard Gallery*

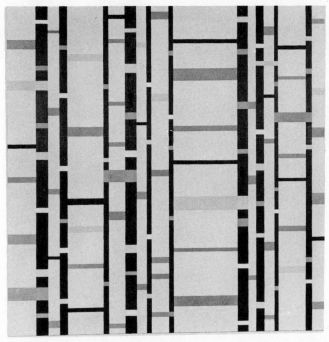

BURGOYNE DILLER   *Nov. 1949   Fried Gallery*

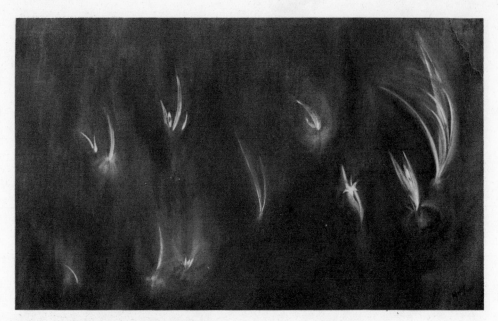

LOREN MACIVER *Oct. 1949 Matisse Gallery*

GEORGE MCNEIL *Feb. 1950 Egan Gallery*

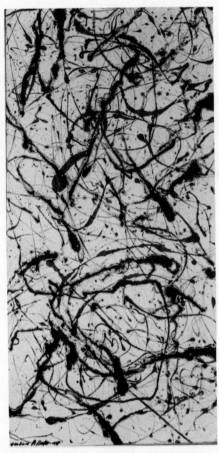

JACKSON POLLOCK *Nov. 1949 Parsons Gallery*

BARNETT NEWMAN *Feb. 1950 Parsons Gallery*

NORMAN LEWIS *Mar. 1950 Willard Gallery*

JAMES CORNELL   *Dec. 1949   Egan Gallery*

JOHN MARIN   *Feb. 1950   American Place*

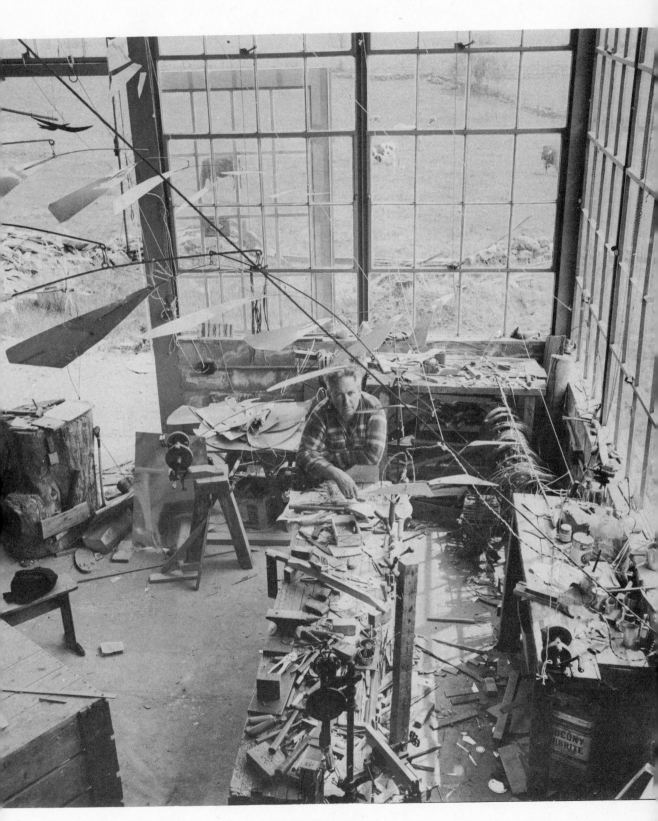

ALEXANDER CALDER

BRADLEY TOMLIN   *May 1950   Parsons Gallery*

REUBEN TAM   *Nov. 1949   Downtown Gallery*

HARRY HOLTZMAN   *1950   Yale University*

MARK ROTHKO *Jan. 1950 Parsons Gallery*

RALPH ROSENBORG *Jan. 1950 Seligmann Gallery*

61

FRITZ BULTMAN   *Feb. 1950   Hugo Gallery*

ADOLPH GOTTLIEB   *Jan. 1950   Kootz Gallery*

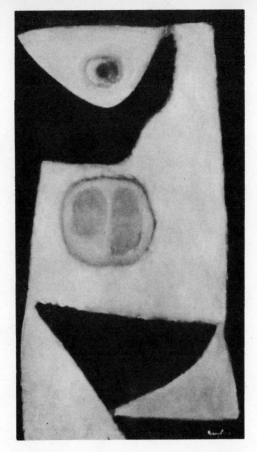

WILLIAM BAZIOTES   *Feb. 1950   Kootz Gallery*

JIMMY ERNST   *Mar. 1950   Laurel Gallery*

ILYA BOLOTOWSKY *Apr. 1950 Fried Gallery*

JAMES BROOKS *Mar. 1950 Peridot Gallery*

LYONEL FEININGER   *Apr. 1950   Buchholz Gallery*

GEORGE CAVALLON   *Mar. 1950   American Abstract Artists Annual*

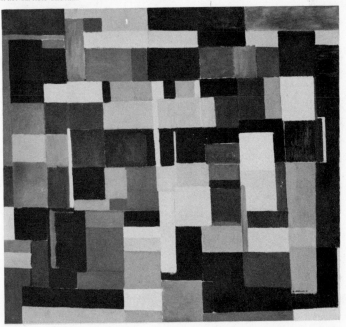

CLYFFORD STILL   *April 1950   Parsons Gallery*

RICHARD POUSETTE-DART   *April 1950   Parsons Gallery*

BUFFIE JOHNSON *Apr. 1950 Parsons Gallery*

GERALD KAMROWSKI *May 1950 Hugo Gallery*

HEDDA STERNE *Feb. 1950 Parsons Gallery*

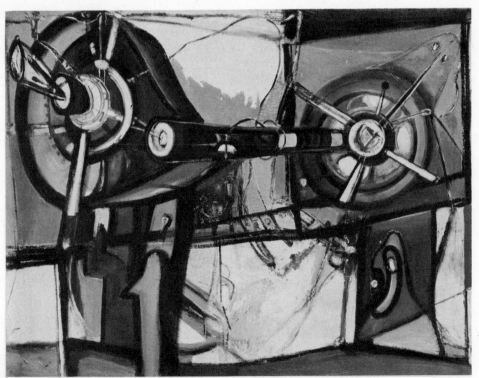

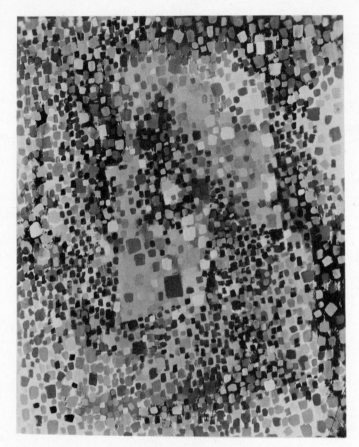

ROBERT JAY WOLFF   *Mar. 1950*   *Museum of Non-Objective Art*

MAURICE GOLUBOV   *Mar. 1950*   *Artists' Gallery*

THEODORE STAMOS   *Dec. 1949*   *Parsons Gallery*

FRITZ GLARNER *1950 Museum of Modern Art*

JOSEF ALBERS *Cincinnati Art Museum 1950*

WILLIAM DE KOONING *Venice Biennale 1950*

MICHAEL LOEW *Nov. 1949 Artists' Gallery*

BALCOMB GREENE *Apr. 1950 B. Schaefer Gallery*

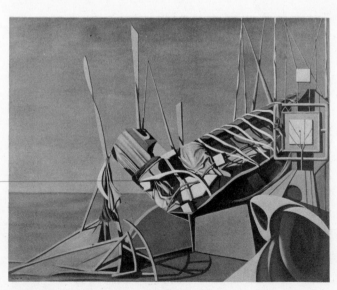

KAY SAGE *Mar. 1950 Viviano Gallery*

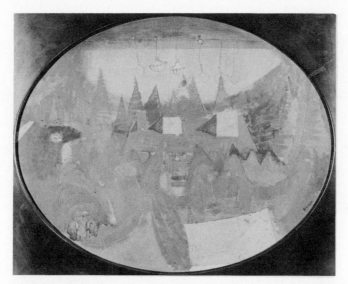

LEE GATCH   *Apr. 1950   Neumann Gallery*

ANTHONY TONEY   *Oct. 1949   A. C. A. Gallery*

MAX SPIVAK *May 1950 Hacker Gallery*

LEE MULLICAN *Feb. 1950 Willard Gallery*

STANLEY HAYTER   *Mar. 1950   Perspectives Gallery*

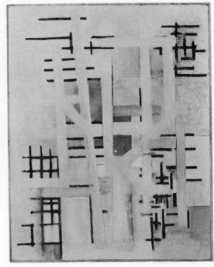

JEAN XCERON   *June 1950   Janis Gallery*

GEORGE L. K. MORRIS   *Mar. 1950   American Abstract Artists Annual*

STUART DAVIS *Virginia Museum* *1950*

KARL KNATHS *Brooklyn Museum* *1949*

A. E. GALLATIN *Jan. 1950 Fried Gallery*   CAMERON BOOTH *Mar. 1950 B. Schaefer Gallery*

YVES TANGUY *Dec. 1949 Matisse Gallery*

KURT SELIGMANN   *1950   Durlacher*

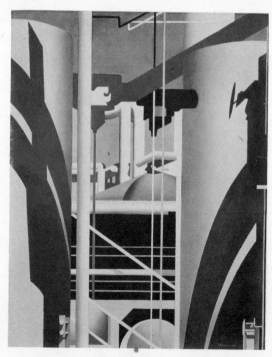

CHARLES SHEELER   *Brooklyn Museum   1949*

NILES SPENCER   *Apr. 1950*   *Downtown Gallery*

CHARLES HOWARD   *1950*   *San Francisco*

RICHARD DIEBENKORN   *Sante Fe, New Mexico   1950*

FRANZ KLINE   *1950   Kootz Gallery*

ALFRED RUSSELL   *Apr. 1950   Peridot Gallery*

EDWARD CORBETT *July 1950 Studio Gallery, Berkeley, Calif.*

FRANK LOBDELL *San Francisco 1950*

HASSEL SMITH *San Francisco 1950*

79

PHILIP GUSTON *1950 Peridot Gallery*

ELMER BISCHOF *1950 San Francisco*

JAMES B. DIXON *1950 San Francisco*

80

WILFREDO LAM *Mar. 1950* *Matisse Gallery*

RALSTON CRAWFORD *Mar. 1950* *Downtown Gallery*

ROBERT DINERO *Talent 1950* *Kootz Gallery*

REGINALD POLLACK *June 1950   Peridot Gallery*

RAYMOND PARKER *New Talent   Museum of Modern Art*

SONIA SEKULA *Artists Under 35   Metropolitan Museum*

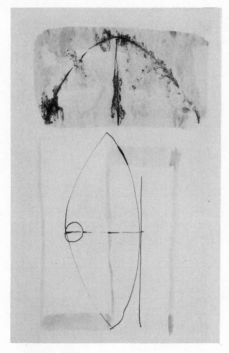

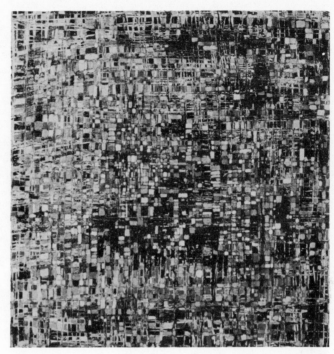

ROBERT NICKLE

CATHERINE HINKLE

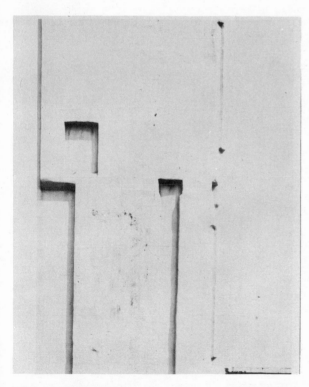

WILLIAM DIFFENDERFER

MARTHA HOSKINS

CARL HOLTY *1950 Neumann Gallery*

HARRY BOWDEN *1950 San Francisco*

84

ESTEBAN VINCENTE *Talent 1950 Kootz Gallery*

GRACE BORGENICHT *Mar. 1950 Laurel Gallery*

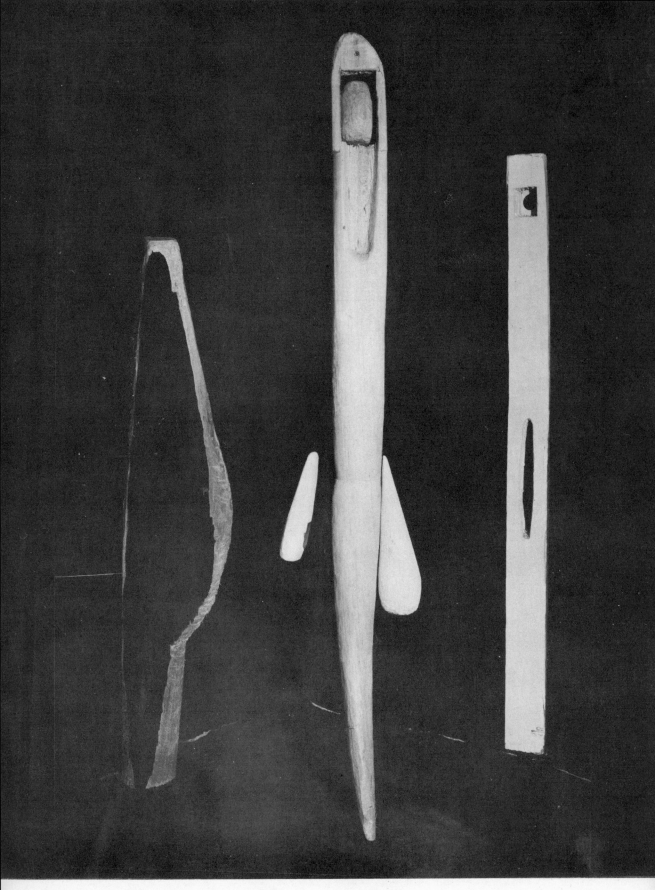

LOUISE BOURGEOIS   *Oct. 1949   Peridot Gallery*

MARY CALLERY *Mar. 1950 Buchholz Gallery*

THEODORE ROSZAK *Museum of Modern Art 1950*

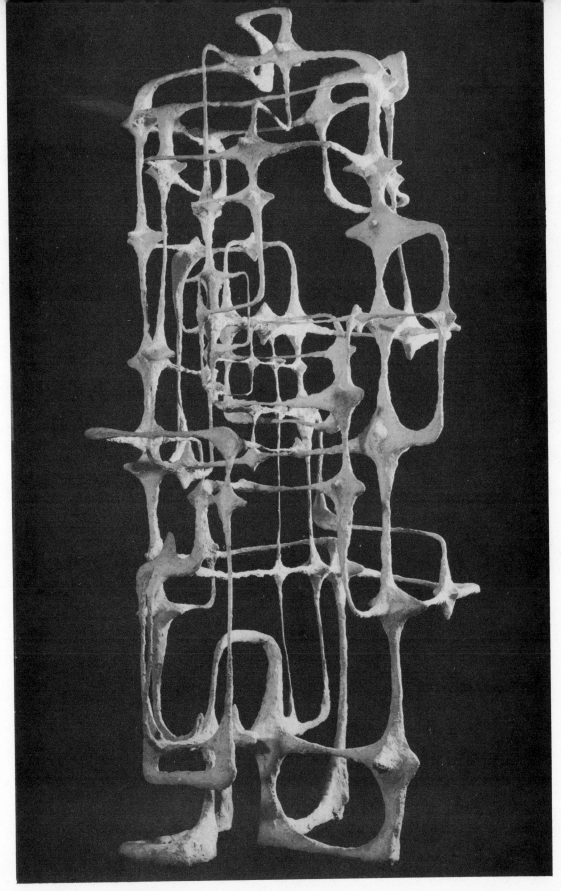

IBRAM LASSAW   *American Abstract Artists   Paris   1950*

ISAMU NOGUCHI   *MAGIC* *May 1950*   *Perspectives Gallery*

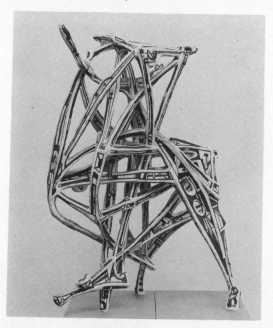

MIRKO   *Apr. 1950*   *Viviano Gallery*

HERBERT KALLEM *Dec. 1949 Roko Gallery*

GUITOU KNOOP   *Dec. 1949   Parsons Gallery*

HELEN PHILLIPS   *Petit Palais   Paris   1950*

HERBERT FERBER *Mar. 1950 Parsons Gallery*

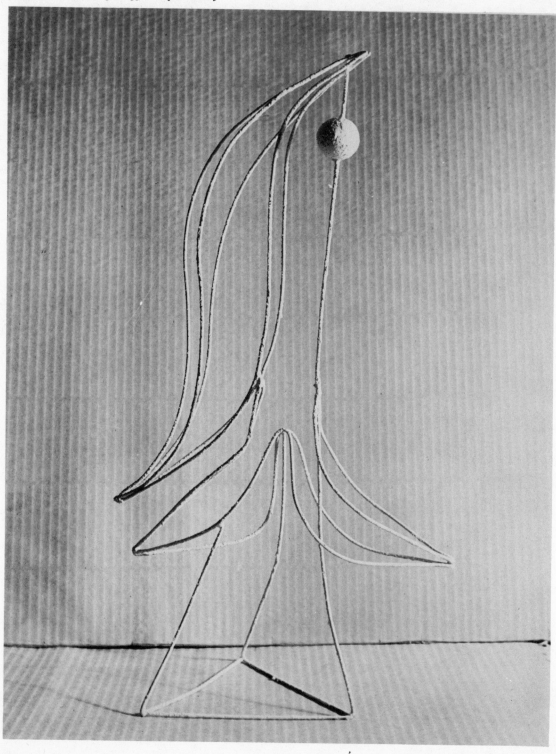

DAVID SMITH *May 1950* *Willard Gallery*

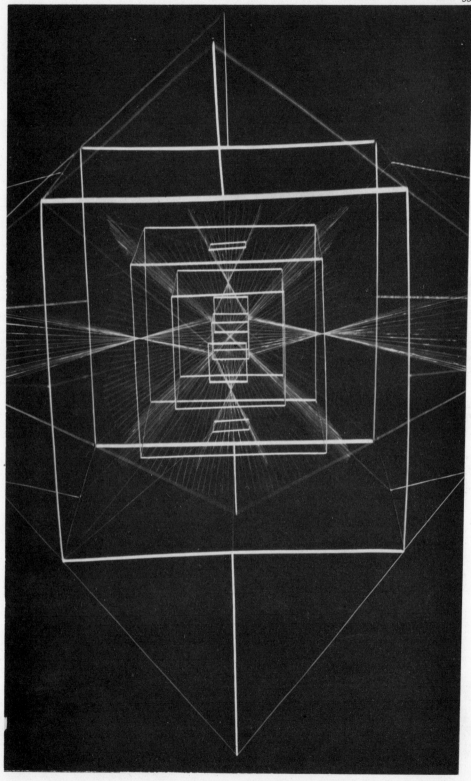

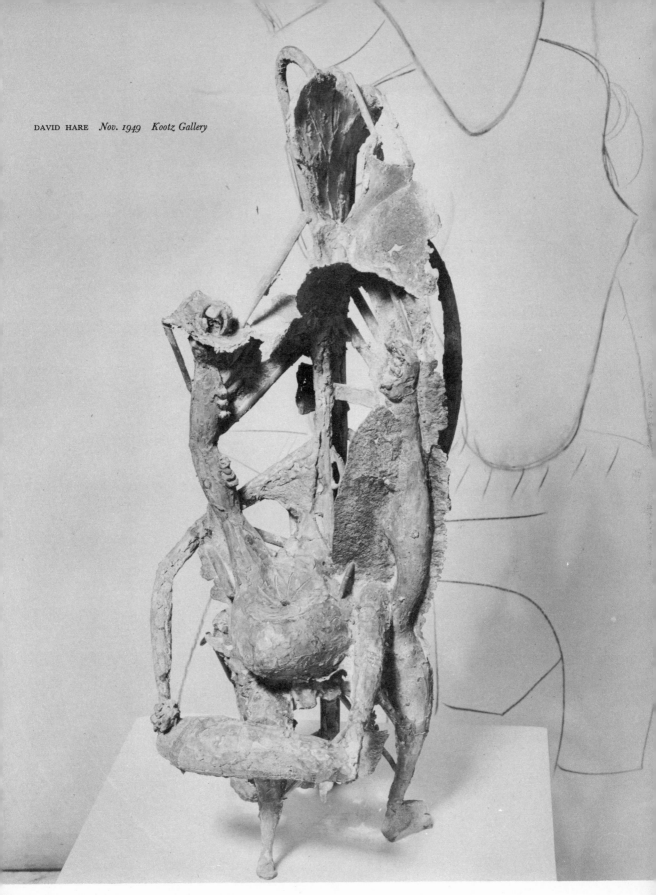

DAVID HARE *Nov. 1949 Kootz Gallery*

EXHIBITIONS

OF ARTISTS IN NEW YORK

GALLERIES

FALL 1949 — WINTER 1950

Note: The symbols used indicate medium as follows:
P Painter;   S Sculptor;   D Draughtsman;
G Graphic Artist.   Where not specified,
the mediums are mixed or unidentified.

Abadi, Fritzie	(P)	Van Diemen-Lilienfeld	Dec 2-15 '49
Abanavas, Constantine	(P)	Contemporary Arts	Jan 2-20 '50
Abbott, Mary	(G)	Ferargil	Apr 24-May 8 '50
Abrams, Ruth	(P)	ACA	Nov 6-25 '50
Adams, Robert	(S)	Passedoit	Apr 3-29 '50
Afro	(P)	Viviano	May 9-June 3 '50
Aguilar		Hugo	Dec 5-31 '49
Albert, Calvin	(S)	Laurel	Nov 6-25 '50
Albrizio, Humbert	(S)	Kraushaar	Nov 13-Dec 2 '50
Alcopley, Lewin	(P)	Pyramid	Feb 9-28 '50
		Passedoit	Nov 20-Dec 2 '50
Allen, Laura Jean		Friedman	May 1-31 '50
Allen, James	(P)	Rehn	Oct 2-21 '50
Ambellan, Harold		Salpeter	Jan 23-Feb 11 '50
Amen, Irving	(G & S)	Argent	Oct 10-22 '49
Amino, Leo	(S)	Clay Club	Oct 23-Nov 29 '49
Anliker, Roger	(P)	Seligmann	Oct 2-21 '50
Arnould, Reynold	(P)	Durand-Ruel	Oct 15-31 '49
Arp, Jean	(P)	Janis	Jan 30-Feb 25 '50
Arpels, Claude		Barzansky	Dec 19-31 '49
Arthur, Revington	(P)	Luyber	Nov 1-19 '49
Ashby, Carl		Pyramid	Feb 9-28 '50
Ault, George		Milch	Jan 30-Feb 18 '50
Auric, Nora	(P)	Hugo	Nov 1-30(?) '50
Austin, Darrel	(P)	Perls	Oct 2-28 '50
Avery, Milton	(P)	Knoedler	June 15-July 15 '50
		Rosenberg	Dec 4-30 '50
Baizerman, Eugenie	(P)	Artists'	Oct 14-Nov 9 '50
Balish, Leonard		Creative	Nov 27-Dec 9 '50
Banks, Virginia	(P)	Grand Central	Mar 7-28 '50
Barker, Kit	(P)	Weyhe	Dec 26-Jan 23 '50
Barnet, Will	(P)	Bertha Schaefer	Oct 17-Nov 5 '49
		Seligmann	Nov 25-Dec 16 '50
Bartlett, Clay	(P)	Macbeth	Oct 10-29 '49
Baskerville, Charles		Ferargil	Dec 12-31 '49
Battaglia, Joseph		Peter Cooper	Dec 6 '50-Jan 8 '51
Baylinson, A. S.	(P)	Laurel	Nov 14-30 '49
Baziotes, William	(P)	Kootz	Feb 7-27 '50
Beal, Gifford		Kraushaar	Apr 3-22 '50
Bean, John		Creative	Dec 12-31 '49
Becker, Maurice		ALA	Oct 31-Nov 19 '49
	(G)	Greiss	Apr 22-May 20 '50
Beckmann, Max	(G & D)	Brooklyn Museum	Oct 11-Nov 27 '49
	(P)	Buchholz	Oct 18-Nov 5 '49
Behl, Wolfgang	(S)	Bertha Schaefer	Oct 23-Nov 11 '50
Bejar, Chano	(P)	Eggleston	Dec 5-17 '49
Bellows, George	(G)	Allison	Dec 4-30 '50
Bemelmans, Ludvig	(P)	Ferargil	Oct 30-Nov 12 '50
Benn, Ben	(P)	Artists'	Oct 29-Nov 17 '49

Bennett, Rainey	(P)	Downtown	Dec 3-31 '49
Beny, Rolof	(G)	Knoedler	May 22-June 9 '50
Ben-Zion		Van Loen	?
Berlowe, Yvette	(P)	Eggleston	Oct 10-22 '49
Berman, Eugene	(P)	Knoedler	Nov 7-26 '49
Bernheimer, Franz	(P)	Argent	April 3-15 '50
Berresford, Virginia	(P)	Levitt	Jan 10-31 '50
Bertram, Abel,	(P)	Brandt	Feb 1-28 '50
Bess, Forrest	(P)	Betty Parsons	Dec 18 '50-Jan 6 '51
Betsberg, Ernestine		Grand Central	Nov 6-21 '50
Biala, Janice	(P)	Carstairs	Feb 7-25 '50
Biddle, George	(P)	Luyber	April 3-29 '50
Bishop, Ben		Charles-Fourth	April 14-May 5 '50
Blackburn, Morris		Luyber	Oct 23-Nov 11 '50
Blaine, Irina	(P)	Eggleston	Nov 7-19 '49
Blair, Streeter	(P)	Carlebach	Oct 23-Nov 11 '50
Blanch, Arnold	(P)	AAA	Oct 3-22 '49
		AAA	Apr 17-May 6 '50
Blatas, Arbit		AAA	Jan 9-28 '50
Bloch, Herbert (Herbloch)	(P)	AAA	May 24-June 10 '50
Block, Dorothy	(P)	Copain	Sept 1-Oct 2 '49
		Copain	Nov 17-Dec 8 '50
Bloom, Martin		Pyramid	Nov 15-Dec 4 '49
Bluestein, Selma	(P)	Artists'	May 25-June 14 '50
Blum, Edith	(P)	Albatross	Apr 10-22 '50
Bodin, Paul	(P)	Laurel	Oct 18-Nov 4 '50
Bodnar, Bertalan	(P)	Binet	Apr 29-May 12 '50
Bohrod, Aaron	(P)	AAA	Dec 5-24 '49
Bolotowsky, Ilya		Pinacotheca	Apr 3-22 '50
Bomar, Bill	(P)	Weyhe	Oct 3-Nov 3 '49
Booth, Cameron	(P)	Bertha Schaefer	Mar 6-Apr 1 '50
Borgenicht, Grace	(P)	Laurel	Mar 11-24 '50
Bosa, Louis	(P)	Kleeman	May 1-31 '50
Bosco, Alfred R.		Friedman	Oct 1-31 '49
Bourgeois, Louise	(S)	Peridot	Oct 3-29 '49
		Peridot	Oct 2-28 '50
Boyko, Fred S.	(P)	Newton	Nov 1-12 '49
Braque, Georges	(P)	Rosenberg	Oct 24-Nov 12 '49
		Rosenberg	Nov 13-Dec 2 '50
Brauner, Victor	(P)	Perspectives	June 13-30 '50
Breeze, Thomas	(P)	Eggleston	Sept 26-Oct 1 '49
Brenson, Theodore	(P)	Newcomb-Macklin	Dec 5-17 '49
Brett, Dorothy		American-British	Mar 27-Apr 15 '50
Brisman, Charles		Eggleston	Dec 4-18 '50
Brittain, Miller	(P)	Binet	Sept 25-Oct 6 '50
Brooks, James	(P)	Peridot	Mar 27-Apr 22 '50
		Peridot	Nov 27-Dec 23 '50
Brown, Carlyle	(P)	Viviano	Nov 14-Dec 2 '50
Browne, Byron	(P)	Grand Central	Feb 21-Mar 4 '50
		Kootz	May 16-June 5 '50
Browne, George	(P)	Grand Central	Feb 14-25 '50

Bruce, Patrick	(P)	Rose Fried	Nov 20-Dec 31 '50
Buffet, Bernard	(P)	Kleeman	Feb 1-28 '50
Bunce, Louis	(P)	Museum of Modern Art	Nov 28-Jan 14 '51
Burchard, Pablo		Bodley	Oct 23-Nov 11 '50
Burchfield, Charles	(P)	Rehn	Apr 10-May 10 '50
Burliuk, David	(P)	ACA	Nov 7-26 '49
Butchkes, Sydney		Friedman	Dec 1-20 '49
Buzzelli, Joseph		Ferargil	Apr 3-15 '50
Cadmus, Paul	(P)	Midtown	Nov 22-Dec 17 '49
Caggle, Charles		Ferargil	Apr 10-22 '50
Calder, Alexander	(S)	Buchholz	Nov 30-Dec 17 '49
Calfee, William	(P)	Weyhe	Dec 5 '49-Jan 4 '50
Callery, Mary	(S)	Buchholz	Mar 14-Apr 2 '50
Campbell, Gretna	(P)	Pyramid	Mar 22-Apr 12 '50
		Artists'	Nov 11-30 '50
Campbell, H. E. Ogden		Little	Aug 1-31 '50
Carewe, Sylvia	(P)	ACA	Oct 9-28 '50
Carreno, Mario		New School	Jan 18-Feb 8 '50
Carton, Norman		Laurel	Oct 9-27 '49
Casanova, Manuel	(P)	Newcomb-Macklin	Nov 8-14 '50
Cerra, Merta		New School	June 8-22 '50
Chagall, Marc	(P)	Van Loen	Sept 15-Oct 15 '50
Chastel, Roger	(G)	Pierre Berès	Sept 27-Oct 18 '50
Chavez, Edward	(P)	AAA	Sept 18-Oct 7 '50
Chiao Ssu-Tu	(P)	St. Etienne	Feb 18-Mar 1 '50
Childs, Frederick		Passedoit	May 1-13 '50
Chochon, André	(P)	American-British	May 22-June 10 '50
Churgin, Leo	(P)	Roko	Nov 14-Dec 3 '49
Cikovsky, Nicolai		AAA	Oct 3-22 '49
Citron, Minna	(P)	Van Diemen-Lilienfeld	Apr 27-May 10 '50
	(G)	New School	Oct 16-30 '50
Clarke, Allan Hugh	(P)	Feigl	Sept 26-Oct 11 '50
Cohen, Hy	(P)	ACA	Dec 12-31 '49
Congdon, William	(P)	Betty Parsons	Apr 17-May 6 '50
Connelly, Brian	(P)	American-British	Nov 2-18 '50
Conover, Garrett B.		Eggleston	Jan 23-Feb 4 '50
Conover, Robert	(P)	Laurel	Feb 25-Mar 10 '50
Constant, George		Ferargil	Mar 27-Apr 8 '50
Constantopoulos		Hugo	Mar 21-April 11 '50
Cook, Lulu Rathbun	(P)	Eggleston	Dec 19-31 '49
Cooper, Rudolf	(P)	Carlebach	May 22-June 15 '50
Corbellini, Luigi	(P)	Portraits	Nov 28-Dec 22 '50
Cornell, Joseph	(S)	Egan	Dec 1-31 '49
		Egan	June 1-24 '50
		Egan	Dec 1 '50-Jan 13 '51
Cotton, Lillian	(P)	Pen & Brush	Jan 23-Feb 9 '50
Cowles, Russell	(P)	Kraushaar	Mar 13-Apr 1 '50
Cramer, Belle	(P)	Van Diemen-Lilienfeld	Mar 9-22 '50

Crane, Stanley W.		Grand Central	Apr 25-May 6 '50
Craske, John W.		American-British	Dec 5-23 '49
Crawford, Ralston	(P)	Downtown	Jan 31-Feb 18 '50
Crespi, Pachita	(P)	Ferargil	Nov 28-Dec 10 '49
Crite, Allan Rohan	(P)	Village Art	Apr 2-9 '50
Crowell, Lucius	(P)	Ferargil	Mar 13-25 '50
Cusumano, Stefano	(P)	Binet	Apr 20-May 15 '50
Cuthbert, Virginia		Contemporary Arts	Oct 31-Nov 18 '49
Dacey, William	(P)	Artists'	June 15-30 '50
Dali, Salvador	(P)	Carstairs	Nov 27 '50-Jan 10 '51
Daly, Norman		Bertha Schaefer	Feb 13-Mar 4 '50
Danzig, Rose	(P)	ALA	Dec 19 '49-Jan 7 '50
Darie	(P)	Carlebach	Oct 25-Nov 5 '49
Davis, Gladys Rockmore	(P)	Midtown	Oct 25-Nov 19 '49
Debree, Oliver		Perspectives	Jan 31-Feb 25 '50
Degas, Edgar	(S)	Silberman	Mar 1-Apr 30 '50
	(P & D)	Rosenberg	Oct 3-22 '49
De Geofroy, Henry	(P)	Demotte	Feb 10-Mar 18 '50
Delaney, Beauford	(P)	Roko	Jan 15-Feb 9 '50
Delbos, Julius		Ferargil	Nov 29-Dec 10 '49
De Martini, Joseph	(P)	Macbeth	Mar 27-Apr 15 '50
De Mejo, Oscar		Carlebach	Oct 4-31 '49
Demonchy, André	(P)	Knoedler	Sept 26-Oct 15 '49
		Knoedler	Sept 18-Oct 15 '50
Demuth, Charles	(P)	Museum of Modern Art	Mar 8-June 11 '50
		Downtown	July 4-28 '50
De Diego, Julio	(P)	AAA	Jan 23-Feb 11 '50
De Voll, F. Usher		Newcomb-Macklin	Mar 20-Apr 1 '50
Di Benedetto, Angelo	(P)	Carlebach	Apr 22-May 6 '50
Dienes, Sari	(P)	Betty Parsons	Nov 6-25 '50
Di Gioia, Frank	(P)	Perls	Jan 30-Feb 25 '50
Diller, Burgoyne	(P)	Pinacotheca	Nov 7-Dec 1 '49
Dobkin, Alexander		ACA	May 8-27 '50
Dodd, Lamar	(P)	Luyber	Oct 2-21 '49
Dohanos, Steven	(P)	Grand Central	Jan 31-Feb 11 '50
Domareki, Joseph	(S)	Contemporary Arts	Nov 6-24 '50
Donati, Enrico	(P)	Rosenberg	Oct 23-Nov 11 '50
Dozier, Otis		Levitt	Mar 27-Apr 15 '50
Drechsler, Leon		Village Art	Dec 18 '49-Jan 6 '50
Drexler, Arthur	(P)	Peridot	Nov 27-Dec 23 '50
Drumlevitch, Seymour	(P)	Museum of Modern Art	Apr 28-June 7 '50
Dubin, Lillian		Bertha Schaefer	May 14-June 2 '50
Dubin, Ralph	(P)	Charles-Fourth	Jan 6-Feb 2 '50
Dubuffet, Jean	(P)	Matisse	Jan 10-28 '50
Duer, Henrietta	(P)	Argent	May 1-13 '50
Dufy, Raoul	(P)	Perls	Oct 30-Nov 25 '50
Duke, Margaret		Ferargil	Oct 31-Nov 12 '49

Eaton, Myrwyn	(P)	Binet	Nov 4-24 '50
Edmiston, Henry	(P)	Milch	Oct 24-Nov 12 '49
Eichenberg, Fritz	(G)	New School	Oct 10-21 '49
Eilshemuis, Louis M.		Kleeman	Feb 1-28 '50
Elser, Elizabeth	(S)	Binet	Apr 10-28 '50
Ember, Oscar		Barbizon-Plaza	Dec 1 '49-Jan 1 '50
Emerson, Ruth Van Cleve		Newcomb-Macklin	Apr 3-15 '50
England, Paul	(P & S)	Bodley	May 22-June 17 '50
Enser, John	(P)	Grand Central	May 9-19 '50
Epstein, Joshua	(P)	Van Diemen-Lilienfeld	Sept 29-Oct 12 '50
Erlanger, Elizabeth	(P)	Marquie	Dec 12-31 '49
Ernst, Jimmy	(G)	Laurel	Mar 25-Apr 7 '50
Ernst, Max	(P)	Perspectives	June 13-30 '50
		Hugo	Nov 7-Dec 31 '50
Esman, Betty	(P)	Contemporary Arts	Oct 2-20 '50
Etnier, Stephen	(P)	Milch	Nov 13-Dec 2 '50
Etting, Emlen	(P)	Midtown	Feb 28-Mar 18 '50
Evershed, Peter	(P & G)	American-British	Jan 9-21 '50
Faggi, Alfeo	(S)	Weyhe	Jan 9-31 '50
Fair, Art		Eighth Street	Oct 23-Nov 5 '50
Faistauer, Anton		St. Etienne	Jan 14-Feb 11 '50
Farr, Dorothy	(P)	Bertha Schaefer	Dec 4-23 '50
Farr, Fred	(S)	Bertha Schaefer	Dec 4-23 '50
Farruggio, Remo	(P)	Salpeter	Oct 17-Nov 12 '49
Fasanella, Ralph	(P)	ACA	Nov 28-Dec 10 '49
Faulconer	(P)	Hugo	Dec 5-31 '49
Fausett, Dean	(P)	Kraushaar	Dec 4-30 '50
Favre, Louis	(G)	Pierre Berès	Sept 25-Oct 14 '50
Feininger, Lux	(P)	Hewitt	Oct 16-Nov 4 '50
Feininger, Lyonel	(G)	Greiss	Feb 4-Mar 4 '50
	(P)	Buchholz	Apr 11-29 '50
Feldman, Hilda	(P)	Argent	Oct 10-22 '49
Ferber, Herbert	(S)	Betty Parsons	Mar 6-25 '50
Fett, William	(P)	Bodley	Oct 2-23 '50
Fetti, Domenico	(P)	Durlacher	Feb 28-Mar 25 '50
Fiene, Ernest		Knoedler	Oct 4-26 '49
Finkelstein, Louis		Pyramid	Nov 15-Dec 4 '49
Firestone, Julien		Regional Arts	Jan 30-Mar 4 '50
Fisher, William	(P)	Eighth Street	Sept 25-Oct 9 '50
Fitzgerald, Harriet	(P)	Barzansky	Feb 13-Mar 8 '50
Fliegel, Leslie		Eggleston	Feb 27-Mar 12 '50
Floch, Joseph	(P)	AAA	Nov 14-Dec 3 '49
Fogel, Seymour	(P)	Levitt	Oct 20-Nov 12 '49
Force, Juliana (In Honor Of)		Whitney Museum	Sept 24-Oct 30 '49
Foujita	(P)	Komor	Nov 10-26 '49
Franck, Frederick	(P)	Van Diemen-Lilienfeld	Nov 2-16 '49
Franck, Rachel	(P)	Argent	Mar 6-18 '50
Franklin, Jenny-Lynn		Regional Arts	Jan 9-29 '50

Franks, Seymour	(P)	Peridot	Feb 27-Mar 25 '50
		Peridot	Nov 27-Dec 23 '50
Frasconi, Antonio	(G)	Weyhe	Mar 13-Apr 12 '50
Fredericksen, William		Emmerick	Dec 1-14 '49
French, Jared	(P)	Hewitt	Dec 19 '50-Jan 6 '51
Freudenberg, Albert	(P)	Carlebach	Oct 3-21 '50
Friedman, Arnold		Jewish Museum	Feb 15-Mar 13 '50
Frisch, Shari		23rd Street	Mar 28-Apr 28 '50
Fulkerson, Idee	(P)	Friedman	Nov 1-30 '49
Fuller, Sue	(S)	Bertha Schaefer	June 5-16 '50
		Seligmann	Nov 25-Dec 16 '50
Gabriel, Ada V.	(P & G)	Allison	Feb 14-Mar 10 '50
Gaertner, Carl	(P & G)	Macbeth	Jan 3-21 '50
Gallatin, A. E.	(P)	Pinacotheca	Jan 3-31 '50
Gans, Joe	(P)	Creative	Jan 16-Feb 11 '50
Garavito, Humberto	(P)	Binet	Oct 29-Nov 18 '49
Gardner, Eugene	(P)	Newcomb-Macklin	Apr 17-29 '50
Garland, Leon		Jewish Museum	Mar 24-Apr 25 '50
Garlock, John		Van Loen	Apr 5-30 '50
Garrison, Eve	(P)	Newton	Sept 25-Oct 7 '50
Gasser, Henry	(P)	Macbeth	Nov 1-19 '49
Gatch, Lee	(P)	New Art Circle	Mar 1-Apr 30 '50
		Little	Aug 1-31 '50
Gatto, Joe	(P)	Barzansky	Oct 2-21 '50
Gauss, Catherine		Newcomb-Macklin	Feb 6-18 '50
Gear, William	(P)	Betty Parsons	Nov 21-Dec 10 '49
Geffen		ALA	Oct 2-15 '49
Gelb, Jan		Weyhe	Apr 21-May 17 '50
Gellert, Jim	(P)	ACA	May 22-June 10 '50
George, Thomas	(P)	Ferargil	Sept 7-20 '50
Gert (Gertrude Lawrence Berger)	(P)	Barbizon-Plaza	Feb 7-27 '50
Gezagnere		Lipton	Feb 1-28 '50
Ghikas, Panos		Binet	June 20-July 10 '50
Giacometti, Alberto	(S)	Matisse	Nov 26-Dec 16 '50
Gibran, Kahlil	(P)	Levitt	Oct 16-Nov 4 '50
Gikow, Ruth	(P)	Grand Central	Sept 20-Oct 6 '50
Gilbert, Jane	(P)	FAR	Nov 15-Dec 15 '49
Gilbert, Michel	(P)	Van Diemen-Lilienfeld	Dec 4-16 '50
Gilbert, Regine		Newton	Jan 4-14 '50
Girard, André		Lipton	Jan 1-31 '50
Glasco, Joseph	(P)	Perls	Jan 30-Feb 25 '50
Gleizes, Albert	(P)	Passedoit	Oct 10-Nov 5 '49
Goertz, Augustus	(P)	Van Diemen-Lilienfeld	Mar 25- Apr 7 '50
Gold, Fay	(P)	Roko	Nov 21-Dec 14 '49
Goldstein, Phyllis		Pyramid	Mar 22-Apr 12 '50
Golubov, Maurice	(P)	Artists'	Mar 25-Apr 13 '50
Gonzalez, Xavier	(P)	Grand Central	Apr 20-29 '50
Goodwin, John		Carlebach	Oct 4-22 '50

Gordon		Pyramid	Feb 1-28 '50
Gordon, Maxwell	(P)	ACA	Jan 16-Feb 4 '50
Gorky, Arshile	(P)	Kootz	Mar 28-Apr 24 '50
Gottlieb, Adolph	(P)	Kootz	Jan 10-30 '50
Goyri, Roberto Gonzalez	(S)	Roko	Mar 26-Apr 20 '50
Grant, Gene	(P)	AAA	Dec 18 '50-Jan 6 '51
Grant, Gordon	(P)	Grand Central	Nov 15-26 '49
Grasso, Elizabeth	(P)	Eggleston	Sept 25-Oct 7 '50
Gray, Cleve	(P)	Seligmann	Oct 24-Nov 26 '49
Greenbowe, Douglas	(P)	Milch	Dec 5-24 '50
Greene, Balcomb	(P)	Bertha Schaefer	Apr 3-22 '50
Greene, Marie Zoe	(S)	Argent	Nov 27-Dec 16 '50
Grimm, Pierre		Knoedler	June 15-July 15 '50
Gris, Juan	(P)	Buchholz	Jan 16-Feb 11 '50
Gromaire, Marcel	(P)	Louis Carré	Dec 6-31 '49
Gross, Sidney	(P)	Rehn	Nov 13-Dec 2 '50
Grosser, Maurice		Knoedler	Jan 23-Feb 11 '50
Groth, John	(P)	Ferargil	Oct 9-22 '50
Gunn, Homer		Creative	Oct 16-28 '50
Gurr, Lena	(P)	ACA	Dec 11-30 '50
Guston, Philip	(P)	Peridot	Nov 27-Dec 23 '50
Gute, Herbert	(P)	Grand Central	Apr 18-29 '50
Guthrie, Ayrie		Argent	Apr 17-29 '50
Halty, Adolfo	(P)	Van Diemen-Lilienfeld	Oct 14-28 '50
Hamar, Irene	(S)	American-British	Oct 9-31 '50
Handly, Avery		Eggleston	Feb 6-18 '50
Hanley, Sarah E.	(P)	Demotte	Oct 14-Nov 12 '49
Hanson, J. M.	(P)	Passedoit	Jan 3-21 '50
Harari, Hananiah	(P)	Laurel	Apr 24-May 6 '50
Hare, Channing	(P)	Grand Central	Nov 28-Dec 11 '50
Hare, David	(S)	Kootz	Dec 6-24 '49
Harmon, Lily		AAA	Mar 27-Apr 15 '50
Harris, Robert E.		Eggleston	Mar 27-Apr 8 '50
Harriton, Abraham	(P)	ACA	Apr 10-29 '50
Hart, George "Pop" Overbury	(P)	Kew Gardens	Mar 20-Apr 30 '50
Hart, Justina	(P)	Newcomb-Macklin	Nov 21-Dec 3 '49
Hartig, Alfred E.	(P)	Regional Arts	Nov 24-Dec 9 '50
Hartley, Marsden	(P)	Rosenberg	Jan 9-28 '50
		Bertha Schaefer	Nov 13-Dec 2 '50
Hayter, Stanley William	(G)	Perspectives	Mar 28-Apr 15 '50
Hebald, Milton	(S)	Grand Central	Nov 29-Dec 10 '49
Heidenreich, Charles	(P)	Salpeter	Sept 26-Oct 15 '49
Heintzelman, Arthur W.	(P)	Binet	Dec 7 '49-Jan 6 '50
Heller	(P)	ALA	Nov 20-Dec 10 '49
Hellman, Edith	(P)	Binet	Nov 19-Dec 6 '49
Henry, E. L.		Graham	Nov 15-Dec 15 '49
Heuseux, Lucette		Van Diemen-Lilienfeld	Feb 21-Mar 6 '50
Heuston, Frank Zell	(P)	Eggleston	Dec 26 '49-Jan 7 '50

Hios, Theo	(P)	Contemporary Arts	Mar 20-Apr 7 '50
Hobbie, Lucille	(P)	Eighth Street	May 29-June 18 '50
		Eighth Street	Oct 9-22 '50
Hofmann, Hans	(P)	Kootz	Nov 15-Dec 5 '49
		Kootz	Oct 24-Nov 13 '50
Hollister, Paul		Village Art Center	Apr 11-28 '50
Holme, Siv		Bertha Schaefer	Apr 24-May 12 '50
Holmes, Mary Jane	(P)	Albatross	Mar 13-25 '50
Holty, Carl	(P)	New Art Circle	Nov 15-Dec 9 '50
Hondius, Gerrit	(P)	Luyber	Jan 16-Mar 4 '50
Hood, Dorothy	(P)	Willard	Oct 10-Nov 4 '50
Hoover, Ellison		Ferargil	Oct 31-Nov 14 '49
		Ferargil	Nov 20-Dec 12 '50
Hoowij, Jan	(P)	Portraits	Apr 11-25 '50
Hopper, Edward	(P)	Whitney Museum	Feb 10-Mar 26 '50
Horn, Margory		Little	Dec 11 '49-Jan 1 '50
Howard, Wing	(P)	Knoedler	Dec 19-31 '50
Howe, Katherine		Little	Mar 2-31 '50
Howland, Isabella	(P)	Midtown	Jan 10-28 '50
Hoyt, Whitney	(P)	Kraushaar	Nov 21-Dec 10 '49
Hugo, John		Hugo	Dec 20 '50-Jan 15 '51
Hulitar, Cosmy	(P)	Friedman	Mar 1-31 '50
Hulse, John C.	(P)	American-British	Feb 20-Mar 4 '50
Humbert, Suzanne	(P)	Brandt	Feb 1-28 '50
Hunt, Lynn Bogue	(P)	Grand Central	Nov 14-26 '49
Huppler, Dudley	(P)	Hewitt	May 1-13 '50
		Hewitt	June 5-17 '50
Ingle, Thomas	(P)	Carlebach	Jan 9-Feb 4 '50
Intarsia, Montici		Knoedler	Dec 7-23 '50
Ipcar, Dahlov	(P)	Wellons	Oct 2-20 '50
Isenberger, Eric	(P)	Knoedler	Nov 27-Dec 16 '50
Jacobsen, Jurgen		Emmerick	Dec 1-14 '49
James, Michael	(S)	Walker	Dec 4-20 '50
Janco, Marcel	(P)	Feigl	Oct 17-Nov 4 '50
Ject-Key, Elsie		Argent	Dec 5-17 '49
Johnson, Buffie		Betty Parsons	Mar 27-Apr 15 '50
Johnson, Frank Tenney	(P)	Grand Central	Jan 26-Feb 11 '50
Johnston, Ynez	(P)	Museum of Modern Art	Nov 28 '50-Jan 14 '51
Junyer, Joan	(P)	Delius	Nov 1-21 '49
Jurgensen, Laurence T.		Eighth Street	Oct 3-16 '49
Kagen, Boris	(S)	Contemporary Arts	Mar 12-18 '50
Kahn, Ely Jacques	(P)	Feigl	Mar 28-Apr 12 '50

EXHIBITIONS

Kahn, Matt	(P)	Konwiser	Aug 21-30 '50
Kallem, Herbert	(S)	Roko	Dec 18 '49-Jan 12 '50
Kalmer, Lee	(P)	Regional Arts	Oct 22-Nov 22 '50
Kamrowski, Gerome	(P)	Hugo	May 8-31 '50
Kantor, Morris	(P)	Rehn	Nov 22-Dec 10 '49
Kaplan, Joseph	(P)	Salpeter	Oct 17-Nov 12 '49
		Salpeter	Nov 13-Dec 2 '50
		Bertha Schaefer	Dec 27 '50-Jan 13 '51
Karasz, Mariska		Downtown	Dec 28 '49-Jan 21 '50
Karfiol, Bernard	(P)	New	Nov 21-Dec 16 '50
Karoly, Fredric	(P)	Luyber	Nov 13-Dec 2 '50
Karp, Leon	(P)	Kennedy	Mar 6-31 '50
Kasimir, Luigi	(G)	Grand Central	Nov 22-Dec 3 '49
Katchadourian, Sarkis	(F)	Binet	Feb 11-Mar 3 '50
Katz, A. Raymond	(P)	American-British	Oct 18-Nov 12 '49
Kauffer, E. McKnight	(P)	Feigl	Nov 15-Dec 3 '49
Kaufmann, Arthur	(P)	Contemporary Arts	Mar 6-24 '50
Kawa, Florence	(P)	Milch	Oct 23-Nov 11 '50
Kayn, Hilde B.	(P)	Creative	Nov 13-25 '50
Kaytor, Albert	(P)	Peridot	Oct 31-Nov 26 '49
Kees, Weldon	(P)	Peridot	Nov 27-Dec 23 '50
		Hugo	Feb 21-Mar 20 '50
Kelly, Leon	(P)	Hugo	Oct 1-31(?) '50
Keogh, Tom		Seligmann	Feb 6-28 '50
Kermes, Constantine		Bertha Schaefer	Sept 5-18 '50
Key-Oberg, Rolf		Kraushaar	Oct 31-Nov 19 '49
Kienbusch, William	(G)	Serigraph Society	Feb 6-Mar 6 '50
Kiley, Robert	(G)	Ferargil	Nov 13-26 '50
King, Clinton	(P)	Museum of Modern Art	Apr 28-June 7 '50
King, William	(S)	Midtown	May 9-27 '50
Kingman, Dong	(P)	Museum of Modern Art	Dec 21 '49-Feb 19 '50
Klee, Paul	(P)	New Art Circle	Jan 2-31 '50 •
		Buchholz	Mar 14-Apr 8 '50
		Buchholz	Apr 25-May 21 '50
		New Art Circle	May 1-June 30 '50
		Little	August 1-31 '50
Kleiber, Hans	(P)	Grand Central	Mar 7-18 '50
Knap, John D.	(P)	Grand Central	Oct 4-15 '49
Knaths, Karl	(P)	Rosenberg	Feb 1-25 '50
		Rosenberg	Dec 4-30 '50
Knoop, Guitou	(S)	Betty Parsons	Dec 13-31 '49
Koch, Samuel		Contemporary Arts	Apr 17-May 5 '50
Koerner, Henry	(P)	Midtown	Mar 21-Apr 15 '50
Kohn, Bernard A.	(G)	Serigraph Society	Feb 6-Mar 4 '50
Kokoschka, Oskar	(P)	Feigl	Dec 7 '49-Jan 14 '50
		Museum of Modern Art	July 19-Oct 4 '49
Kollwitz, Kathe	(P)	St. Etienne	Nov 30-Dec 23 '49
Konzal, Joseph	(S)	ALA	Nov 20-Dec 10 '49
		Contemporary Arts	May 8-25 '50
Kopf, Maxim		Van Diemen-Lilienfeld	Feb 4-17 '50
Kopman, Benjamin	(P)	Milch	Oct 2-21 '50

Krause, Glen	(P)	Levitt	Apr 17-May 6 '50
Krauskopf, Bruno		Feigl	Dec 7 '49-Jan 14 '50
Kruckman, Herbert	(P)	ACA	Oct 23-Nov 11 '50
Kuniyoshi, Yasou	(P)	Downtown	Apr 4-22 '50
Kupferman, Lawrence	(P)	Levitt	Nov 15-30 '49
Lachaise, Gaston	(D)	Knoedler	Apr 17-May 6 '50
Laks, Victor	(P)	Penthouse	Nov 28-Dec 20 '50
Lam, Wilfredo	(P)	Matisse	May 2-20 '50
La More, Chet	(P)	Carlebach	Feb 6-25 '50
Lanan, Bernard	(S)	Regional Arts	Nov 28-Dec 15 '49
Lane, Leslie	(P)	Luyber	May 22-June 15 '50
La Salle, Toni		Pinacotheca	May 23-June 15 '50
Laske, Oskar	(P)	St. Etienne	Oct 1-31 '50
Lavalle, John	(P)	Ferargil	May 15-28 '50
La Villeon, Elaine	(P)	Brandt	Feb 1-28 '50
Lawrence, Jacob	(P)	Downtown	Oct 24-Nov 11 '50
Lax, David	(P)	Grand Central	Nov 8-19 '49
Lazzari, Pietro	(P)	Betty Parsons	Sept 19-Oct 8 '49
		Betty Parsons	Mar 6-25 '50
Lebrun, Rico	(P)	Seligmann	Mar 27-Apr 22 '50
Lechay, James	(P)	Macbeth	Oct 9-28 '50
Lee, Amy		Betty Parsons	Jan 23-Feb 11 '50
Lee, Doris	(P)	AAA	Nov 6-25 '50
Lee, Robert J.		Ferargil	Jan 15-28 '50
Léger, Fernand	(P)	Buchholz	Nov 6-Dec 2 '50
Lehman, Irving	(P & S)	Salpeter	Jan 2-21 '50
	(P)	Salpeter	Oct 17-Nov 12 '49
Lehmann, Lotte	(P)	Schaeffer	Jan 23-Feb 15 '50
Lenney, Annie	(P)	Argent	Oct 10-22 '49
Lensen, Michael	(P)	Laurel	Jan 28-Feb 11 '50
Leonard, Jack	(S)	Peridot	Nov 28-Dec 28 '50
Leonid (Leonid Berman)		Durlacher	Jan 3-28 '50
Lerner		Jewish Museum	Feb 19-Mar 19 '50
Lester, William	(P)	Passedoit	Jan 23-Feb 11 '50
Leventhal, Ethel S.	(P)	Argent	Oct 10-22 '49
Levi, Julien	(P)	Downtown	Nov 14-Dec 2 '50
Levin, Abraham	(P)	Eggleston	Nov 21-Dec 3 '49
Levine, Jack	(P)	Downtown	Jan 17-Feb 17 '50
Levine, Stanley		Village Art	Apr 11-28 '50
Levy		Egan	June 5-24 '50
Lewis, Norman		Willard	Mar 21-Apr 15 '50
Leydenfrost, Robert		Binet	June 20-July 10 '50
Lion, Ronnie		Creative	Feb 27-Mar 11 '50
		Creative	Dec 25 '50-Jan 6 '51
Lipman-Wulf, Peter	(S & G)	New School	Jan 3-16 '50
Lippold, Richard	(S)	Willard	Feb 28-Mar 21 '50
Lipton, Seymour	(S)	Betty Parsons	Oct 17-Nov 4 '50
Lishinsky, Saul		44th Street	May 1-31 '50

Lissitzky, El		Pinacotheca	Oct 6-31 '49
Litwak, Israel		New Art Circle	Apr 1-30 '50
Livingston, Charlotte	(P)	Eighth Street	Feb 19-Mar 5 '50
Lockspeiser, Eleanore		Village Art	Dec 18 '49-Jan 6 '50
Loew, Michael	(P)	Artists'	Nov 19-Dec 8 '49
Longo, Vincent		Regional Arts	Dec 16 '49-Jan 6 '50
Lorian, Dolia	(P)	Greiss	Feb 4-Mar 4 '50
Love, Jane	(S)	Barbizon-Plaza	Jan 4-Feb 5 '50
Low, Howard	(S)	Wittenborn	Aug 1-31 '50
Lowengrund, Margaret	(P)	Seligmann	Nov 25-Dec 16 '50
Lurie, Boris	(P)	Creative	Mar 13-25 '50
		Barbizon-Plaza	May 15-31 '50
Lutz, Dan		Barbizon-Plaza	Nov 1-30 '49
Macbryde, Robert	(P)	Durlacher	Jan 31-Feb 25 '50
McCobb, Paul		Laurel	Sept 11-30 '50
McFee, Henry Lee	(P)	Rehn	Jan 10-28 '50
MacIver, Loran	(P)	Matisse	Oct 11-29 '49
MacKendrick, Lillian	(P)	Levitt	Sept 27-Oct 15 '49
McKinley, Hazel		Laurel	June 12-30 '50
MacMurray, Helen		Eggleston	Oct 16-28 '50
McNeill, George	(P)	Egan	Feb 6-25 '50
McQuillan, Frances	(P)	Argent	Oct 23-Nov 4 '50
Major, Henry		Levitt	Mar 6-25 '50
Malbandian, Karnig	(P)	Newton	Nov 13-25 '49
Malouf, Carl		Copain	Oct 3-25 '49
Manacher, Frances	(P)	Passedoit	Mar 6-25 '50
Mané-Katz	(P)	Binet	Mar 4-24 '50
Mangor, Lisa	(P)	ALA	Dec 26 '50-Jan 13 '51
Manning, Michaele		Village Art	Apr 11-28 '50
Manso, Leo	(P)	Levitt	Sept 18-Oct 14 '50
Marca-Relli, Corrado di	(P)	Niveau	Nov 15-Dec 1 '49
Margo, Boris	(P)	Betty Parsons	Nov 6-25 '50
		Seligmann	Nov 25-Dec 16 '50
Marin, John	(P)	American Place	Nov 20 '49-Feb 18 '51
		American Place	Mar 20-May 6 '50
		Downtown	Dec 27 '50-Jan 27 '51
Marini, Marino	(S)	Buchholz	Feb 14-Mar 11 '50
Maroger, Jacques	(P)	Grand Central	Oct 31-Nov 12 '49
Marren, Janet	(G)	Greiss	Apr 22-May 20 '50
	(P)	Roko	Sept 17-Oct 11 '50
Marsh, Reginald	(P)	Rehn	Nov 1-30(?) '50
Martin, Florence	(P)	Binet	Mar 25-Apr 8 '50
Martone, J.		ALA	Apr 2-22 '50
Marx, Milton	(P)	Copain	Sept 12-Oct 15 '50
Masson, André	(P)	Buchholz	Nov 8-26 '49
		Perspectives	June 13-30 '50
Matisse, Henri	(P)	Rosenberg	Oct 24-Nov 12 '49
Matson, Greta	(P)	Pen & Brush	Apr 13-28 '50

Maurer, Alfred	(P)	Whitney Museum	Nov 5-Dec 11 '49
		Bertha Schaefer	Nov 28-Dec 23 '49
		Bertha Schaefer	Nov 13-Dec 2 '50
Mayers, Myron	(P)	Roko	Oct 23-Nov 16 '49
Mays, Maxwell		Ferargil	Nov 14-26 '49
Medearis		Kende	June 5-17 '50
Melcarth, Edward		Durlacher	Mar 28-Apr 22 '50
Meltsmer, Paul	(P)	Barzansky	May 1-15 '50
Mendes, Marion Desola	(P)	Argent	May 1-13 '50
Menken, Marie		Betty Parsons	Oct 31-Nov 19 '49
Meyer, Fred	(P)	Midtown	Oct 4-22 '49
Michaux, Henri		Perspectives	Mar 1-18 '50
Michelson, Leo	(P)	AAA	Apr 24-May 13 '50
Mildwoff, Ben	(G)	Greiss	Apr 22-May 20 '50
Miles, Jean		Betty Parsons	May 8-27 '50
Millington, Halla		Eggleston	May 1-13 '50
Minewski, Alex		Contemporary Arts	Apr 3-21 '50
Mira, Alfred	(P)	Grand Central	Nov 29-Dec 10 '49
Mirko	(S & G)	Viviano	Apr 11-May 6 '50
Miro, Joan	(G)	Perspectives	Oct 4-23 '49
	(P, G & S)	Matisse	Dec 6-31 '49
Mitchell, Peter Todd	(P)	American-British	Nov 15-Dec 3 '49
Mitchell, Wallace	(P)	Bertha Schaefer	Jan 3-21 '50
Miyamoto, Kaname	(P)	Laurel	Jan 2-14 '50
Modigliani, Amedeo	(P)	Rosenberg	Nov 13-Dec 2 '50
Moholy-Nagy, Laszlo	(P)	Pinacotheca	Apr 24-May 19 '50
Moller, Hans	(P)	Kleeman	Jan 4-31 '50
		Seligmann	Nov 25-Dec 16 '50
Mondrian, Piet	(P)	Janis	Oct 10-Nov 12 '49
Monod, Vivette	(S)	Lipton	Nov 1-30 '49
Montagu, Richard J.	(P)	Eggleston	Oct 24-Nov 5 '49
Montgomery, Frank		Regional Arts	Oct 24-Nov 12 '49
Moore, Susan	(P)	Contemporary Arts	Oct 16-Nov 3 '50
Moose, Philip		Ferargil	Mar 6-19 '50
Moreing, David Burr		Milch	Feb 20-Mar 11 '50
Morgan, Randal	(P)	New Art Circle	Apr 1-30 '50
Morgan, Wallace		Ferargil	Jan 3-15 '50
Morgenrath, Selig		Contemporary Arts	Jan 23-Feb 10 '50
Morris, Helen		Regional Arts	Mar 5-25 '50
Morrison, George	(P)	Grand Central	May 2-13 '50
Moses, Grandma	(P)	American-British	Jan 24-Feb 11 '50
		St. Etienne	Nov 15-Dec 31 '50
Moskowitz, Ira	(G)	Kennedy	Nov 1-30 '49
Motherwell, Robert	(P)	Kootz	Oct 4-22 '49
		Kootz	Nov 14-Dec 4 '50
Moy, Seong	(P)	Hacker	May 31-June 30 '50
Mullican, Lee	(P)	Willard	Feb 1-27 '50
Munch, Edvard	(G)	Kleeman	June 1-30 '50
	(P & G)	Museum of Modern Art	June 29-Aug 13 '50
Mundt, Ernest	(S)	Museum of Modern Art	Nov 28 '50-Jan 14 '51
Munsell, Richard		Ferargil	Oct 17-29 '49

Nadelman, Elie	(D)	Knoedler	Nov 29-Dec 10 '49
	(S)	Hewitt	Nov 28-Dec 16 '50
Nagler, Fred	(P)	Midtown	Nov 28-Dec 23 '50
Nakian, Reuben	(S)	Egan	Apr 1-30 '50
Nalbandian, Karnig		Newton	Nov 14-26 '49
Neagoe, Anna	(P)	Feigl	Mar 7-22 '50
Neal, Frank		44th Street	Apr 4-29 '50
Neal, ?		Copain	Dec 8 '50-Jan 2 '51
Negret, Edgar	(S)	Peridot	May 15-June 10 '50
Nelson, Martin	(P)	Roko	Dec 10 '50-Jan 4 '51
Nesch, Rolf		Kleeman	Oct 1-31 '49
Neufeld, Woldemar		Grand Central	Feb 21-Mar 4 '50
Newman, Barnett	(P)	Betty Parsons	Jan 23-Feb 11 '50
Newswanger, Christian	(P)	Binet	Oct 16-Nov 3 '50
Newswanger, Kiehl	(P)	Binet	Oct 16-Nov 3 '50
Nichols, Hobart	(P)	Grand Central	Mar 14-25 '50
Noailles, Marie Laure de		Hugo	Nov 14-Dec 5 '49
Nordfeldt, B. J. O.	(P)	Passedoit	Oct 30-Nov 11 '50
Noreen, Sister Mary	(P)	Demotte	Jan 2-31 '50
Oenslager, Donald	(P)	Ferargil	Sept 25-Oct 15 '49
O'Keeffe, Georgia	(P)	American Place	Oct 16-Nov 25 '50
Olds, Elizabeth	(P)	ACA	Jan 2-21 '50
Orban, George		44th Street	Mar 7-28 '50
Ossaye, Roberto	(P)	Roko	Mar 26-Apr 20 '50
Pace, Stephan	(P)	Greiss	Feb 4-Mar 4 '50
Pailes, Isaac		Carstairs	Mar 7-31 '50
Palazzo, Tony	(P)	Friedman	Mar 1-31 '50
Palmer, William C.	(P)	Midtown	Oct 31-Nov 25 '50
Park, Edwin Avery	(P)	Levitt	Apr 17-May 6 '50
Parker, Raymond	(P)	Museum of Modern Art	Apr 28-June 7 '50
Peisley, Wilfred John		Barbizon-Plaza	Mar 24-Apr 14 '50
Peloso, Fred R.		23rd Street	Jan 1-Feb 28 '50
Pels, Albert		Brown	Oct 4-22 '49
Penney, James		Kraushaar	Jan 30-Feb 18 '50
Perham, Jr., Roy Gates		Newcomb-Macklin	May 1-13 '50
Peri, Eve	(P)	Hacker	Apr 18-May 6 '50
Perlman, Amalia	(P)	Creative	Oct 2-14 '50
Persons, Simmons	(P)	Rehn	Mar 6-31 '50
Picabia, Francis	(P)	Pinacotheca	Feb 15-Mar 31 '50
Picasso, Pablo	(S)	Perspectives	Sept 24-Oct 2 '49
	(P)	Rosenberg	Oct 24-Nov 12 '49
	(P)	Louis Carré	Jan 9-31 '50
	(P & G)	Museum of Modern Art	Jan 25-Mar 19 '50
	(P)	Rosenberg	Nov 13-Dec 2 '50
Piper, John	(P)	Buchholz	Oct 17-Nov 4 '50

Pleasants, Blanche	(P)	Grand Central	Nov 1-12 '49
Pleissner, Ogden M.	(P)	Macbeth	Oct 31-Nov 18 '50
Pollack, Reginald	(P)	Peridot	Sept 8-Oct 1 '49
		Peridot	Nov 27-Dec 23 '50
Pollock, Jackson	(P)	Betty Parsons	Nov 21-Dec 10 '49
		Betty Parsons	Nov 28-Dec 16 '50
Pousette-Dart, Richard	(P)	Betty Parsons	Mar 27-Apr 15 '50
Prassinos, Mario		Perspectives	Jan 31-Feb 25 '50
Prendergast, Maurice	(P)	Kraushaar	Jan 3-28 '50
Presser, Josef	(P)	Roko	Nov 13-Dec 7 '50
Pressman, Meichel	(P)	Jewish Museum	Dec 1-31 '50
Preston, Malcolm		Eggleston	Feb 20-Mar 4 '50
		Eggleston	Apr 10-22 '50
Prestopino, Gregorio	(P)	ACA	Apr 24-May 13 '50
Price, Clayton S.		Willard	Nov 29-Dec 23 '49
Price, Evan	(P)	Ferargil	Nov 13-25 '49
Price, Melville		Peridot	Jan 28-Feb 25 '50
Priebe, Karl		Perls	Oct 3-29 '49
Prins, Warner	(P)	Carlebach	Mar 1-31 '50
Propper, Ganz	(P)	Salpeter	May 15-June 10 '50
Putnam, Wallace		Passedoit	May 15-June 15 '50
Pytlack, Leonard	(G)	Serigraph Society	Oct 17-Nov 12 '49
Quanchi, Leo	(P)	Salpeter	Sept 29-Oct 20 '50
Quistgaard, Johan Waldemar			
de Rehling	(P)	Newcomb-Macklin	Oct 3-20 '49
Racz, André	(P & G)	Laurel	Oct 31-Nov 12 '49
Radenkovitch, Yovan		Albatross	Feb 27-Mar 11 '50
Rager, Edward		Village Art	Dec 18 '49-Jan 6 '50
Ranson, Nancy	(P)	Binet	Jan 7-24 '50
Rasha	(P)	Albatross	Mar 27-Apr 8 '50
Raskin, Saul	(P)	Jewish Museum	Feb 19-Mar 19 '50
Ratkai, George	(P)	Babcock	Nov 13-Dec 2 '50
Rattner, Abraham	(P)	Rosenberg	Feb 1-25 '50
		Rosenberg	Apr 3-22 '50
		Rosenberg	Dec 4-30 '50
Ray, Rudolf		Willard	Oct 4-29 '49
Redein, Alex	(P)	Salpeter	Oct 17-Nov 12 '49
		Salpeter	Oct 23-Dec 2 '50
Reed, Martha	(P)	Eggleston	Nov 13-25 '50
Refregier, Anton	(P)	ACA	Oct 17-Nov 5 '49
Reinhardt, Ad	(P)	Betty Parsons	Oct 31-Nov 19 '49
Reisman, Philip	(P)	ACA	Feb 20-Mar 11 '50
Renoir, Auguste	(P)	Rosenberg	Oct 3-22 '49
		Wildenstein	Mar 22-Apr 29 '50
Revzan, Daniel	(P)	Artists'	Feb 11-Mar 2 '50

Reynal, Jeanne	(Mosaic)	Hugo	Mar 15-Apr 1 '50
		Hugo	Oct 16-Nov 7 '50
Richards, Joe		AAA	Oct 4-22 '49
Richardson, Constance	(P)	Macbeth	Jan 23-Feb 11 '50
Richardson, Gretchen	(S)	Pen & Brush	Jan 23-Feb 9 '50
Riesenfeld, Victor	(P)	Wildenstein	Nov 16-Dec 3 '49
Ripley, A. Lassell	(P)	Grand Central	Oct 8-29 '49
Ritter, Chris		Laurel	May 23-June 10 '50
Robertson, T. W.		Ferargil	Nov 27-Dec 11 '50
Robins, Louise		Ferargil	Jan 3-15 '50
Robinson, Mary Turlay	(P)	Binet	Jan 25-Feb 10 '50
Roche, Marguerite		Demotte	Oct 9-28 '50
Rogers, Gertrude	(P)	American-British	Sept 25-Oct 7 '50
Romano, Umberto	(P)	AAA	Mar 6-25 '50
Rood, John	(S)	AAA	Oct 16-Nov 4 '50
Rose, Francis	(P)	Passedoit	Nov 8-20 '49
Rosenbauer, Wallace	(S)	Wellons	Nov 13-30 '50
Rosenfeld, Edward	(P)	Babcock	Nov 14-Dec 3 '49
Rosenthal, Bernard	(S)	AAA	Nov 27-Dec 16 '50
Rostow, Julius	(P)	Jewish Museum	May 1-Aug 6 '50
Rouault, Georges	(P)	Binet	Oct 1-28 '49
		Perls	Oct 31-Nov 26 '49
Routhenstein, Florence		Pyramid	Jan 19-Feb 7 '50
Rowan, Lynn	(P)	Roko	Sept 26-Oct 19 '49
		Bodley	Sept 15-30 '50
Roy, Pierre		Carstairs	Nov 30-Dec 31 '49
Ruggles, John	(P)	Artists'	Sept 25-Oct 12 '50
Russell, Alfred	(P)	Peridot	Apr 24-May 13 '50
		Peridot	Nov 27-Dec 23 '50
Russell, Morgan	(P)	Rose Fried	Nov 20-Dec 31 '50
Ruvulo, Felix	(P)	Viviano	Mar 13-Apr 1 '50
Ryan, Anne	(P)	Betty Parsons	Sept 26-Oct 14 '50
Ryan, Sally	(P)	American-British	May 8-20 '50
Sadron	(P)	ALA	Nov 15-Dec 10 '49
Sage, Kay	(P)	Viviano	Feb 21-Mar 11 '50
Salemme, Antonio	(P)	Van Diemen-Lilienfeld	Nov 17-30 '49
Salemme, Martha	(P)	Van Diemen-Lilienfeld	Nov 17-30 '49
Saltonstall, Elizabeth	(P)	Pen & Brush	Apr 12-28 '50
Salzer, Liezel	(P)	Emmerick	Nov 9-23 '49
Samstag, Gordon	(P)	Milch	Jan 9-28 '50
San Yu	(P)	Passedoit	May 15-June 15 '50
Sandberg, Judith	(P)	Creative	Feb 13-25 '50
Saperstein, Fannie	(P)	Argent	Nov 27-Dec 16 '50
Sasson, Ingrid		Ferargil	Dec 12-24 '50
Schachter, Judy		Argent	Feb 6-18 '50
Schaeffer, H. Bella	(P)	Artists'	Oct 8-27 '49
Schames, Samson	(P)	Carlebach	Feb 28-Mar 18 '50

Schanker, Louis	(P & G)	Hacker	May 8-27 '50
	(P & G)	Willard	Jan 3-28 '50
Schatia, Doris	(S)	Argent	Nov 7-19 '49
Schatz, Bezalel	(P)	Bodley	Nov 13-Dec 2 '50
Scheinman, Hortense	(P)	Argent	Nov 7-19 '49
Schnakenberg, Henry	(P)	Kraushaar	Oct 23-Nov 11 '50
Schrag, Karl		Kraushaar	Feb 20-Mar 11 '50
Schreiber, George	(P)	AAA	Oct 24-Nov 12 '49
Schubart		Charles-Fourth	Mar 17-Apr 13 '50
Schucker, Charles	(P)	Macbeth	Nov 21-Dec 10 '49
Schwartz, June	(P)	Marquie	Oct 17-29 '49
Schwieder, Arthur		Rehn	Feb 13-Mar 4 '50
Seligmann, Kurt	(P)	Durlacher	Nov 7-Dec 2 '50
Sennhauser, John	(P)	Artists'	Mar 4-24 '50
Sepeshy, Zoltan	(P)	Midtown	Jan 31-Feb 25 '50
Serger, Frederick	(P)	Van Diemen-Lilienfeld	Apr 11-24 '50
Serneels, Clement	(P)	Van Diemen-Lilienfeld	Oct 17-31 '49
Sexton, Henry		Pyramid	Jan 19-Feb 7 '50
Seyffert, Jr., Leopold		Grand Central	Feb 28-Mar 11 '50
Shadbolt, J. L.	(P)	Laurel	Sept 19-Oct 7 '49
Shahn, Ben	(P)	Downtown	Oct 25-Nov 12 '49
Shapira, Abraham J.	(P)	Jewish Museum	Sept 6-30 '50
Shaw, Charles	(P)	Passedoit	Sept 13-Oct 4 '50
Shayn, John	(P)	Newton	Dec 5-23 '50
Shelton, Alphonse J.	(P)	Grand Central	Apr 11-22 '50
Shotwell, Helen Harvey	(P)	Argent	Nov 7-19 '49
Shul, Philip		ALA	Mar 5-Apr 1 '50
Sideris, Alexander	(P)	Newton	Mar 13-25 '50
Sievan, Maurice	(P)	Salpeter	Oct 17-Nov 12 '49
Silver		ALA	Jan 15-Feb 4 '50
Simon, Bernard	(S)	ACA	May 22-June 10 '50
Simon, Sidney		Niveau	Dec 7-30 '49
Sinclair, Mary	(P)	Van Diemen-Lilienfeld	Sept 29-Oct 12 '50
Slote, Edna		Village Art	Dec 18 '49-Jan 6 '50
Small, Hannah	(S)	Passedoit	Oct 9-28 '50
Smith, David	(S)	Willard	Apr 18-May 13 '50
Smith, John	(S)	Barzansky	Sept 27-Oct 15 '49
Smith, Judson	(P)	Hacker	Nov 14-Dec 2 '50
Smith, Sibley	(P)	Willard	Nov 7-25 '50
Snaith, William T.	(P)	Contemporary Arts	Oct 17-Nov 4 '49
Snyder		Friedman	Sept 1-30 '50
Solakian, Setta	(P)	Argent	Oct 23-Nov 4 '50
Solman, Joseph	(P)	ACA	Oct 30-Dec 9 '50
Sopo, Miguel		New School	Oct 24-Nov 4 '49
Soutine, Chaim	(P)	Feigl	Jan 19-Feb 28 '50
		Museum of Modern Art	Nov 1 '50-Jan 7 '51
		Rosenberg	Nov 13-Dec 2 '50
Spivak, Max	(P)	Hacker	May 8-27 '50
Springhorn, Carl	(P)	Macbeth	May 8-27 '50
Staehle, Albert		Friedman	Feb 1-28 '50
Stamos, Theodoros	(P)	Betty Parsons	Dec 13-31 '49

Stea, Cesare	(P & S)	Artists'	Dec 2-21 '50
Stefanelli, Josef	(P)	Artists'	Apr 15-May 4 '50
Steig, Joseph		Roko	May 21-June 14 '50
Steig, Laura		Roko	May 21-June 14 '50
Stephan, John	(P)	Betty Parsons	Sept 26-Oct 14 '50
Sternberg, Harry	(P)	ACA	Mar 13-Apr 1 '50
		ACA	Sept 18-Oct 7 '50
Sterne, Hedda	(P)	Betty Parsons	Feb 13-Mar 4 '50
		Betty Parsons	Dec 18 '50-Jan 6 '51
Sterner, Harold	(D)	American-British	June 12-Aug 25 '50
Stevens, Edward John	(P)	Weyhe	Feb 4-Mar 8 '50
Stewart, Jack		Binet	June 20-July 10 '50
Still, Clyfford	(P)	Betty Parsons	Apr 17-May 6 '50
Stillman, Ary	(P)	Bertha Schaefer	Jan 23-Feb 11 '50
		Seligmann	Nov 25-Dec 16 '50
Storm, Nicolaj		Roko	Apr 21-May 18 '50
Strater, Henry	(D)	Laurel	Nov 27-Dec 9 '50
Streeter, Muriel	(P)	Hewitt	Sept 25-Oct 14 '50
Strickland, Edward		44th Street	Oct 4-31 '49
Stuempfig, Walter	(P)	Durlacher	Nov 29-Dec 24 '49
Sturgis, Katherine	(P)	Kraushaar	Apr 24-May 13 '50
Sullivan, Gene	(P)	Ferargil	Sept 19-Oct 1 '49
Tacke, R. R.	(P)	Binet	Nov 25-Dec 15 '50
Taddei, Luigi	(Mosaic)	Newton	Dec 5-15 '49
Taeuber-Arp, Sophie	(P)	Janis	Jan 30-Feb 25 '50
Talbert, Anne		Eggleston	May 15-20 '50
Tam, Reuben	(P)	Downtown	Nov 15-Dec 3 '49
Tamayo, Rufino	(P)	Knoedler	Apr 24-May 13 '50
Tanguy, Yves	(P)	Matisse	Apr 4-22 '50
Taubes, Frederic	(P)	AAA	Feb 13-Mar 4 '50
	(D)	AAA	Nov 20-Dec 9 '50
Tavelli, Louis	(P)	Hacker	May 8-27 '50
		Hacker	Sept 12-30 '50
Taylor, John	(P)	Macbeth	Mar 6-25 '50
Teichman, Sabina	(P)	Salpeter	Nov 21-Dec 10 '49
Terenzio, Antony	(P)	Creative	Dec 11-23 '50
Tevan, Roszi	(S)	Laurel	Jan 2-14 '50
Thon, William	(P)	Midtown	Apr 18-May 6 '50
Tilburne, Albert R.		Eggleston	Feb 13-25 '50
Tobey, Mark	(P)	Willard	Nov 1-26 '49
		Willard	Nov 28-Dec 30 '50
Tofel, Jennings	(P)	Artists'	Jan 21-Feb 9 '50
Tomlin, Bradley Walker	(P)	Betty Parsons	May 8-27 '50
Toney, Anthony	(P)	ACA	Sept 26-Oct 15 '49
Topolski, Feliks		American-British	June 12-30 '50
Toran, A. T.	(P)	Creative Studio	Oct 1-30 '49
		Creative Studio	Feb 2-25 '50
		Creative Studio	June 10-Sept 30 '50

Torres-Garcia, Joaquin		Janis	Mar 27-Apr 24 '50
Tortosa, Francisco	(P)	Tribune	Mar 1-31 '50
Toulouse-Lautrec, Henri de	(G)	Knoedler	Mar 21-Apr 18 '50
	(P)	Kleeman	Oct 9-30(?) '50
	(P)	Knoedler	Nov 6-25 '50
Treiman, Joyce	(P)	Hewitt	Nov 6-25 '50
Trivigno, Pat	(P)	Luyber	Oct 2-21 '50
Tromka	(P)	ACA	Mar 27-Apr 15 '50
Truxell, Ann		Village Art	Apr 11-28 '50
Tschamber, George	(P)	Eighth Street	May 29-June 18 '50
Tunnard, John	(P)	Durlacher	Oct 10-Nov 4 '50
Utrillo, Maurice	(P)	Feigl	Jan 19-Feb 28 '50
		Niveau	Oct 14-Nov 11 '50
Van Gent, Cock		Weyhe	Oct 16-Nov 15 '50
Van Gogh, Vincent	(P)	Metropolitan Museum	Oct 21 '49-Jan 15 '50
Van Leyden, Karin		American-British	Nov 20-Dec 9 '50
Van Loen, Alfred	(S)	Village Art	Sept 23-Oct 14 '49
Vansier, Boris	(P)	Kleeman	Sept 19-Oct 1 '49
Vaughan, Keith		Durlacher	Jan 31-Feb 25 '50
Vicente, Esteban	(P)	Peridot	Oct 30-Dec 23 '50
Vilas, Faith	(P)	Pen & Brush	Jan 23-Feb 9 '50
Vivin, Louis	(P)	Janis	Dec 27 '49-Jan 28 '50
Vlaminck, Maurice de	(P)	Van Diemen-Lilienfeld	Jan 3-31 '50
Von Wicht, John	(P)	Passedoit	Feb 13-Mar 4 '50
		Seligmann	Nov 25-Dec 16 '50
Vytlacil, Vaclov	(P)	Feigl	Oct 26-Nov 12 '49
		Feigl	Dec 7 '49-Jan 14 '50
Waehner, Trude	(P)	Emmerick	Jan 26-Feb 11 '50
Walkowitz, Abraham	(P)	Jewish Museum	Oct 5-31 '49
Watkins, Franklin C.	(P)	Museum of Modern Art	Mar 22-June 11 '50
Weber, Max	(G)	Rosenberg	Nov 14-Dec 10 '49
	(P)	Rosenberg	Feb 1-25 '50
	(G)	Greiss	Feb 4-Mar 4 '50
	(P)	Rosenberg	Dec 4-30 '50
Weidl, Seff	(P)	Kleeman	Nov 1-30 '50
Weihs, Erika	(P)	Roko	Oct 16-Nov 9 '50
Weissmann, Gerald	(P)	Salpeter	Dec 12-31 '49
Wenger, John	(P)	Grand Central	Sept 19-30 '49
Werner, Max	(S)	ACA	Jan 30-Feb 18 '50
Weston, Harold	(P)	Babcock	Feb 13-Mar 4 '50
White, Charles	(D)	ACA	Feb 12-25 '50

White, Robert H.		Newcomb-Macklin	Feb 13-25 '50
White, Robert	(P & S)	Artists'	May 6-24 '50
Whorf, John	(P)	Milch	Apr 3-22 '50
Wild, Roger		Lipton	Oct 1-31 '49
Wilde, John	(D)	Hewitt	May 15-June 30 '50
Wilson, Ben		Salpeter	Mar 5-25 '50
Wilson, "Scottie"	(P)	Passedoit	Dec 5-31 '49
Wilson, Sol		Babcock	Mar 6-25 '50
Winik, Leon		Friedman	Apr 1-30 '50
Winter, Luman Martin		Salpeter	Feb 13-28 '50
Wolf, Ben	(P)	Babcock	Oct 23-Nov 11 '50
Wolins, Joe	(P)	Contemporary Arts	Oct 3-21 '49
Woolman, Eugene		Argent	Dec 5-17 '49
Wright, S. MacDonald	(P)	Rose Fried	Nov 20-Dec 31 '50
Wyeth, Andrew	(P)	Macbeth	Nov 21-Dec 9 '50
Xavier, Hector	(D)	Weyhe	Nov 7-30 '49
Yashima		Modreal	Oct 14-31 '50
Yano, Ben		Regional Arts	Sept 27-Oct 15 '49
Yunkers, Adjo	(G)	Kleeman	Apr 1-22 '50
Zeid, Princess	(P & G)	Hugo	Jan 9-29 '50
Zorach, William	(S)	Art Students League	Nov 5-30 '50
Zouté, Leon		Levitt	Feb 6-26 '50
Zuckerman, Jack	(P)	Hacker	Oct 3-21 '50

INTRODUCTORY NOTE

In 1951 Art d'aujourd'hui, *the monthly magazine of modern art published in Paris under the editorship of André Bloc, devoted its June issue to "Painting in the United States," the most complete and perhaps just representation of avant-garde painting in America that has appeared abroad. The work of some 75 American artists was reproduced, as well as more personal photographs, e.g., the late Piet Mondrian at an exhibition in New York with some of his friends, Morgan Russell and his wife standing in front of an enormous abstract picture that was exhibited at the Salon des Indépendants in Paris in 1914, and Jackson Pollock working on the floor of his studio on Long Island; there also appeared in translation the talks delivered at the Museum of Modern Art in New York by five American painters, Stuart Davis, Fritz Glarner, Willem de Kooning, George L. K. Morris and Robert Motherwell (the sixth artist, Alexander Calder, was omitted, as a sculptor, in an issue devoted solely to painting), on the occasion of the Museum's large exhibition, "Abstract Art in America," organized by Andrew C. Ritchie.*

But the main text, in many respects the most interesting to us in America, in this number of Art d'aujourd'hui *is that by the man who is responsible for the issue, having made a trip from Paris especially for the purpose, Michel Seuphor, author of the standard work in Europe on* L'art abstrait *(Paris, 1949), who is perhaps the first European to deal in his article (a translation of which follows) sympathetically and understandingly with the history and present status of American avant-garde art, and with tacit acceptance of the fact so often denied or ignored in Europe, that we too have contributed to that international tradition in modern art that nothing has been able to smother, wherever artists have been independent, which indeed might be called the art of independents.*

PARIS NEW YORK 1951

by Michel Seuphor

"What you must never forget," Marcel Duchamp said to me as we were dining in the Donati's fashionable apartment, "what you must never forget, my friend, is that only a century ago Twenty-third Street was open country, and I do mean open country." Today the heart of New York City extends from Thirty-second to Fifty-seventh Street, forming a rectangle centered around Rockefeller Center, the Museum of Modern Art and Times Square, skirted to the south by the Empire State Building, to the North by the rows of art galleries on Fifty-seventh Street. The skyscraper bastion of Wall Street is way down at the very tip of the island, far, very far from New York's daily life. But even this bastion has existed for less than a half century. Indeed forty years ago the Singer Building was the highest of the skyscrapers, while today one hardly notices it; it is eclipsed by the multitude and the bulk of its neighbors. This district of high finance has turned out to be the most ancient part of New York. I walked in those very narrow and somber streets, the only non-rectilinear ones of New York, much as in Paris a tourist would walk in the Rue de la Huchette.

Imagine a Paris of 1850, still restricted to the Latin Quarter and Saint-Germain-des-Près, and having become in one hundred years what it is today but with these original districts completely transformed and rebuilt in height during this lapse of time. Such is the prodigy of New York.

Art always arrives last. It appears when wealth has been acquired. It is a luxury, a dessert. But it outlasts riches. If it has subsisted through them and has sometimes worked for them, its spirit is elsewhere. Art's essential quality is not indebted to wealth, does not repay wealth. It is a world ever new in the old world of greed; it is disinterestedness, gratuity, creation

through sheer delight of creation. To a grey universe encumbered by the useful, it brings the one indispensable uselessness: spirit. And suddenly everything is brightened by sunlight.

Is this why Fifty-seventh Street has always seemed to me so drenched in sunlight, even on a snowy day? Or is it Sidney Janis' smile, Wittenborn's animated voice, Egan's veiled humor, or, just around the corner on Madison Avenue, the ever cordial welcome of Kootz? This street of the art trade has very wide pavements; there is room for everyone. Although the houses are high, they are bright outside as well as within. Space and light for all. Besides, artists and art galleries are less numerous here than in Paris. For a hundred in New York we have a thousand in Paris, and yet it seems there is not enough space for everyone. Let those who are not pushers take care. Among the modest, the non-intriguing, who will have a chance? I get the impression that in New York everyone gets his chance. Although there too it passes, perhaps, even more quickly than elsewhere.

It is only in the past five or six years that modern painting has begun to live. I mean it has entered the ranks of society, it is talked about. Formerly everything was imported, at least all the art in the galleries and museums. Nearly all the original conceptions came from Paris. Today Paris maintains a very great prestige in the eyes of most Americans, but the opinion is that their young painters equal ours. Certain individuals, lightly tinged with nationalism, go so far as to say that their painters are much stronger than those of blood-drained Europe, a senile continent doddering to its end. They are of course wrong. A certain American painter visiting Paris a few months ago had only criticism for the paintings he saw. Yet he had the opportunity to see excellent exhibitions and large Salons where there was both good and bad; but nothing, absolutely nothing, found grace in his eyes. All subtlety he called weakness or antiquated romanticism, all strength lacked that very quality. Meanwhile he never stopped singing the praises of American painting, extolling its powerfulness, virginality and its multiple audacities. I have just seen all this on the spot, I have made a thorough round of New York's art world, I have sniffed in every corner, and I admit that there is indeed a young American art that is attracting a great deal of attention by its sometimes very pure, sometimes very violent accents, but I can not state that what I saw there is either superior or inferior to the avant-garde movements in Paris. The diverse trends manifested here are also seen over there, the problems the artists give themselves are the same, the quality of the paintings is often very similar. Sidney Janis demonstrated this authoritatively in a recent exhibit where twelve New York painters were confronted with twelve from Paris. Whereupon my nationalist exclaimed that the works of the Paris painters were the best of the respective artists, while the Americans were badly chosen! You see impassioned individuals always have an answer for everything; they make their fixation dance and so fill the world with their folly.

I said earlier that young American painting made its entry into the world only a few years ago. However, it has had a long pre-history that is also a long and serious education. In this field the influence of Marcel Duchamp has been predominant ever since the famous exhibition at the Armory in 1913. In 1920 Kathérine Dreier collaborated with Duchamp and Man Ray in founding the "Société Anonyme," a prodigious collection that at present contains the works of all the painters who have won distinction in abstract art between 1910 and 1945. Since its first aim was didactic, a part of this collection is always on tour in some part of the United States, in this way familiarising the remote university circles with the most typical artistic expressions of our time.

It was approximately at about the same time (1920) that A. E. Gallatin began the collection, which is likewise very important, that was later to be called the Museum of Living Art. It is now in the Philadelphia Museum.

A third collection which cannot be slighted is the one sponsored by the Guggenheim Foundation (The Museum of Non-Objective Painting) directed by Hilla Rebay. This museum seems to have been founded exclusively for Rudolf Bauer and Kandinsky, although some works of other painters also hang there.

Last in chronological order, but already tending to surpass the others in importance, is the collection of the Museum of Modern Art. Founded in 1929, this museum acquired its building only ten years later. At the present time it owns about nine hundred works of which only one sixth can be exhibited at one time.

But it is the "Société Anonyme" that remains the richest in diverse, authentically modern art products. If this were merged with the private collection of Miss Dreier, we would have the largest collection in the world for the study of avant-garde art of the first half of this century. In its present state today in New Haven, at the Museum of Yale University, this collection already represents sixty-nine artists from twenty-three countries with over five hundred works, most of them abstract.

To give an example of America's discernment in the field of art, I need only say that each of these four museums has owned for a long time important canvases by Mondrian, a painter absent from the museums of France where he spent twenty-four years of his life, a very inconspicuous one, to be sure. Yet this did not stop Miss Dreier, Gallatin, and still other Americans from discovering him and buying his canvases more than twenty years ago. Miss Dreier's signal accomplishment is that as early as 1926 she dared write, "Holland has produced three great painters who, while being the logical expression of their nation, surpassed it by the vigor of their personality. The first was Rembrandt, the second van Gogh, the third is Mondrian." Thus it is that a visiting American was capable of recognizing, more than a quarter of a century ago, what the French art critics are only beginning to surmise.

But man is the same everywhere, and in America as elsewhere, the theory that no one is a prophet in his own country is at times verified. MacDonald-Wright and Morgan Russell, for instance, were cutting a figure as pioneers in Paris in 1913, and at the same period exhibited in New York at the Armory Show. In spite of a long analysis of their work in Willard Huntington Wright's book, published in New York in 1915, in which their art (Synchronism) is analysed at length, they remained in oblivion until the past few months. Rose Fried's gallery is the one that was first to exhibit, in November of 1950, the early works of these two great precursors; in the same exhibit the gallery fittingly added Patrick Bruce, another American painter whose life was quite obscure and who died in New York in 1937. I knew Bruce in Paris in about 1930. I remember him as a melancholy and taciturn man; he occupied a somber studio in the Place de Furstemberg that seemed empty and inhospitable. Henri-Pierre Roche, who knew him at that time saved a part of his work from destruction.

Even though it is true that an Association of Abstract American Painters, founded by G. L. K. Morris, has been organizing exhibits since 1936, I have a very clear impression that it was during the winter of 1950–1951 that abstract American Art entered into what might be called its apogee. Several remarkable exhibits took place in various galleries, culminating at the end of January in the exhibition called "Abstract Painting and Sculpture in America" at the Museum of Modern Art.

On the fifth of February, the same day that Sidney Janis inaugurated a magnificent exhibition of Mondrian, there took place in this museum an evening symposium at which five painters and one sculptor answered the question, "What does abstract art mean to me?" These six were chosen by Mr. Ritchie as being the most representative of the diverse tendencies in abstract American art. They are: Morris, Motherwell, Glarner, de Kooning, Calder, Stuart Davis. Below you will find the essential train of thought in each of these talks.

The great lecture hall of the Museum was filled with people eager to hear these gentlemen, but I must say that the public discussion following these statements was not of a higher intellectual level than that at similar discussions in Paris.

After this very solemn and impressive session a reception was held at the Penthouse of the Museum. Being engaged in a conversation, concerning Mondrian of course, with Mme. Charmion Wiegand, I found it natural for her to accompany me upstairs. But friendly voices seemed to oppose this, and the word "official" was pronounced several times. Mme. Wiegand, not being "officially" invited, had to leave the elevator midway, interrupting a conversation that was concerned with the precise aim of my trip to America. I was dismayed to such a point that, when I reached the top floor, I was incapable of joining the select few right away. I went to meditate for a while on the terrace, facing the lights of Rockefeller Center. I thought of Mondrian's very humble life, and of the difficult times endured by abstract art, which had upon this very day become official in New York.

An angry voice had exclaimed loudly in the elevator: "When things become official they are dead." Such an obviously exaggerated notion stems from our long tradition of fighting against the State's impingement on the realm of art; against the stipends and awards and dignitary honors, in other words, against the official world. In other epochs, for example in the Italian Renaissance, this same officialdom was magnanimous, discriminating, even audacious in its tastes; and no one dreamed of questioning its sanctions.

"Officials" are, after all, human beings, and it is on the excellence of these gentlemen's quality of mind, on their clairvoyance, that everything depends. Is it the distorting influence of being a foreigner that gives me such a favorable impression of American officials? All those I have had the pleasure of meeting, Barr, Wheeler, Ritchie, Clifford, have seemed to me to be so generous, hospitable by nature, well-informed—so much so that an art protected by them could have no better guarantee of not falling into a sterile academicism, and of freely developing according to the infinite variety of talents and modes of expression.

The art of today,—by which I mean in substance abstract art, is a universal language in which every individual can forge his own style with as much originality, felicity and force as his talent and personality allow. Everyone is invited, everyone is called (this must certainly be admitted), but as in the past, it is only the tenaciously persevering, the great self-conquerers, those who are ready to undergo any sacrifice rather than make the slightest compromise, who are elected—this too must be admitted.

It seems to me that many American painters are endowed with these qualities; and it is a great marvel to see that the Museum of Modern Art (which there is truly worthy of its name) knows these artists, exhibits and buys their work, and requests their presence at such great official gatherings.

In exoneration of the French "officials," I might say that in Paris, artists (even abstract) are so numerous that it would be impossible to let everyone speak. Furthermore, we are so used to free-for-alls! What would become of the French "critical sense" if we had to stop tripping each other up, even for a day. "I had him on the spot. . . . He got a taste of it. . . . It wouldn't hurt him to wait a while. I am going to knock that

into his head. . . ." Woe to the fellow who doesn't hurt anyone. You win friends here in exact proportion to the slandering you do. The existence of an enemy camp is the only raison d'être of a bond of friendship. In France, generosity and a conciliatory disposition do not pay: one must be against. To be against or not to be.

During my stay there were two other important exhibitions: at the Eighth Street Whitney Museum (Contemporary American Painting) and at the Metropolitan Museum (American Painting Today). Both were brilliant proof that it is indeed abstract art that holds first place in the States, both for the number and the quality of the works. This is not only true in New York City, but throughout the country. At the Metropolitan I saw abstract paintings of unquestionable worth from 13 different states. This was a surprise to me, for young painters had spoken of this as being an uninteresting grouping of out-of-date art. By chance I got there anyway. I have made a memorandum of the names of the painters whose work (always abstract) struck me as particularly interesting: Magafan, Drumlevitch, Slutzky, Alston, Vytlacil, Salemme, Scarlett and Ruvolo (all from New York State), Vavruska, Guy, Takehita, Koppe and Chermayeff (Illinois), Conway (Missouri), Day and Mueller (Wyoming), Norris (Hawaii), Burkhardt and Armer (California), Meigs (Nebraska), Thrall and Knipschild (Michigan), Fogel (Texas), Stuart (North Carolina), Atherton (Vermont), Phoutrides (Washington) and Parker (Minnesota).

At the Whitney Museum there was an equally large number of paintings which could not leave one indifferent. Some names: Robert Conover, Fred Conway, Willem de Kooning, Jimmy Ernst (son of Max), Lyonel Feininger, Fritz Glarner, Adolph Gottlieb, Philip Guston, J. M. Hanson, Stanley William Hayter, Josef Albers, William Baziotes, Ilya Bolotowsky, Fritz Bultman, Boris Margo, John Marin, George L. K. Morris, Robert Motherwell, Seong Moy, I. Rice Pereira, Jackson Pollock, Richard Pousette-Dart, Ad Reinhardt, Mark Rothko, Bradley Tomlin, Esteban Vincente, Jean Xceron, Max Weber and John von Wicht.

In the same museum, this exhibit was followed by a retrospective showing of the work of Arshile Gorky, who died three years ago. If one could put aside the Gorky influenced by Picasso, the Gorky aping Léger and Miro, there would still remain an authentic Gorky, of an erotic-surrealistic vein, but highly sensitive and individualized, unquestionably abstract. In my opinion his work is important enough for him to be considered a very great painter who will leave an imprint on American Art.

I shall try to sketch in a few strokes the principal patterns of present-day painting in America. This classification is by nature incomplete and arbitrary. But one cannot give an overall picture of anything without resorting to simplification. So here is a homemade plan of the various headquarters of painting over there.

1. An abstract-fauve or neo-expressionistic trend, preferring to use lines and spots expressing natural disorder, spasms, violence. Examples: de Kooning, Pollock, Tomlin, Clifford Still.

2. An abstract-geometric trend. Successors of Mondrian and Van Doesburg. Examples: Glarner, Diller, Bolotowsky, Leon Smith.

3. An abstract-impressionistic trend. It puts all the stress on expression through color alone, on pure harmony of tones, with the deliberate exclusion of all definite line or form. Examples: Rothko, Stamos.

4. A romantic-objective or semi-abstract trend borrowing its motifs and sometimes even its inspiration from primitive art and popular wall drawings. Examples: Gottlieb, Tamayo.

5. Surrealistic trend. Examples: Seligmann, Kay Sage.

6. An abstract trend stemming from surrealism. Preference given to the curving line. Examples: Baziotes, Gorky, Donati.

7. An abstract-cubistic trend. Preference given to straight and angular line. Examples: Stuart Davis, Morris, Xceron.

8. A figurative-expressionistic trend. The best of these painters are visibly influenced by abstraction; to it they owe their freedom of expression and the freshness of their inspiration. Examples: Feininger, Marin.

It is not necessary to add that certain painters can be said to belong to two or three schools at one time. The art of Motherwell, for instance, is often a definite mixture of surrealistic and cubistic tendencies, with still another element evident which is pure Motherwell.

Hans Hofmann, in the past few years, has shown a very decided desire to conciliate the chaotic morphology of his early work with rectilinear geometric forms to which are sometimes added constructions of fluid lines; the whole is merged into a lyricism whose vigor of expression conceals a very great refinement of thought.

Shall I sketch a few portraits?

Stuart Davis is a sulky rebel, gin drinker as well as painter. Wears very red suspenders on a very blue shirt. Talks out of the corner of his mouth, making no effort to make himself heard. Pretty young wife who at one time danced with Mondrian, but his steps were too tricky for her. New York accent not much more intelligible than her husband's. I spent the evening between a tender mewing and a muffled barking. No paintings to be seen. Davis is presently reading a book, "The Human Use of Human Beings," which is much more important than painting. The fact is that Davis misused my "being." Instead of paintings, he showed me "Miarka, the Bear's Daughter."

You could not imagine a more striking contrast to this stocky proletarian than the person of George L. K. Morris, an aristocrat to his finger-tips, with a body as long as a breadless day. But here bread is not lacking, nor any desired delicacy. Good breeding, perfect manners, a very enviable collection of masters. We dined in the company of Braque, Picasso, Léger, Klee, in their highest spirits, with a view of the East River and the Queensboro Bridge.

Mrs. Morris is known as Frelinghuysen. She paints and sings. When she sings, you don't know she is a painter and vice versa. No, she doesn't dance.

Glarner is short and square. Stones move slowly. They think first, at great length. They are of one piece. This particular stone smokes a pipe, rather it spends the day lighting its pipe and burning its fingers. A very human stone. Seems to know what it wants. Surely it must contain a lot inside. And it laughs easily, making its belly shake. He who laughs will not be punished. Laughter gives the indispensable tone to the harmony of life. And Glarner knows how to harmonize a canvas to perfection. His is painting that laughs seriously.

Pollock is sullen. What loads does this man carry on his shoulders? What is the remorse that gnaws at him so? Only once, for only an instant have I seen him brighten: at the end of the showing of a color film in which he is seen painting under a blue sky in the way a peasant tills, sows, works.

Motherwell looks very gentle. Is he really as gentle as all that? Civilized. Too much so? A bit of decadence could not harm an art as subtle as his, like a rare viand gamy to just the right degree. He is impulsive, low-voiced, speaks a finical English. What is he dreaming of while he talks of other things?

Diller, indolent athlete, taciturn, more at ease in his painting than in his own skin. Variations on a neo-plastic theme with avowed preference for the pizzicato.

De Kooning, quicksilver, frank, enthusiastic, every day torn with some new anguish, which every day's act of painting relieves. Owns a rumpled second-floor studio on Fourth Avenue that almost merges with the life of the street.

Reinhardt observes the world and speaks not, while a very slight smile floats on his round face. There is a hidden humor behind the wilfully indifferent glance.

Xceron, hurried, frightened, intimidated, with a heart full of friendship. Who has beaten this good man? Who feels ill-disposed towards this honest and straightforward human being?

The Hulbeck apartment is so vast that all the members of the family paint at great distances from each other. They borrow nothing from one another, never are jealous of each other. Beate and Richard cooperated in the creation of Tom, whose height is exactly that of Beate and Richard put together. She tears papers with rage and pastes them up again with love; he paints as one would play lotto, to forget that he is Richard Hülsenbeck, Dada poet, medical doctor and Tom's father.

In Connecticut, one hour's driving distance from New York, Calder owns a great birdcage filled with metal birds where you sometimes hear the sound of a gong. Fifty yards away, there is another cage filled with green birds, or if you prefer, with a mass of varied plants, some of them climbing ones. He works in the former, lives in the other. A grand piano is almost hidden under the greenery. But resonant accompaniment is furnished by the crackling of the logs in the fireplace whose yawning maw violently contrasts with all the surrounding green. Outside, it is snowing.

Of all the artists in New York, Kiesler lives the highest. Probably because he is the smallest, the most . . . modest! According to the Gospel, "Be humble and ye shall be lifted high." He reigns as a master—what am I saying, as an emperor, over Greenwich Village. Noblesse oblige. He is so good to his subjects that he has earned the right, even in this life, to live on high. From the top of his lofty paradise, New York certainly looks like the capital of the world, which is a very little thing in the eyes of the works of Frederick John Kiesler.

Very near to Kiesler (very far from here in the vertical sense) Evsa Model lives in a sort of mezzanine that he has decorated with great red, black and yellow squares with a surprising effect. His art consists of unceasingly repeating New York houses in the manner of a house painter in love with vivid colors. Being afraid that it might be taken for abstraction, he takes care to put two or three little men on each canvas. He really paints them in, doesn't cut them out of a magazine. The canvases are very big and the men tiny. Model speaks French. All of us (living and dead) knew him in Montparnasse in days gone by. In truth, he has never left Bohemian Montparnasse, as American as he may be.

Stamos swarms in all directions in feverish search of . . . what?

Richter is the man who knows best how to preside at a table. He judges the living and the dead. He has all the qualities of a judge: a temperament easily incited to anger (the anger is often feigned) and a heart of gold full of juvenile yearnings. He owns a country house with a little lake in a spot that I shall dream of for a long time, a charming wife and numerous cigars.

Did Donati sell his soul to the devil or to surrealism? In any case he is the owner of a quivering stone that is one of the three marvels of New York, the other two being the Empire State Building and the tame squirrels in Central Park.

Rothko? Gallatin? Gottlieb? Holtzmann? Cavallon? Seliger? Holty? Morgan Russell? I shall speak of them another time. Our visit must not become too tiring. Let's get an orange drink at the corner drugstore.

Paris is velvet, silk, soft clinging woolen stuff. New York is made of cutting metal. In its better moments, it is a diamond with a thousand facets in which the moon is sometimes mirrored. The night sky of New York is the greatest beauty of this city. The scintillating carpet stretched overhead invites lyricism, intoxicates to the point of exaltation. I have never met anyone who has not been more or less bewitched by it. Seen from the top of a skyscraper it is the ecstasy of earth comparing itself with the calm sky. The most extravagant of dreams can become reality in this festival of light. A light that is both orderly and wildly scattered.

Paris beats the measure; New York moves in rhythms. Paris has its gait; New York walks.

Paris has secrets; its ear is open to obscure lives that are bound up in it—that will not be heard about until later; in New York everybody is famous, everybody figures on the first page, aggrandizement is killed by publicity.

Everything is open in this city, everything is easy to know and get into. The generosity and hospitality of Americans is proverbial, but I never thought the proverb so true until I began to get acquainted with these qualities. Houses are open everywhere, very hospitable ones. But what is even better is the open hearts and minds of their occupants. When everything is open

there is not much mystery, there is not much to discover, but there is also less intrigue. In the artistic circles, the groups do not fight and do not consider themselves exclusive, do not wave doctrinaire banners. There are no airtight partitions; all the artists know each other and see each other. This does not mean that there is no competition, but it is not ferocious. It is a matter of taking your place; there is a place for everyone in this round world where everyone is on top. On the other hand, in Paris everyone is preoccupied with keeping the other fellow from getting any place whatsoever. For in Paris to be sure, there could not be room enough for everybody. Where would we go if everyone had to have a place—his place in the sun and there was not enough sun?

Therefore the literary and artistic life of Paris is rotten with intrigues, trickery, wire pulling, sordid calculation, murderous gossip. And no one profits much from it; jealousy and bitterness reign over all.

I have not told you much about painting. Alas, I have neither the keen mind nor the caustic wit of our acknowledged art critics who would bring back more judgments from such a trip. All the talent of the critic lies in quick, definitive, unimpeachable judgment. But are there any such critics now (except Charles Estienne and Léon Degand of course) who have this talent? As for me I feel I am very aloof where these qualities are concerned. I am even afraid of judging. I am timid before a work of art. But I think that in not judging I have rarely been mistaken. I am glad to exist, to harm no one, to help where I can. Live and let live, that also is an American motto. As to the work, it will be judged by time.

"Paintings should be seen and not heard about," said Henry Clifford. That is why it is better for the moment to illustrate this article with photographs, even if merely black and white ones, hoping that one of these days the Museum of Modern Art will be able to bring to Paris the remarkable collection of abstract American art that it has just hung on its walls. It would be impossible to adequately multiply cultural exchanges between the two poles—between the two capitals—of the Western World.

(Translated by Francine du Plessix and Florence Weinstein)

ART D'AUJOURD'HUI

LA PEINTURE AUX ÉTATS-UNIS

"The most significant gift of the year is that of the Louise and Walter Arensberg Collection of Twentieth Century and pre-Columbian art, the title to which, at the close of the year 1950, passed from the Francis Bacon Foundation to" the Philadelphia Museum of Art. Since 1914, the collection represents the pioneer spirit and selective interest of Mary Louise Stevens, a musician, and Walter Conrad Arensberg, a poet. These views show the paintings and sculptures installed in the Arensberg house, Hollywood. Outstanding for its examples by Constantin Brancusi and Marcel Duchamp, it includes the work of 51 modern artists and almost 200 paintings, sculptures, prints, drawings and "objects," exclusive of the art of primitive cultures. On the occasion of a major exhibition at the Art Institute of Chicago (October-December 1949), the Arensberg Collection was described as "the most discriminating single group of twentieth century paintings and sculpture in existence."

All the following photographs of the Arensberg residence are reproduced through the courtesy of Fred R. Dapprich, photographer, Los Angeles.

MUSEUM

ACQUISITIONS

A SELECTED LIST OF
MODERN WORKS OF ART
ADDED TO AMERICAN PUBLIC
COLLECTIONS

FALL 1949 —— WINTER 1950

ADLER, Jankel: TWO RABBITS, Oil on canvas
(1942), Museum of Modern Art, 1949
AFRO (BASALDELLA): CONCERTINO, Oil and
watercolor (1948), Albright Art Gallery,
1949
ALBERS, Josef: TENAYUCA (DARK), Oil on
canvas, Cincinnati Art Museum, 1949
ALBRIGHT, Ivan Le Lorraine: AMONG THOSE
LEFT, Oil on canvas (1928-29), Carnegie
Institute, 1950; HEAVY THE OAR TO HIM
WHO IS TIRED, HEAVY THE COAT,
HEAVY THE SEA, Oil on canvas, Art In-
stitute of Chicago, 1949
ARNEST, Bernard: VIEW OF THE CITY
THROUGH SIGNS, Oil on canvas (1950),
Walker Art Center, 1950
AULT, George C.: FESTUS YAYPLE AND HIS
OXEN, Oil on canvas, Cleveland Museum
of Art, 1949
AVERY, Milton: CLEANING FISH, GASPE, Oil
on canvas, Whitney Museum, 1950; GASPE
BAY, Oil on canvas, Houston Museum of
Fine Arts, 1949

BAIZERMAN, Saul: SLUMBER, Hammered
Copper, Whitney Museum, 1949
BARKER, Walter: THE EARTH RECEIVING
THE DEAD, City Art Museum of St. Louis
BARLACH, Ernst: WITCH, Woodcut, Allen
Memorial Art Museum, 1949
BARNET, Will: SMALL TOWN, Drypoint, Wor-
cester Art Museum, 1949
BAYER, Herbert: BLUE MOVEMENT, Oil on
canvas (1945), San Francisco Museum of
Art, 1949
BAZIOTES, William: GREEN FORM, Oil on
canvas, Whitney Museum, 1949
BECKMANN, Max: HOTEL LOBBY, Oil on can-
vas, Albright Art Gallery, 1950; THE
MILL, Oil on canvas (1947), Portland Art
Museum, 1950; STILL LIFE WITH CAN-
DLES, Oil on canvas (1949), Museum of
Modern Art, 1950; STILL LIFE WITH
LILLIES, Oil on canvas (1949), Detroit In-
stitute of Arts, 1950; BEAULIEU, Univer-
sity of Illinois; NUDE, Drypoint, DANCERS,
woodcut, Allen Memorial Art Museum,
1949; Two lithographs from series "DAY
AND DREAM", Brooklyn Museum, 1949

BELLING, Rudolf: PORTRAIT OF ALFRED
FLECHTHEIM, Bronze, (1927), Museum of
Modern Art, 1950
BELLOWS, George: EDITH CAVELL, Oil on
canvas, Springfield (Mass.) Art Museum,
1949
BENTON, Thomas Hart: BOOM TOWN, Roch-
ester Memorial Art Gallery, 1950; SHAL-
LOW CREEK, Lithograph, Montclair Art
Museum, 1949
BÉRARD, H. M.: CLAIR OBSCUR, Oil on can-
vas, San Francisco Museum of Art, 1949;
SUR UN THÈME DE J. S. BACH, Oil on
canvas, San Francisco Museum of Art,
1949; THE MADWOMAN OF CHAILLOT,
Costume studies, Brush and ink, (1945)
Museum of Modern Art, 1950
BERMAN, Eugene: TOBIAS AND THE ANGEL
study, Ink drawing (1938), Detroit Institute
of Arts, 1949; COSTUMED FIGURE, Ink
(1943), Allen Memorial Art Museum, 1949
BOCCIONI, Umberto: MUSCULAR DYNAMISM,
Charcoal (1913), UNIQUE FORMS OF CON-
TINUITY IN SPACE, Bronze (1913), Mu-
seum of Modern Art, 1950
BOHROD, Aaron: KIOSK, PARIS, Gouache,
Allen Memorial Art Museum, 1949
BONNARD, Pierre: LE BAIN, Lithograph, Allen
Memorial Art Museum, 1949; THE DES-
SERT, Oil on canvas (1920), Cleveland Mu-
seum of Art, 1949; IN THE DINING ROOM,
Art Institute of Chicago, 1950; STREET
SEEN FROM ABOVE, Lithograph, John
Herron Art Institute, 1950
BOOKATZ, Samuel: THE REST (EUDORA),
Pencil (1949), Corcoran Gallery of Fine
Arts, 1949
BORÈS, Francisco: THE FITTING, Oil on can-
vas (1934), Museum of Modern Art, 1949
BOSA, Louis: END OF THE FESTIVAL, Oil on
canvas, University of Illinois, 1949; HAL-
LOWE'EN, Worcester Art Museum, 1949
BOUCHÉ, Louis: RAILROAD CROSSING, Oil on
canvas, Cincinnati Art Museum, 1949
BOUNEAU, Emile: LA CONCORDE, Oil on can-
vas, John Herron Art Institute, 1949
BOURGEOIS, Louise: SLEEPING FIGURE, Bal-
sa wood (1950), Museum of Modern Art,
1950
BRANCUSI, Constantin: FISH, Marble, (1930),
Museum of Modern Art, 1950

MUSEUM ACQUISITIONS

BRAQUE, George: STILL LIFE WITH FISH, Oil
on canvas (1943), Toledo Museum, 1949;
HELIOS, Color lithograph (1947), Portland
Art Museum, 1949

BRAUNER, Victor: PANTACULAR PROGRES-
SION, Encaustic (1948), Museum of Modern
Art, 1949

BRICE, William: PALM SHEATH, Crayon,
brush and ink (1947), Museum of Modern
Art, 1950

BROWNE, Byron: WOMAN WITH BIRD, Oil on
canvas, Whitney Museum, 1949

BRYEN, Camille: IMAGINARY STRUCTURE,
Watercolor, pen and ink (1948), Museum of
Modern Art, 1950

BUFFET, Bernard: STILL LIFE WITH FISH II,
Oil on canvas (1949) Museum of Modern
Art, 1950

BUNCE, Louis: GARDEN NO. I, Serigraph,
Portland Art Museum, 1949

BURCHFIELD, Charles: CHURCH BELLS
RINGING, RAINY WINTER NIGHT, Water-
color, Cleveland Museum of Art, 1949;
PIPPIN HOUSE, EAST LIVERPOOL, OHIO,
Watercolor (1920), Museum of Modern Art,
1950; SPHINX AND THE MILKY WAY,
Munson-Williams-Proctor Institute

BURFORD, Byron: STILL LIFE, Oil on canvas, Walker Art Center, 1949

BURLIUK, David: THE WHITE COW, Oil on
canvas, Whitney Museum, 1949

CALDER, Alexander: POMEGRANATE, Sheet
metal, Whitney Museum, 1950; STEEL
FISH, (1934) Virginia Museum of Fine
Arts, 1949

CALLAHAN, Kenneth: CHALLENGE AND RE-
SPONSE, University of Washington, LAND-
SCAPE NO. 5, SERIES 2, Ink, Portland Art
Museum, 1950

CÉZANNE, Paul: CHESTNUT TREES AT JAS
DE BOUFFAN, Oil on canvas (1885-87),
Minneapolis Institute of Arts, 1949; HOUSE
IN PROVENCE, Oil on canvas, (1885-86),
John Herron Art Museum, 1949; LAND-
SCAPE, Watercolor, Newark Museum,
1950; LE VIADU À L'ESTAQUE, Oil on
canvas (1882-85), Allen Memorial Art Mu-
seum, 1949; VICTOR CHOQUET, Oil on

canvas (1878-80), Columbus Gallery of
Fine Arts, 1950

CHAGALL, Marc: THE FATHER'S GRAVE,
Etching, Allen Memorial Art Museum,
1949; THE FLYING FISH, Oil on canvas
(1948), Albright Art Gallery, 1949; CIR-
CUS RIDER, Oil on canvas, Art Institute of
Chicago, 1950

CHAPMAN, Howard E.: THE COVE, Gouache
(1949), Corcoran Gallery of Fine Art, 1949

CHIRICO, Giorgio de: HORSE AND ZEBRA ON
A BEACH, Oil on canvas, Newark Museum,
1949; SACRED FISH, Oil on canvas (1917?),
Museum of Modern Art, 1950; DISTURB-
ING VOYAGE, Oil on canvas (1913), Mu-
seum of Modern Art, 1950

CIKOVSKY, Nicolai: SPRING MELODY, Oil on
canvas (1948), Corcoran Gallery of Fine
Art, 1949

CITRON, Minna: MEN SELDOM MAKE PASSES,
Color etching, Worcester Art Museum,
1949

COLQUHOUN, Robert: WOUNDED SCOTSMAN
AND THE MATCH SELLER, Transfer
drawing (1945), Museum of Modern Art,
1950

CONSTANT, John: UNTITLED (Seated Nude
Woman), Watercolor, San Francisco Museum of Art, 1949

CONWAY, Fred: DANCER, Oil on canvas, Uni-
sity of Illinois, 1949; WITCHERY, Oil on
canvas (1948), Corcoran Gallery of Fine
Art, 1949

CORNELL, Joseph: CENTRAL PARK CAR-
ROUSEL — 1950, IN MEMORIAM, Construction (1950), Museum of Modern Art,
1950

CORINTH, Lovis: SELF PORTRAIT, Oil on
canvas (1924), Museum of Modern Art,
1950

CRAWFORD, Ralston: AIRCRAFT FACTORY,
Oil on canvas, Cincinnati Art Museum,
1949; THIRD AVENUE EL, Oil on canvas
(1949), Walker Art Center, 1950; WHITE-
STONE BRIDGE, Rochester Memorial Art
Gallery, 1950

DALI, Salvador: HONEY IS SWEETER THAN
BLOOD, Oil on canvas, Santa Barbara Mu-

seum of Art; MAE WEST, Gouache, Art Institute of Chicago, 1950; ST GEORGE AND THE DRAGON, Etching, Detroit Institute of Art, 1949

DARIE, Sandu: COMPOSITION IN RED, Gouache, ink and wax (1946), Museum of Modern Art, 1950

DAVID, Hermine: ALGIERS, Watercolor, University of Michigan Museum of Art

DAVIS, Stuart: GARAGE LIGHTS, Rochester Memorial Art Gallery, 1950; LITTLE GIANT STILL LIFE, Virginia Museum of Fine Arts

DEGAS, Edgar: AFTER THE BATH, Lithograph, Fogg Art Museum, 1949; GALLOPING HORSE, Bronze, Toledo Museum of Art, 1950; MANET, etching (1864), Metropolitan Museum of Art, 1949; MARY CASSATT AT THE LOUVRE, etching and aquatint (1865), John Herron Art Institute, 1950

DE CHIRICO see CHIRICO

DEMUTH, Charles: TWO GIRLS, Watercolor (1917), University of Michigan Museum of Art; VAUDEVILLE, Watercolor (1917), Museum of Modern Art, 1950

DOESBURG,Theo van: COMPOSITION (THE COW), Oil on canvas (1917?), Museum of Modern Art, 1949

DODD, Lamar: THE COTTON PICKERS, Oil on canvas, Wilmington Society of Fine Arts, 1949; FROM THIS EARTH, Oil on canvas (1945), Rochester Memorial Art Gallery, 1949

DOVE, Arthur: CARS IN SLEET STORM, Rochester Memorial Art Gallery, 1950

DRUMLEVITCH, Seymour: THE ARCHANGEL, Oil on canvas (1948), Albright Art Gallery, 1949

DU BOIS, Guy Pène: RACE TRACK, DEAUVILLE, Oil on canvas (1927), Carnegie Institute, 1949

DUFY, Raoul: THE FLEET AT VILLE-FRANCHE, Oil on canvas (1926), Museum of Modern Art, 1950

ENSOR, James: L'HOTEL DE VILLE D'AUDENARDE, Etching, Brooklyn Museum, 1949; LA MULTIPLICATION DES POISSONS, Etching (1891), Brooklyn Mu-

seum, 1949

EPSTEIN, Jacob: MARCHESA CASATI, Bronze (1918), Allen Memorial Art Museum, 1949

ERNST, Jimmy: CALLIGRAPHICA, NO. 2, Watercolor, Whitney Museum, 1949; PERSONAL HISTORY, Oil on canvas, Whitney Museum, 1950; A TIME FOR FEAR, Oil on canvas, Museum of Modern Art, 1950

FAGGI, Alfeo: BLANCHE GUZZI HECHT, Oil on canvas, Whitney Museum, 1949

FALKENSTEIN, Claire: SEED DISPOSAL, Plastic sculpture (1947) San Francisco Art Association, 1949

FEININGER, Lyonel: MANHATTAN CANYON (1942), STUDY IN SPACE IV (1947) THURINGIO (1948), Watercolors, Baltimore Museum of Art, 1950

FERBER, Herbert: PORTRAIT OF J. P., Lead, (1949), Museum of Modern Art, 1949

FINE, Perle: SUB-MARINE, Watercolor, Whitney Museum, 1949

FLANNAGAN, John: ASS, Granite, Newark Museum, 1950

FLOCK, Wyatt: MALEFACTOR, Los Angeles County Museum, 1949

FOUGERON, Andre: STUDIES OF A DEAD COCK, Brush and ink wash (1947), Museum of Modern Art, 1950

FRASCONI, Antonio: DON QUIXOTE AND ROCINANTE, NO. 14 (1949), RAIN,(1948), Woodcuts, Brooklyn Museum, 1949

FULLER, Sue: BAT, YOUNG BIRD, Engraving and soft-ground etchings, Brooklyn Museum, 1949

GATCH, Lee: BATTLE WAGON, Oil on canvas (1946), Museum of Modern Art, 1949

GAUGUIN, Paul: L'ESPRIT MODERNE ET LE CATHOLICISME, Monotypes and manuscript (1897-1902), City Art Museum of St. Louis, 1949; TAHITIAN LANDSCAPE, Oil on canvas, Minneapolis Institute of Arts, 1949; TWO TAHITIAN WOMEN, Metopolitan Museum, 1950

GELLER, Todros: STRANGE WORLDS, Oil on canvas, Art Institute of Chicago, 1949

GIACOMETTI, Alberto: CITY SQUARE (LA PLACE), Bronze (1948), Museum of Modern Art, 1950; MAN POINTING, Bronze, Baltimore Museum of Art, 1949; SLAUGHTERED WOMAN (FEMME ÉGORGÉE), Bronze (1932), Museum of Modern Art, 1950

GLARNER, Fritz: RELATIONAL PAINTING 1947-48, Oil on canvas, Museum of Modern Art, 1949

GLASCO, Joseph: BIG SITTING CAT, Pen and ink (1949), Museum of Modern Art, 1950

GLICKER, Benjamin: HARLEQUIN MUSICIAN, Oil on canvas, Detroit Institute of Art, 1949

GOGH, Vincent van: CYPRESSES, Oil on canvas, Metropolitan Museum of Art, 1949; LANDSCAPE, Oil on canvas (1889), John Herron Art Museum, 1949; STILL LIFE: FRUIT, Art Institute of Chicago, 1950; SUNFLOWERS, Oil on canvas, Metropolitan Museum of Art, 1949

GOLDIN, Leon: STILL LIFE, Oil on canvas, Los Angeles County Museum, 1949

GORKY, Arshile: AGONY, Oil on canvas (1947), Museum of Modern Art, 1950; THE BETROTHAL, NO. 2, Oil on canvas, Whitney Museum, 1950; COMPOSITION—HORSE AND FIGURES, Oil on canvas (1928), Museum of Modern Art, 1950

GOTTLIEB, Adolph: VIGIL, Oil on canvas, Whitney Museum, 1949

GRAHAM, Ellwood: MY STORY, Oil on panel (1947), San Francisco Museum of Art, 1949

GRANT, Gordon: THE LAST WORD, Etching, Detroit Institute of Art, 1949

GRAVES, Morris: BAT DANCING FOR A SLUG, Watercolor (1943), Museum of Modern Art, 1950; BIRD DEPRESSED BY THE LENGTH OF THE WINTER OF 1944, Oil on canvas, Fogg Art Museum, 1950; CEREMONIAL BRONZE TAKING FORM OF A BIRD, Gouache, Seattle Art Museum, 1949; PORTRAIT OF BILL CUMMINS, Oil on canvas, Portland Art Museum, 1949; WOUNDED IBIS, Worcester Art Museum, 1949

GREENE, Balcomb: EXECUTION: FIRST VERSION, Oil on canvas (1948), Museum of Modern Art, 1950

GREENE, Stephen: BURIAL, Oil on canvas, Whitney Museum, 1949

GRIS, Juan: THE CAFÉ TABLE, Art Institute of Chicago, 1950

GROSZ, George: DISPUTE BY MOONLIGHT, Brush and ink (c1920), Museum of Modern Art, 1950; STORM CLOUDS, CAPE COD, Lithograph, Allen Memorial Art Museum, 1950; THE WANDERER, Oil on canvas, Rochester Memorial Art Gallery, 1950

GUTTUSO, Renato: BULL, MINE CAR, Wash drawings (1949), Museum of Modern Art, 1950; MELON EATERS, Oil on canvas (1948), Museum of Modern Art, 1949

GUGLIEMI, Louis: CITYSCAPE WITH FIGURES, Oil on canvas, Whitney Museum, 1949

GWATHMEY, Robert: FOLK SONG, Ink on rice paper (1947), Museum of Modern Art, 1950; NON-FICTION, Rochester Memorial Art Gallery, 1950; SOWING, Oil on canvas, Whitney Museum, 1949

HANSON, J. M.: NOCTURNAL ENCOUNTERS, Oil on canvas (1949), Museum of Modern Art, 1950

HARKAVY, Minna: THE LAST PRAYER, Bronze, Whitney Museum, 1950

HARTLEY, Marsden: DUCK, Oil on canvas, Detroit Institute of Art, 1949; END OF STORM, Rochester Memorial Art Gallery, 1950: NORTHERN SUMMER WINDOW, Oil on canvas (1936), University of Michigan Museum of Art

HASELTINE, Jane W.: WITHIN, Linoleum cut, Portland Art Museum, 1950

HAWTHORNE, Charles W.: THE FISH AND THE MAN, Dallas Museum of Fine Arts

HAYTER, Stanley William: VICTIM, City Art Museum of St. Louis; WORK IN PROGRESS, Drawing, Whitney Museum, 1949

HELIKER, John: MEDITERRANEAN LANDSCAPE, University of Nebraska; STUDY, Pastel and ink, Whitney Museum, 1950

HOFER, Karl: TWO GIRLS EMBRACING, Watercolor, University of Michigan Museum of Art; WOMAN AT A TABLE, Ink and wash, Allen Memorial Art Museum, 1949

HOFMANN, Hans: ELEGY, Oil on canvas (1950), Walker Art Center, 1950; CONSTRUCTION, Gouache, Whitney Museum, 1950

HOFMANN, Robert: THE SCULPTOR IVAN MESTROVIC, Pastel, Syracuse Museum of Fine Arts, 1949

HOGUE, Alexander: AVALANCHE BY WIND, University of Arizona

HOPPER, Edward: SEVEN A.M., Oil on canvas, Whitney Museum, 1950

HOWARD, Charles: THE PROGENITORS, Oil on canvas, California Palace of the Legion of Honor, 1949

ISENBURGER, Eric: ROMANTIC FIGURE, Oil on canvas (1948), Corcoran Gallery of Fine Arts, 1949

JACKSON, Martin: HARBOR IN THE NIGHT, Oil on canvas (1948), Corcoran Gallery of Fine Arts, 1949

JAMIESON, Mitchell: BROTHER AND SISTER, Crayon drawing, Portland Art Museum, 1949

JOHNSTON, Ynez: SHIP AND STORM, Los Angeles County Museum, 1949

JUNYER, Joan: FIGURES FOR A CORNER, Pencil on cardboard, washed with white gouache (1948), Museum of Modern Art, 1950

KANDINSKY, Wassily: THE BLACK CIRCLE, Watercolor (1924), Museum of Modern Art, 1950; CHURCH AT MURNAU, Oil on cardboard (1909), Museum of Modern Art, 1950; LANDSCAPE WITH POPLARS, Oil on canvas (1911), Museum of Modern Art, 1950; ABSTRACTION IN RED, BLUE AND BLACK, Lithograph, Brooklyn Museum, 1949

KIRCHNER, Ernst Ludvig: THE CONCERT, Woodcut on paper, Fogg Art Museum, 1949; SELF PORTRAIT AS A SOLDIER, Oil on canvas (1915), Allen Memorial Art Museum, 1950; STREET, Oil on canvas (1907), Museum of Modern Art, 1950

KLEE, Paul: EQUALS INFINITY, Oil on canvas (1932), Museum of Modern Art, 1950; IN

THE SPIRIT OF HOFFMANN, Color lithograph, Smith College Museum of Art; LAUGHING GOTHIC, Watercolor (1915), Museum of Modern Art, 1950; VIRGIN IN TREE, Etching (1903), Brooklyn Museum, 1949

KNATHS, Karl: DUCK FLIGHT, Oil on canvas, Whitney Museum, 1949; SALT FLATS, Oil on canvas (1949), Walker Art Center, 1950

KOLBE, George: SELF PORTRAIT, Bronze (1926), City Art Museum of St. Louis, 1950: STANDING NUDE, Bronze, Portland Art Museum, 1950

KOLLWITZ, Kathe: THE HAPPY MOTHER, Lithograph, Fogg Art Museum, 1949; PLOWERS, Aquatint, Allen Memorial Art Museum, 1949

KUHN, Walt: CLOWN, Rochester Memorial Art Gallery, 1950; CLOWN IN HIS DRESSING ROOM, Oil on canvas, Whitney Museum, 1950

KUPFERMAN, Lawrence: THE FABULOUS CRUSTACEAN, Boston Museum of Fine Arts

LACHAISE, Gaston: GEORGIA O'KEEFFE, Alabaster, THE MOUNTAIN, Bronze, Metropolitan Museum of Art, 1950

LA FRESNAYE, Roger de: STUDIES OF A CLARINETIST, Pencil (c1918), Museum of Modern Art, 1950

LASANSKY, Mauricio: PIETA, Etching (1947), Brooklyn Museum, 1949

LAURENS, Henri: FEMME AGENOUILLÉE, Baked clay, Albright Art Gallery, 1949

LAWRENCE, Jacob: SEDATION, Casein (1950), Museum of Modern Art, 1950

LEBRUN, Rico: FIGURE IN RAIN, Oil on canvas (1949), Museum of Modern Art, 1950; MOCKING SOLDIER, Oil on canvas, University of Illinois, 1949; STUDY FOR A SOLDIER, Watercolor and gouache, Los Angeles County Museum, 1949

LEGER, Fernand: THE BLACK ROOT, Color lithograph, Smith College Museum of Art; THE CIRCUS, 5 lithographic illustrations, prints, John Herron Art Institute, 1950; DECORATIONS (2), Oil on canvas (1941), Museum of Modern Art, 1950; THE CRE-

ATION OF THE WORLD (BALLET NEGRÉ), Set designs, Pencil (1922), Museum of Modern Art, 1950

LEHMBRUCK, Wilhelm: STANDING WOMAN, Bronze (1910), City Art Museum of St. Louis, 1950

LEPRI, Stanislao: BANQUET, Gouache (1945), Museum of Modern Art, 1950

LEONID: MALAMOCCO, Oil on canvas (1948), Museum of Modern Art, 1950; SPANISH MOSS, Pencil, Detroit Institute of Art, 1949

LEVINE, Jack: RECEPTION IN MIAMI, Oil on canvas (1948), Whitney Museum, 1949

LIPCHITZ, Jacques: RAPE OF EUROPA IV, Gouache (1941), Museum of Modern Art, 1950; SAILOR WITH GUITAR, Bronze cast (1914), Philadelphia Museum of Art, 1950; SKETCH FOR PROMETHEUS, Bronze, SKETCH FOR SACRIFICE, Bronze, Portland Art Museum, 1950

LIPPOLD, Richard: VARIATION NO. 7: FULL MOON, Nickel chromium wire and thin brass rods (1949-50), Museum of Modern Art, 1950

LITVINOVSKY, P.: DISCUSSION, Oil on canvas, Los Angeles County Museum, 1949

LUKS, George: LONDON CABBY, Oil on canvas, Rochester Memorial Art Gallery, 1950

MacBRYDE, Robert: STILL LIFE, Oil on canvas (1948), Albright Art Gallery, 1949; STILL LIFE, SLICED CUCUMBERS IN DISH, Oil on canvas, Toledo Museum of Art, 1950

McCLELLAN, Douglas: CROWN OF THORNS, Drawing, Los Angeles County Museum, 1949

MACDONALD-WRIGHT, Stanton: SYNCHROMY, Oil on canvas (1917), Museum of Modern Art, 1949

MacGINNIS, Henry R.: DECEMBER MISTS, Oil on canvas, John Herron Art Institute, 1949

McINTOSH, Robert: THREE FIGURES, Watercolor and gouache, Los Angeles County Museum, 1949

MacIVER, Loren: THE CIRCUS, Walker Art Center; VENICE, Oil on canvas, Whitney Museum, 1949

MAILLOL, Aristide: CHAINED ACTION, Sketch for the bronze figure, Allen Memorial Art Museum, 1949; THE RIVER, Lead (1938-43), Museum of Modern Art, 1949; THE THREE NYMPHS, Bronze (1936), Minneapolis Institute of Arts, 1950

MANESSIER, Alfred: EVOCATION OF THE ENTOMBMENT, Watercolor, (1948), Museum of Modern Art, 1950

MANSHIP, Paul: EUROPA AND THE BULL, Bronze, John Herron Art Institute, 1950

MARCKS, Gerhard: ORPHEUS, Portfolio of woodcuts based on Ovid, Detroit Institute of Art, 1949

MARECAK, Edward: THE SAINT, Colorado Springs Fine Arts Center

MARGULES, Hirsh: PORTRAIT OF JOSEPH STELLA, Oil on canvas, Whitney Museum, 1949

MARIN, John: FROM THE BRIDGE, NEW YORK CITY, 1933, Wadsworth Atheneum; MARIN ISLAND — SMALL POINT MAINE, Rochester Memorial Art Gallery, 1950; REGION OF BROOKLYN BRIDGE FANTASY, Watercolor, Whitney Museum, 1949

MARINI, Marino: CAVALIER, Bronze, HORSEMAN, Lithograph, Portland Art Museum, 1949; PORTRAIT OF LAMBERTO VITALI, Bronze (1945), Museum of Modern Art, 1950

MARTINI, Alberto: DAEDALUS AND ICARUS, Bronze (1934-35), Museum of Modern Art, 1950

MASSON, André: MEDIATION ON AN OAK LEAF, tempera, pastel and sand on canvas (1942), Museum of Modern Art, 1950; THERE IS NO FINISHED WORLD, Oil on canvas, Baltimore Museum of Art, 1949

MATISSE, Henri: DANCER RESTING, Oil on canvas (1940), Toledo Museum of Art, 1949; FLOWERS, Brush and ink (1947), Museum of Modern Art, 1950; NUDE RECLINING, Lithograph (1929), Brooklyn Museum, 1949; THE RED STUDIO, Oil on canvas (1911), Museum of Modern Art, 1949; VASE OF ANEMONES, Oil on canvas (1918), San Francisco Museum of Art, 1949; STILL LIFE, Monotype, Allen Memorial Art Museum, 1949

MAURER, Alfred: YOUNG WOMAN IN KIMONO, Oil on canvas (1901-03), Corcoran Gallery of Art, 1950

MENKES, Sigmund: GIRL WITH FRUIT BOWL, Walker Art Center

MEZA, Guillermo: LA CAMISA BLANCA, Philadelphia Museum of Art

MIRO, Joan: COMPOSITION NO. 3, Etching, Brooklyn Museum, 1949; COW AND DOG, Color stencil, Smith College Museum of Art

MILLES, Carl: PEGASUS, Bronze, Des Moines Art Center, 1949

MODIGLIANI, Amedeo: RECLINING NUDE, Oil on canvas (1918?), Museum of Modern Art, 1950; STONE HEAD (1919), Philadelphia Museum of Art, 1950

MONDRIAN, Piet: COLOR SQUARES IN OVAL, Oil on canvas (1915), Museum of Modern Art, 1950; COMPOSITION C, Oil on canvas (1920), Museum of Modern Art, 1949; COMPOSITION IN BROWN AND GRAY, Oil on canvas (c1914), Museum of Modern Art, 1950; COMPOSITION — GRIS ROUGE, Oil on canvas, (1935), Art Institute of Chicago, 1950

MOORE, Henry: FAMILY GROUP, Bronze (1945-49), Museum of Modern Art, 1950; RECLINING FIGURE, Silk screen on linen, San Francisco Museum of Art, 1949

MORANDI, Giorgio: STILL LIFE, Oil on canvas (1938), Museum of Modern Art, 1950

MOTHERWELL, Robert: THE RED SKIRT, Oil on canvas, Whitney Museum, 1949; WESTERN AIR, Oil on canvas (1946-47), Museum of Modern Art, 1950

MOY, Seong: THE OLD CITY, Woodcut (1949), Brooklyn Museum, 1949

MUNCH, Edvard: PORTRAIT OF DR. MAX LINDE, Drypoint (1902), Brooklyn Museum, 1949

MURCH, Walter Tandy: THE CIRCLE, Oil on canvas, Brooklyn Museum, 1949

NASH, Paul: FRENCH FARM, Oil on canvas, Toledo Museum of Art, 1950; LANDSCAPE OF THE MEGALITHS, Watercolor (1937), Albright Art Gallery, 1949

NAUEN, Heinrich: HARVESTERS, Watercolor (1909), University of Michigan Museum of Art

NEPOTE, Alexander: SECLUDED, Oil on canvas (1948), San Francisco Museum of Art, 1950

NESCH, Rolf: GOD FATHER, Panel of four prints, Portland Art Museum, 1950

NICHOLSON, Ben: STILL LIFE, Oil on canvas (1945), Albright Art Gallery, 1949

NICOT, Louis Henri: GREYHOUND, Bronze, John Herron Art Institute

NOGUCHI, Isamu: MISS EXPANDING UNIVERSE, Aluminum (1932), Toledo Museum, 1949; PORTRAIT OF MY UNCLE, Terra Cotta (1931), Museum of Modern Art, 1950

NOLDE, Emil: AMARYLLIS AND ANEMONE, Watercolor, Museum of Modern Art, 1950; DER SÄNGER, Woodcut, Allen Memorial Art Museum, 1950

NORDFELDT, B. J. O.: FLOOD, Oil on canvas (1948), Corcoran Gallery of Fine Art, 1949; THE SWALLOWS, Oil on canvas, Wilmington Society of Fine Arts, 1949

O'KEEFFE, Georgia: JAWBONE AND FUNGUS, Rochester Memorial Art Gallery

OSVER, Arthur: CHIMNEYS AND BUILDINGS, Oil on canvas, University of Illinois, 1949; THE CLUSTER, Oil on canvas (1947), University of Michigan Museum of Art; TANKS AND BILLBOARDS, Colorado Springs Fine Arts Center

PALAZZOLA, Guy: ALLIUM SATIVUM, Oil on canvas, Detroit Institute of Art, 1949

PARKER, Raymond: HELICOPTER, Oil on canvas, Walker Art Center, 1949

PASCIN, Jules: GROUP OF WOMEN, Lithograph, John Herron Art Institute, 1950

PECHSTEIN, Max Hermann: SELF PORTRAIT WITH PIPE, Woodcut, Brooklyn Museum, 1949

PENNEY, James: OPEN WINDOW, Oil on canvas, Springfield (Mass.) Museum of Fine Arts, 1950

PERLIN, Bernard: THE STREET, Springfield (Mass.) Museum of Fine Arts, 1950

PEVSNER, Antoine: DEVELOPABLE COLUMN, Oxidized tin on brass (1942), Museum of

Modern Art, 1950

PHOUTRIDES, Evan: UNTITLED OIL, University of Washington

PICASSO, Pablo: HARLEQUIN, Oil on canvas (1915), Museum of Modern Art, 1950; HEAD OF THE ACROBAT'S WIFE, Drawing?, Art Institute of Chicago, 1950; SEATED BATHER, Oil on canvas (1929), Museum of Modern Art, 1950; SELF PORTRAIT (1906), Philadelphia Museum of Art, 1950; STILL LIFE WITH MANDOLIN, Oil on canvas (1938), Museum of Modern Art, 1950; THE THREE MUSICIANS, Oil on canvas (1921), Museum of Modern Art, 1949; WOMAN WITH A FAN, Ink (1905), Allen Memorial Art Museum, 1949; YOUNG PAINTER AND HIS MODEL, Pen and ink drawing (1926), San Francisco Museum of Art, 1949

PIGNON, Edouard: OSTEND, Watercolor (1948), Museum of Modern Art, 1950

POLLOCK, Jackson: NO. 1, Oil on canvas (1948), Museum of Modern Art, 1950; NO.4, Oil on paper (1948), Museum of Modern Art, 1949

POUSETTE-DART, Richard: NO. 7: A PRESENCE, Oil on canvas, Museum of Modern Art, 1950; NO. 11, Oil on canvas, Museum of Modern Art, 1950

PRENDERGAST, Maurice: BEACH, ST. MALO, Oil on canvas, Cleveland Museum of Art, 1949

PRENDERGAST, Charles: WORLD'S FAIR, 1939, Oil on canvas, Whitney Museum, 1949

PRICE, Clayton S.: BLACK COW, Lithograph, Portland Art Museum, 1949; THE RIVER, Oil on canvas, Portland Art Museum, 1950

QUANCHI, Leo: FISHERMAN, Oil on canvas, Whitney Museum, 1949

REDON, Odilon: THE EYE, LIKE A STRANGE BALLOON, DIRECTS ITSELF TOWARD THE INFINITE, Lithograph (1882), Rhode Island Museum of Art, 1950

REFREGIER, Anton: THE STAIRCASE, Oil on canvas, Whitney Museum, 1949

RENOIR, Auguste: FRUIT, Oil on canvas (1895), John Herron Art Institute, 1950

RIVERA, Diego: DRAWING (1930), San Francisco Museum of Art, 1949

ROMANO, Umberto: FRIGHTENED HORSES, Lithograph, Montclair Art Museum, 1949

ROSZAK, Theodore: SPECTRE OF KITTY HAWK, Welded and hammered steel brazed with bronze and brass (1946-47), Museum of Modern Art, 1950

ROUAULT, George: CLOWN, Oil on canvas (c1907), Museum of Modern Art, 1950; HEAD OF CHRIST, Oil on canvas, Albright Art Gallery, 1950; THE JUDGE, Oil on canvas, Toledo Museum, 1949; CHRIST, Oil on canvas, Newark Museum, 1950; TWO NUDES, Watercolor, Metropolitan Museum of Art, 1950; WOMAN SEATED WITH CHIN IN HAND, Etching, aquatint and heliogravure (not in "Miserere et Guerre"), Brooklyn Museum, 1949

ROUSSEAU, Henri-Julien: THE JUNGLE, Oil on canvas (1908), Cleveland Museum of Art, 1949; THE SAWMILL, OUTSKIRTS OF PARIS, Art Institute of Chicago, 1950

SARKISIAN, Sarkis: STILL LIFE WITH GRAPES AND FIGS, Oil on canvas, Detroit Institute of Art, 1949

SCHMID, Elsa: FATHER D'ARCY, Mosaic and modeled fresco (1948-49), Museum of Modern Art, 1950

SCHMIDT-ROTTLUFF, Karl: LANDSCAPE WITH A TOWER, Watercolor (1922), Museum of Modern Art, 1950; SUNRISE, Woodcut, Allen Memorial Art Museum, 1949

SCHWITTERS, Kurt: PICTURE WITH LIGHT CENTER, Paper collage and oil paint on cardboard (1919), Museum of Modern Art, 1950

SEPESHY, Zoltan: AT SEA, Oil on canvas (1949), Walker Art Center, 1950; INVARIABLES, Tempera (1947), University of Michigan Museum of Art; THEY WAIT, William Rockhill Nelson Gallery

SEURAT, Georges: PORT OF GRAVELINES, Oil on canvas (1890), John Herron Art Museum, 1949

SHAHN, Ben: BOY, Tempera (1944), University of Michigan Museum of Art; OHIO MAGIC, Oil tempera on panel, California Palace of the Legion of Honor, 1949; PACIFIC LANDSCAPE, Tempera on composition board (1945), Museum of Modern Art, 1950; THE PASSION OF SACCO AND VANZETTI, Oil on canvas, Whitney Museum, 1950; SUMMERTIME, Oil on canvas, Addison Gallery

SHEELER, Charles: INCANTATION, Oil on canvas (1946), Brooklyn Museum, 1949

SHEETS, Millard: CAMEL WOMAN, Watercolor (1944), Carnegie Institute, 1949

SINTENIS, Renée: DAPHNE, Bronze (1930), City Art Museum of St. Louis, 1950

SIQUEIROS, Alfaro: BY THE PRISON GATE, Oil on canvas (1920), San Francisco Museum of Art, 1949; HANDS, Duco (1949), Museum of Modern Art, 1950

SKOLLE, John: SARGASSO SEA, Dallas Museum of Fine Arts

SLOAN, John: THE CHINESE RESTAURANT, Oil on canvas, Rochester Memorial Art Gallery, 1950; NURSE MAIDS, MADISON SQUARE, University of Nebraska

SMITH, David: TAHSTVAAT, Cast iron and forged fabricated steel (1946), University of Michigan Museum of Art

SORENSON, Donald E.: AT THE BEACH, Oil on canvas, Portland Art Museum, 1950

SOYER, Raphael: BLUE SHAWL, William Rockhill Nelson Gallery

SPONENBURGH, Mark: THUNDERBIRD, Cedar, Portland Art Museum, 1950

SPRUCE, Everett: OLD TREE, Oil on canvas, Walker Art Center, 1950

STAËL, Nicolas de: PAINTING, Oil (1947), Museum of Modern Art, 1950

STAMOS, Theodoros: COMPOSITION WITH BRAIDED ROPE, Wadsworth Atheneum

STEINBERG, Paul: Drawings (24) for MODERN LIVING EXHIBITION, India ink, Detroit Institute of Art, 1949

STILLMAN, Ary: RHYTHMIC VARIATIONS, Oil on canvas, Houston Museum of Fine Arts, 1949

STUEMPFIG, Walter: TWO HOUSES, Oil on canvas, Corcoran Gallery of Fine Art, 1950; WEST WILDWOOD, Oil on canvas, California Palace of the Legion of Honor, 1949

SUTHERLAND, Graham: MAIZE, Color lithograph, John Herron Art Institute, 1950; WOOD END, Etching, Detroit Institute of Art, 1949

TAL COAT, René Pierre: LA MARSEILLAISE, Oil on canvas (1944), Museum of Modern Art, 1950

TAM, Reuben: EDGE OF PLACE, MONHEGAN AFTERNOON, Oil on canvas, Albright Art Gallery, 1950

TANGUY, Yves: FEAR, Oil on canvas, Whitney Museum, 1949; FROM ONE NIGHT TO THE OTHER, Oil on canvas, California Palace of the Legion of Honor, 1949

TCHELITCHEW, Pavel: THE GREEN LION, Santa Barbara Museum of Art

THOMPSON, William R.: LOW TIDE, Oil on canvas (1949), Corcoran Gallery of Fine Arts, 1949

TIBBLE, Geoffrey: HAIRDRESSING, NO. 3, Oil on canvas (1948), Albright Art Gallery, 1949

TOBEY, Mark: ODALISQUE, Oil on canvas (1927), Museum of Modern Art, 1950

TOMKINS, Margaret: LINEAGE, Tempera on panel, Seattle Art Museum, 1949

TOMLIN, Bradley Walker: ARRANGEMENT, Oil on canvas, University of Illinois

TONEY, Anthony: ENTRANCE, Oil on canvas, University of Illinois

TOULOUSE-LAUTREC, Henri de: FOLLETTE, Oil on canvas (1890), Philadelphia Museum, 1950; YAHNE ET ANTOINE DANS L'AGE DIFFICILE, Lithograph (1895), Brooklyn Museum, 1949

TSCHACBASOV, Nahum: THE CLOWN, Oil on canvas, Whitney Museum, 1949; THE MATRIARCH, Oil on canvas, Whitney Museum, 1949

TUNNARD, John: FLOWERS FOR 1945, Tempera (1945), Albright Art Gallery, 1949

UBAC, Raoul: TWO PERSONS AT A TABLE, Oil on canvas, (1950), Museum of Modern Art, 1950

MUSEUM ACQUISITIONS

URTEAGA, Mario: THE WAKE, University of
Arizona
UTRILLO, Maurice: SACRÉ-COEUR DE MONT-
MARTRE, Gouache, John Herron Art In-
stitute, 1950

VAN DOESBURG see DOESBURG
VAN GOGH see GOGH
VAN ROGGER, Roger: DESCENT FROM THE
CROSS, Oil on canvas (1946-48), Museum
of Modern Art, 1950
VAUGHAN, Keith: BATHERS BY A GREY SEA,
Oil on canvas (1947), Albright Art Gallery,
1949
VESPIGNANI, Renzo: ROOF TOPS, Pencil, De-
troit Institute of Art, 1949
VILLON, Jacques: THE SHIP MODEL, Etching,
Brooklyn Museum, 1949
VLAMINCK, Maurice de: MONT VALÉRIEN, Oil
on canvas (1903), Museum of Modern Art,
1949; STILL LIFE, Waltercolor and gouache
(c1910), Museum of Modern Art, 1950
VUILLARD, Edouard: Lithographs (2), Brook-
lyn Museum, 1950

WADE, Bennett: GIRL WITH BOWL, Sculpture,
Los Angeles County Museum, 1949
WALKOWITZ, Abraham: FLOWERS IN A VASE,
Oil on canvas (1927?), University of Michigan Museum of Art; 40 drawings (1905-
1932?), 6 Watercolors (1902-1911?), University of Michigan Museum of Art

WARSHAW, Howard: BUILDINGS, Oil on can-
vas, GOLGOTHA, Oil on canvas, WRECKED
AUTOMOBILES, Watercolor and gouache,
Los Angeles County Museum, 1949
WATKINS, Franklin C.: ANGEL OF THE RES-
URRECTION, Oil on canvas, Detroit In-
stitute of Art, 1949
WEBER, Max: DISCOURSE, Rochester Mem-
orial Art Gallery, 1950; FIGURE, color
woodcut, Allen Memorial Art Gallery;
TORSO, Gouache, San Francisco Museum
of Art, 1950; MUSIC, Munson-Williams-
Proctor Institute
WEDDIGE, Emil: THE COLOSSEUM, Color
lithograph, Detroit Institute of Art, 1949
WEIDENAAR, Reynold H.: INSURGENTES
MARKET, Etching, Detroit Institute of Art,
1949
WENGENROTH, Stow: BLACK EAGLES, Litho-
graph, Detroit Institute of Art, 1949
WYETH, Andrew: THE OIL LAMP, Oil on can-
vas, Houston Museum of Fine Art, 1949

YUNKERS, Adja: THE PINK FISHES, Color
woodcut, Worcester Art Museum, 1949

ZADKINE, Ossip: TORSO, Ebony (c1920-23),
Museum of Modern Art, 1949
ZERBE, Karl: THREE MASKS, Gouache (1950),
Walker Art Center, 1950; TROUPERS,
Rochester Memorial Art Gallery, 1950
ZORACH, William: GIRL AND CATS, Terra
cotta, Detroit Institute of Arts, 1950

ART IN THE WORLD

OF EVENTS

A CALENDAR

OF EXCERPTS

1946 —— 1950

PART ONE

"What Is Past Is Prologue"

PART TWO

"The Stage Is Set"

EDITORIAL NOTE The original plan for this section, "Art in the World of Events",

contemplated full reprinting of texts from the daily press,

magazines and catalogs representative of the recent season in

art. Isolation of the significant statements and prejudices of the

year, as expressed in the written words on art, would serve

to intensify whatever pattern underlay the sequence of happenings.

Meanings would be revealed by reproduction of the actuality in

print, exhibited without commentary.

In view of serious limitations — some economic, some diplomatic

— which arose during the process of compilation, it has been

necessary to curtail this plan of self-clarification. Abridgments

indicate the core of the item selected, or its relevance to other

events similarly recorded. In most instances, the complete force

of the statement is conveyed only by the original documents

in toto.

The success of such a method of exposition presupposes — as

with the work of art itself — that communication is the result

of a process of active participation.

"I am accused often of much experimentation,

but what else should I do when all other factors

of man are in the same condition? Shall any

member of the body exist independently of the

rest? I thrust forward into space as science and

the rest do. My activity is the same, therefore

my end will be similar. The gods of the past

are as dead today as they were when Christianity

overcame the Pagan world. The time is similar,

only the arena is the whole world."

Mark Tobey

"In the face of vast social pressure there is a

very great need for that conscience toward

medium to which an earlier age affixed the

reproachful title 'art for art's sake'. In an age

steadily becoming more collective, art remains

one of the few means through which the

individual will can assert itself; its function

is not to record what we all now like taken

together but to affirm the creative differences

among us from which all will eventually gain.

For this purpose a free climate is essential."

James Thrall Soby

"WHAT IS PAST IS PROLOGUE"

March 1946

AN ART PROGRAM FOR NEW YORK STATE, by James Thrall Soby. Magazine of Art, v.40, p.29, Jan. 1947.

> Comment on the proposals of a committee to consider a state art program, followed by the text of bill no. 2706 (int. 2423, In Assembly, Mar. 6, 1946) introduced by Mr. Mitchell: "An act to amend the education law, in relation to creating in the University the division of painting, sculpture and graphic arts; providing for the appointment of a supervisory board; defining its powers and duties, and making an appropriation therefor."

May 1946

MUSEUMS AND WORLD PEACE, by Archibald MacLeish. The Museum News, v. 24, p. 6-8, June 1, 1946.

> "We are no longer concerned with the decisions of directors and boards of trustees and curators solely from the point of view of the museum visitor. We are concerned with their decisions as citizens of a new and dangerous world who have been compelled by events beyond our control, or any man's, to reexamine our institutions with a view to deciding how far and in what way they can help us to survive." Reprinted in Magazine of Art, v. 40, p. 32-34, Jan. 1947.

January 1947

AMERICANS ABROAD, by John D. Morse. Magazine of Art, v.40, p.21-25.

> "The exhibitions briefly illustrated on the following pages mark its [the U. S. Department of State] first step towards expanding the "public relations level" for American paintings to include the entire world." Additional comment titled "We regret" published in the May 1947 issue (p. 169) on the cancellation of the Department's exhibition "Advancing American Art."

1947

ADVANCING AMERICAN ART. [Prague, American Embassy, 1947].

> From a letter of transmittal: "The catalog . . . was prepared at the American Embassy in Praha, Czechoslovakia, for use in exhibiting a collection of oil paintings sent abroad by the Department [of State, U. S.] in response to requests for examples of work by the modern school in America. The collection was recalled in the summer of 1947, however, because of criticism in this country of the inclusion of this type of material in the Department's informational and educational exchange program. . . . The paintings in question were delivered to [the War Assets] Administration for sale as surplus property."

1947

MONA LISA'S MUSTACHE, by T. H. Robsjohn-Gibbings. New York, Knopf, 265 p.

> Extensively reviewed by Margaret Miller in the Magazine of Art (January and March 1948, v. 41, p. 34, 36, 116-118), the review is prefaced by the following "Editor's note": "Mr. Robsjohn-Gibbings' association of 'modern art' and 'Fascism' is taken apart. . . . We have given space to this review because we believe the raising of irrelevant issues and the reduction of all artistic values to the level of "horse-sense" is an attack not alone upon modern art but upon art as such. The purported argument of this book on art is only verbal; it is without illustration of works of art and nowhere mentions or dis-

cusses individual works of painting, sculpture or architecture." The reveiwer indicates that "wilful distortion, suppression of evidence, paralyzing repetitions and irrational argument" manifest "the author's hostility towards artists as a class ... not restricted to the painters and architects of the twentieth century." His indictment of modern art as a fascist conspiracy of an élite is nowhere validated, either by his hysterical evidence or the objective facts.

December 1947

MODERN ART AND MUDDLED THINKING, by George Biddle. The Atlantic Monthly, v. 180, no. 6, p. 58-61.
An examination of "the cause which may explain this all-out trend toward extreme Modernism or non-objective art in America today" which this American painter attributes to "war neuroses, a dealer-rigged market, snobbism, and an association of Modernism with up-to-dateness." "The critical thinking which is the basis for healthy experimentation" can not be based on "modernists who advocate a social or Marxian approach; who believe in expression through the subconscious; who believe that art should have no intellectual content; who advocate the subjective-expressionistic approach; who proclaim the mathematical architectonics of the abstract." It must incorporate another artistic credo: "A restatement ... or experience of life, expressed in a given medium with a certain rhythm. ... Life is the artist's raw material. ... Those arts which appeal to the greatest number of people and which deal with basic human emotions will survive the longest and exercise the most influence." "Extreme Modernism ... offers nothing by way of content other than technical experimentation."

February 1948

FREEDOM OF THE BRUSH, by Daniel Catton Rich. The Atlantic Monthly, v. 181, p. 47-51, 1948.
"American painting is facing a major change. ... Tradition is being challenged by the growth of a new American school of non-representational painting." Referring to the 58th Chicago Art Institute annual of abstract and surrealist art, the article surveys the influences affecting non-academic art in America, as well as the criticism suffered by the advance-guard. Includes the text of President Truman's letter commenting adversely on "modernism."

February 1948

"MODERN ART" AND THE AMERICAN PUBLIC, a Statement by the Institute of Contemporary Art, formerly the Institute of Modern Art. Boston, February 17, 4 p. (leaflet).
"Like all revolutionary movements, modern art had its imaginative leaders and brilliant apologists, its struggle with reaction. ... Now that a full generation has passed since its inception, it has become imperative to re-appraise the movement. ... The artist gradually withdrew from a common meeting-ground with the public. ... This cult of [bewilderment] rested on the hazardous foundations of obscurity and negation, and utilized a private, often secret, language. ... Today, however, "modern art" describes a style which ... has become both dated and academic." A Statement of Principles includes "the need for interpretation," the proclamation of "standards of excellence which the public may comprehend," the exercise by the artist of "his historic role of spiritual leadership," a conviction that "maximum public service lies in endorsement of that art which is the full embodiment of the artist's creative impulse and draws strength both from experiment and tradition." "In order to give full emphasis to these objectives, and in order to dissociate the policy and program of this institution from the widespread and injurious misunderstandings which surround the term "modern art," the Corporation has today changed its name from The Institute of Modern Art to the Institute of Contemporary Art ... James S. Plaut, Director."

March 1948

REPORT OF THE PANEL DISCUSSION SPONSORED BY THE MODERN ARTISTS GROUP OF BOSTON, Modern Artists Group of Boston, March 25, mimeographed, 10 p.
> "The Institute's highly sensational manifesto is a fatuous declaration which misinforms and misleads the public concerning the integrity and intention of the modern artist. By arrogating to itself the privilege of telling the artists what art should be, the Institute runs counter to the original purposes of this organization whose function was to encourage and to assimilate contemporary innovation." Statements by H. W. Janson, Karl Knaths, Lawrence Kupferman.

May 1948

MODERN ARTISTS SPEAK, by Ralph M. Pearson. The Art Digest, May 15, v. 22, no. 16, p. 16, 30.
> A report of the symposium at the Museum of Modern Art protesting a variety of current attacks on the modernists. Includes quotations from speeches. In addition, the Digest printed a rebuttal by a critic, Miss Genauer (p. 17), an editorial (p. 7), and a statement by the director of the Boston Institute of Contemporary Art (p. 5).

July 1948

A PLATFORM FOR ARTISTS, the Federal Fine Arts Program of the New York State Art Division, National Council of the Arts, Sciences and Professions. [14] p.
> Booklet, supplemented by inserts and by a Sept. 17 release of the same title (3 p., mimeographed). Signed by Ben Shahn and Paul Strand, co-chairman, Art Division, "We call for a Department of Education, Arts and Sciences, with a Secretary of Cabinet rank . . . whose function shall be the promotion of all the arts as an expression of the spirit of the American people, and, toward the enrichment of the people's lives, to make the arts available to all."

July 1948

RETIRED AMERICAN ART. Newsweek, v. 32, p. 68, July 5, 1948.
> "The final chapter was written last week on one of the most controversial art stories of recent times. What was once titled "Advancing American Art"—the collection of 79 oil paintings and 38 watercolors which the State Department had brought and planned to exhibit abroad—was finally disposed of by the War Assets Administration." Additional reports are contained in "M K R Art Outlook" (New York), for October 14, 1946, December 9, 1946, April 21, 1947, May 12, 1947, (all reprinted in the Akron Art Institute Summer Activities Number 1947). Also articles in the New York Journal-American, November 19, 1946 and April 6, 1947; Look Magazine February 18, 1947, p. 80-81; the New York Times April 7, May 6, May 11, May 18, 1947, June 25, 1948; a pamphlet of the Art Division, New York State Progressive Citizens of America titled The State Department and Art [12]p. 1947; a column by Samuel Grafton in the New York Post, May 19, 1947, p. 20: a June 1947 mimeographed release of the San Francisco Museum of Art called "An Important Notice!", and Robert M. Coates' articles in the New Yorker, v. 24, no. 15, p. 78-80, June 5, 1948 on "The State Department Collection."

August 1948

AN INSTITUTE IS AN INSTITUTE IS AN INSTITUTE, a Symposium about the statement by the Institute of Contemporary Art in Boston on " 'Modern Art' and the American Public," by members of the faculties of Bard College, Bennington College, Goddard College, Olivet College. Published at Bard College, Annandale-on-Hudson, New York, August 1, 1948. 8 p., mimeographed.
> Foreword: "The business of any non-profit Institute of Art—ancient, modern or contemporary—is art and education. Our own business is art and education and we are

minding it." The opinions expressed by the "artist-teachers" include the following. "Every aging generation of officials has risen in high dudgeon over those youngsters who caused art to go to the dogs by disregard of tradition: lunatics, radicals, poor citizens who spread confusion and bewilderment among a defenseless public. . . . The search must be one for the causes of the alleged confusion in contemporary artistic standards and not one for convenient scapegoats. . . . The Institute suggests that the level of its standards of excellence should be set at the public's comprehension. It would appear to be more to the point that the work of art set whatever level necessary. . . . We do not feel that the attitude of the artist toward the world necessarily makes him a good or bad artist. . . . This kind of purposive confusion in an authoritative guise is usually more widespread in social-political practices than in art, where choice and determination of principles are so much more a matter of individual struggle. . . . Modern art is in the process of diffusion. For better or worse, this is the artistic idiom of our day, call it modern or contemporary."

October 1948

THE STATE OF MODERN PAINTING, by Lincoln Kirstein. Harper's Magazine, v. 197, p. 47-53.
"The new opposition, unlike Philistia, in no way opposes the use of unhampered imagination, experiment in new method or material, or what is loosely called distortion. This new opposition does, however, oppose improvisation as method, deformation as a formula and painting (which is a serious matter) as an amusement manipulated by interior decorators and high-pressure salesmen. The new opposition deplores a basic lack of general culture, historical and scientific, on the part of most of our painters, and their lack of stable technical processes and rational craftsmanship. . . . What painting lacks today is what bad painting always lacks: adequate intellectual capacity and manual skill." Excerpts published in American Artist, v. 13, p. 37 ff, February 1949; editorial by Peyton Boswell in The Art Digest, v. 23, no. 3, p. 7, November 1, 1948, with extracts.

November 1948

CHALLENGE AND PROMISE: MODERN ART AND MODERN SOCIETY, by René d'Harnoncourt. Magazine of Art, v. 41, p. 251-2.
"Widespread preoccupation with the social functions of art indicates a growing popular awareness of the importance of art as a factor in our lives . . . but we cannot remain insensible to the peculiarly vindictive temper of many of the criticisms of modern art and modern artists. . . . In an era tortured by doubts and by fears for the very survival of civilization, people desperately call for leadership — not only political but spiritual. . . . The now too prevalent assumption that a painter lacks a sense of social responsibility because his work cannot be readily understood by all the people or even by many people is a conclusion reached in despair: but it is illogical and has no foundation in fact. . . . Unique in the art of today . . . is the simultaneous existence of many art forms that are, at least stylistically, entirely unrelated. . . . The art of the twentieth century has no collective style, not because it has divorced itself from contemporary society but because it is part of it. . . . The dilemma of our time cannot be solved by a denial of experimentation whether by directive or by pressure. . . . To expect a diversified society to produce a uniform, universally understood art is a measure of our true fear of facing the results of our own advances. . . . A good name for such a society is democracy. . . . Modern art in its infinite variety and ceaseless exploration is its foremost symbol."

December 1948

MODERN ART AND THE DIGNITY OF MAN, by Henry Francis Taylor. The Atlantic Monthly, v. 182, no. 6, p. 30-36.
"Art for [the intelligentsia] has ceased to have any moral or religious significance; they

have divorced it from the area of common human experience and made it a form of private communication—when it communicates at all—whereby abstract associations of form and color convey intimacies scarcely less cryptic than those revealed on the psychoanalyst's couch. The innocent layman, visiting the national exhibitions, may be forgiven for suspecting that the chief purpose of American art is to illustrate the Kinsey report. . . . To humiliate and patronize the masses with an art which can be deciphered only by an intellectual elite—the fashionably initiated—must inevitably arouse a people's antagonism and their indignation. . . . The issue for our generation is not so much one of principle as it is one of the degree of communicability versus incommunicability. And, while no sensible person would wish to turn back the clock, there are many who might wish to read its face without having to take its works apart. . . . In the sense that it announces the sterility and the intellectual vacuum of twentieth-century America or Europe, [the art of today] will have at least that questionable validity; it will be recognized as the product of its time. . . . Absorption in technical experiment and the influence of psychiatric and physical investigation have completely engrossed the larger and more experimental minds. What started in Picasso to be a revelation and, indeed, a revaluation of the art of seeing has come through excessive introspection and cynicism to be a terrible dis-service to younger artists who lack his extraordinary talent and mercurial virtuosity. . . . Man and artist have become the victims of the scientific world they have created, and in their common fear for the future have lost contact with one another. . . . How, then, the reader may well ask, is the artist to proceed in the intellectural and moral vacuum of the present day? Each artist of good will and personal integrity must work this problem out for himself. First of all he must be willing to communicate his meaning in terms of universal human experience. . . . If the public must respect the artist's freedom of creation, then in the same way the latter must acknowledge the public's freedom of acceptance or rejection.''

February 1949

MINIVER CHEEVY AND THE DIGNITY OF MAN, by Robert Goldwater, Magazine of Art v. 42, p. 57, 72.

"The question," says Mr. Taylor significantly, "is no longer one of technique or taste but revolves about the problem of reality." But this exactly is the problem with which the modern artist is concerned, in his own visual and psychological terms. If his solutions are not those of the past, is that surprising? If his findings are personal and various, that is part and parcel of a democratic development to be reversed only at a risk of which the arts (to speak only of the arts) of Germany and Russia are a warning. If the answers he arrives at are not always to our liking, is he to be accused of insincerity and lack of integrity? The religious concern of a Mondrian or a Kandinsky for the understanding and translation of new kinds of visual reality; the stoic devotion of a Beckmann or a Giacometti to the faithful portrayal of the emotional impact of the modern world, are these to be dismissed because they do not match a pleasant, preconceived "reality"? Is Rouault to be condemned for the agony of his religion? Was it Picasso who bombed Guernica? No nostalgia for the past, however strong, however keening, will bring it back to life.

But with all his regrets for what has gone before, with all his condemnation rather than encouragement of the present, we are permitted to wonder if Mr. Taylor really longs for the art of the past. Nowhere does he give any sign that painting and sculpture are for him not merely the approximate, inconvenient bearers of a didactic message, but sources of life and vitality. For a work of art is not simply the record of a prefabricated philosophy, but a sensuous and material thing; it is something new in the world, and something made; it not only records, it creates reality. . . .

"THE STAGE IS SET"

March - October 1949

THE CONGRESSIONAL RECORD. Proceedings and Debates of the 81st Congress, First Session. March 11, p. 2364-65: Mr. Dondero "Communist art in government hospitals;" March 25, p. 3297-98: Mr. Dondero "Communists maneuver to control art in the United States;" April 29, Extension of remarks of Jacob K. Javits "Art exhibits for paraplegics;" Extension of remarks of Charles A. Plumley, June 16: "Artists Equity;" May 17, p. 6487-90: Mr. Dondero "Communism in the heart of American art—what to do about it;" August 19, p. 1181-14, Mr. Dondero "Modern art shackled to communism;" Extension of remarks of Mr. Dondero, October 13: "Is Harper's Magazine biased?" Editorials on these remarks were published by Peyton Boswell, Jr. in The Art Digest v. 23, no. 12, p. 7, March 15, 1949 ("Assassination by Implication") and v. 23, no. 17, p. 7, June 1, 1949 ("A Plea for Tolerance"). A final editorial, v. 23, no. 19, p.3, 23, August 1, 1949 ("It Can Happen Here") consists largely of a letter by Alfred H. Barr, Jr., of the Museum of Modern Art, New York City.

April 1949

THE CUBIST WITCH, by R. B. Beaman. South Atlantic Quarterly, v. 48, no. 2, p. 204-212. "Witches thrive best in periods of insecurity and fear. . . . Even modern art is by now a "hostile act." . . . The repeated Soviet criticism of all the modern arts is like that of the usual American objections, that art must be based upon "realism," that any distortions spell "art for art's sake" if not paranoia. . . . "Realism" seems to mean a neo-photographic naturalism combined with literary content. . . . Conservative Russian and American judgment of modern art nowhere shows any real appreciation for any content to art other than the verbal, the ideological. That the formal, that is the design values of art, which both groups denounce, can speak powerfully in their own language rather than in literary terms and that this is the peculiar purpose of the arts is an idea which receives only lip service at best, because the real meaning requires too much actual eye-ear training to become apparent." Extracts, and additional commentary on this viewpoint was published by Howard Devree in the New York Times, Sept. 11, 1949 ("Modernism under fire"). The Soviet views have been published in V O K S Bulletin no. 52, p. 29-36, 1947.

April 1949

PAINTING TODAY. San Francisco round table (White, Mundt, Bothwell, Varda, Horn). Arts & Architecture, April 1949, p. 16-21. "I disagree, the layman is very real, he is not an abstraction. He could be a threat to freedom of expression; he is dangerous because he is desperate. If he does not understand, he is vicious in his grudges." (Prof. Walter Horn)

July 1949

A GOING IN THE MULBERRY TREES, by James Thrall Soby. Saturday Review of Literature, July 2, p. 30-31. "The entire history of repression in the arts of our time has followed the same melancholy pattern: those who cannot create poison the minds of those who cannot understand; and art becomes merely something which the former can achieve, the latter accept."

September 1949

STILL LIFE WITH RED HERRING, by Emily Genauer. Harper's Magazine, v. 199, p. 88-91. Commentary on the views of Representative Dondero, to which he issued a rebuttal in his extension of remarks to the Congressional Record (81st Congress, Oct. 13), a reply also published, in part, in the "letters" section of Harper's Magazine, v. 199, p. 18-20, 22, Dec. 1949 with corrective remarks by the editor.

November 1949

WE NEED U. S. COMMISSION TO STUDY STATE OF ART AND MUSIC IN AMERICA, by Maurice J. Tobin, Secretary of Labor. Allegro, v. 24, p. 7-8.

"We in America don't want government, any government, to dictate to us the terms of our cultural development. . . . It is my hope that government, where it can without intruding on the area of freedom, will help further this growth."

December 1949

PROPOSAL FOR AN INTERNATIONAL CONVENTION OF ARTISTS AND INTERNATIONAL EXHIBITION OF ART, by Theodore Brenson. December 7, 1949, 1 p., mimeographed.

Designed to implement a 1952 convention in New York City, this is a seven point initial statement by the co-chairman of the Committee on International Cultural Relations of Artists Equity Association. "The special feature of this project would lie in the fact that the convention would be called by the artists and would work for the artists . . . (enabling) us to put into action the natural dynamism which . . . so far has not been fully utilized in an organized way. . . ." (Supplemented by an extensive outline of March 24, 1950).

January 1950

IN FREEDOM'S SEARCH, AN EXHIBITION . . . Museum of Fine Arts, Springfield, Mass., January 15 through February 19, 1950. [12]p. illus.

"The selection has been made to serve, at the least, as a partial answer for some people, to the question, "In the search for freedom of expression, to what extent may the painter disregard the generally accepted canons of painting and yet continue to have his work be considered as part of that tradition?" Catalog foreword by Frederick B. Robinson, director, largely reprinted in the museum's current bulletin.

March 1950

A STATEMENT ON MODERN ART, by The Institute of Contemporary Art, Boston; The Museum of Modern Art, New York; Whitney Museum of American Art, New York. 4 p. March [27].

"We oppose any attempt to make art or opinion about art conform to a single point of view. . . . We believe that a primary duty of a museum concerned with contemporary art is to be receptive to new tendencies and talents. . . . We believe that the so-called "unintelligibility" of some modern art is an inevitable result of its exploration of new frontiers. . . . We recognize the humanistic value of abstract art, as an expression of thought and emotion and the basic human aspirations toward freedom and order. . . . Contrary to those who attack the advanced artist as anti-social, we believe in his spiritual and social role. . . . We hold that American art which is international in character is as valid as art obviously American in subject matter. . . . We also reject the assumption that art which is esthetically an innovation must somehow be socially or politically subversive, and therefore un-American. We deplore the reckless and ignorant use of political or moral terms in attacking modern art. . . . A museum's proper function, in our opinion, is to survey what artists are doing, as objectively as possible, and to present their works to the public as impartially as is consistent with those standards of quality which the museum must try to maintain. We acknowledge that humility is required of those who select works of art, as it is of those who create them or seek to understand them. We believe that there is urgent need for an objective and open-minded attitude toward the art of our time, and for an affirmative faith to match the creative energy and integrity of the living artist."

March 1950

A DEFENSE OF MODERN ART. New York Times, March 28.
    An editorial on the tri-museum statement on modern art. "The stand which opposes a narrowly chauvinistic approach to art and one which rejects the notion that all esthetic innovations are somehow politically subversive and 'un-American', is particularly welcome in the face of recent confused and often reckless attacks."

March 1950

THE 19TH CENTURY HERITAGE. Loan exhibition, Paul Rosenberg & Co., New York, March 7 to April 1. (Catalog 69).
    Introduction by Alexandre P. Rosenberg, p. 13-24. "This subordination of the content and primacy granted to structural researches tended to bend creative activity toward formal problems. Thereafter the center of gravity of painting lay not with descriptive accuracy but with invention of shapes. . . . The slightest subject matter could then provide enough ground for an exploration of the world which virtually encompasses the totality of human experience. . . . The end of painting was no longer to attain particular objects or even their qualities, but to resolve the ultimate foundations and most general conditions of reality: light and space."

March 1950

OUTLINE OF THE PROGRAM FOR THE INTERNATIONAL CONVENTION OF ARTISTS TO BE HELD IN NEW YORK CITY IN 1952. 3 p. mimeographed.
    Prepared March 24, 1950 by Theodore Brenson for the program committee of the United States Commission for Unesco as a result of a proposal to the general conference in Florence. "To obtain an overall picture of the situation of the artist, both within his culture as well as in his relation to the world as a whole, and to prepare in the light of this information for his future activities." Proposed program included "the artist and his social environment," "the economic condition of the artist," "conditions of work," "professional protection," "international cultural communication (exchanges of thought, of works, of artists)," "collaboration with associations," "creation of an international council of artists. (Probable results: A national convention in New York in January 1952; later an international in Venice).

Spring 1950

QUERY ON FREEDOM AND WORKING CONDITIONS OF THE ARTIST. 6 p. mimeographed. Board of Directors, Artists Group of Bay Area Associated, San Francisco.
    A questionnaire undertaken in relation to "a conference on artists' problems in relation to Unesco, sponsored nationally by Artists Equity Association."

April 1950

AMERICAN PAINTING 1950. An exhibition directed by James Johnson Sweeney at the Virginia Museum, April 22 through June 4. Foreword by Leslie Cheek, Jr., director. [24]p. illus. Richmond, Va., 1950.
    From the text by J. J. Sweeney titled "Americans, 1950:" "All poetic language is the language of pictorial expression. . . . Any painter who thinks in paint must have similar needs beyond the existing categories of his artistic language. What gives a living artist interest is his success in keeping his language as fictile as possible, in expanding the frontier of expression by directing a certain fluid force against circumstance; through conception, rather than mere reflection and observation. A realization of this need to see that the language of painting does not petrify and of the importance of preparing for new advances along the lines of true metaphor is what has strikingly characterized American painting during the last ten years."

ART IN THE WORLD OF EVENTS

April 1950

MR. SWEENEY—A MACABRE HUMORIST? Richmond Times-Dispatch, Richmond, Va., April 23, p. 20.

>An editorial in the Sunday issue, commenting on the current Virginia Museum exhibit, "American painting, 1950." Special articles published by Ross Valentine, April 25 ("Apollinaire's famous warning"), April 30 (" 'Modern art' on its last legs"), May 1 (" 'Bourgeois' dollars and 'modern art' "). Extensive publication of letters in the "Voice of the people" column, April 27, etc.

May 1950

RESOLUTION ADOPTED BY THE BOARD OF DIRECTORS OF THE EBELL CLUB OF LOS ANGELES. Thursday, May 4. mimeographed.

>A protest about the 1950 Annual Exhibition of Artists of Los Angeles and Vicinity at the Los Angeles County Museum. "WHEREAS, The Art Department of the Museum appears to be presenting works of Art of a radical nature in un-equal representation to the exhibition of paintings from other schools of Art; and WHEREAS, The Ebell of Los Angeles stands firmly for a policy of true Americanism and the educational advancement of the public relative to all phases of living expressive of the American way of life; and, WHEREAS, our great club advocates a policy of equalization representative of traditional art as compared with contemporary art; now, therefore, BE IT RESOLVED, That the Ebell of Los Angeles requests the Los Angeles County Board of Supervisors to instruct the Director [James B. Byrnes, Curator of Contemporary Art], and the jury for the selection of Exhibits, [Dr. Alfred M. Frankfurter, Donald Bear, Jermayne MacAgy] to appear for interrogation before said County Board of Supervisors for the purpose of stating their procedure. . . ." A memo of May 15 signed by members of artists', women's and other groups (American Legion, Chamber of Commerce, etc.) was submitted, and said, in part: "We believe that the greater percentage of the public is not in sympathy with painting that is not understandable to the normal mind and that Museum visitors are entitled to see at least an equal number of works of an ennobling character, based on the fundamentals of beauty. We object also to public monies being allotted for prizes for mediocre art and the importing of eastern "intellectuals" to judge California art. We firmly urge you, as representatives of the tax paying public, to establish a policy of equitable representation of traditional art that can properly hang in the homes of true Americans." In his answer of June 25, Mr. Byrnes made a rebuttal of charges and defended the position of the Museum, addressing his reply to Mr. Duncan Gleason, Chairman, Coordinating Committee of Traditional Art, Los Angeles. These, and similar documents, have been made public in mimeographed or duplicated copies.

May 1950.

OPEN LETTER TO ROLAND L. REDMOND. President of the Metropolitan Museum of Art, May 20. 1 p. mimeographed.

>Eighteen painters and ten sculptors protest the organization of the national exhibition planned "at the Metropolitan Museum of Art next December." The director of the Metropolitan had issued "A report on American Art" in the Museum Bulletin, January 1950, outlining its procedure in respect to the exhibition. The New York Herald Tribune published an editorial May 23 commenting on the protest of "The irascible eighteen." One of the signers, Weldon Kees, reprinted the protest in The Nation, v. 170, p. 556-7, June 3, with additional commentary.

May 1950

RESOLUTION OF AN INTERNATIONAL CONGRESS OF THE ARTS. Approved by the Unesco General Conference, Florence, May 26.

"The Director-General is authorized to plan in 1951 an international congress of the arts to be held in 1952, with the special reference to the freedom of the artist, the contribution of the artist to the work of Unesco, and the widest international use of what is produced by creative workers in all fields of art." Item 8.5 of the agenda, substituted for resolution 4.213 proposed by the American delegation.

June 1950

STATEMENT OF THE AMERICAN DELEGATION AT THE INTERNATIONAL ASSOCIATION OF ART CRITICS. Published in New York Times, sect. X, p. 9, June 25. Dated "June 17, Venice, Italy."

"In view of continued sporadic attacks on art, especially on unfamiliar expressions in pictures and sculptures, the members of the A. I. C. A. unanimously feel it an urgent duty to publish the following statement: 1. We believe that the artist is entitled to the same freedom in the creation, exhibition and publication of his works as is enjoyed by writers in the tradition of a free press; 2. We believe in the right of free individuals to disagree in matters of taste and that this right implies a reciprocal obligation of tolerance toward explorations in the arts which may provoke such disagreement; 3. With examples in mind of art under political restrictions, we deplore the imposition on the artist or on the exhibition of his work of restraints based on considerations extraneous to art." In the Unesco Courier. v. 3. no. 6-7, p. 4, July-August, 1950, this viewpoint was stated as follows: "The creation of new philosophical, artistic or literary work, should be fostered by the assertion and défence of the independence of the thinker, writer and artist. Unesco seeks to promote international cooperation in order to insure respect for this independence throughout the world."

June 1950

100 AMERICAN PAINTERS OF THE 20th CENTURY. New York, Metropolitan Museum of Art, 1950. xxiii p., 111 plates.

"The modern artist is the greatest eclectic of all time [and] asks that, in order to enjoy his pictures, we be familiar with the sources from whence they come. . . . But this at once brings up the grave question as to how much we must give in order to receive. Certainly there is little pleasure in the world as it is and little to be gained from blind and unreasoning eyes. . . . We should understand the art of our times, for it is still, as it has always been, the mirror of ourselves. If our art seems violent it is because we have perpetrated more violence than any other generation. If it deals with weird dreams it is because we have opened up the caverns of the mind. . . . We live in the fear of some monstrous event. . . . The artist is in part a prophet. We should not complain if the shadows that have lately haunted us have been for some time visible upon his canvas." Text by Robert Beverly Hale, associate curator of American art, which prefaces these "works selected from the collections of the Metropolitan Museum."

July 1950

WORLD AGREEMENT WILL ABOLISH DUTIES ON ART; FILMS, AND MUSEUM MATERIALS. 2p. mimeographed. Unesco, MC/RO/1; Paris, 31 July.

An international proposal to facilitate exchanges of cultural materials approved by 59 member states attending the Unesco general conference in Florence. Ratification required to render the convention effective, and to lift from artistic and cultural items the limitations of "commodities."

ART IN THE WORLD OF EVENTS

July 1950

PEYTON BOSWELL, JR., 1904-1950 [an obituary], by C. J. Bulliet. The Art Digest v. 24, no. 18, p. 5.
"Art was art for Boswell, something eternal, subject to its own evolutions and revolutions, but not at the call of every Tom, Dick and Harry who had a political or a personal axe to grind." Bulliet comments on the last major issue ["intolerable Federal restrictions on art"] which had engaged the vigorous protest of the editor of The Art Digest.

August 1950

THE DECADENCE OF MODERN ART, by Salvador Dali. The American Weekly, Aug. 20.
A syndicated article published in the New York Journal American, the Philadelphia Bulletin, the Washington Times Herald, etc. "Here are the reasons for the dizzy decline of modern art: The lack . . . of every vestige of technique, skill and craftsmanship . . . (which) threatens to plunge an entire generation into the darkest artistic barbarism. . . . As soon as painting ceases to be realistic and starts to become abstract, it becomes decorative. . . . Another reason . . . is the total lack of the culture of artists today. A young painter of the present day is . . . a new barbarian. . . . On reaching this point the reader may feel a trifle ill at ease for this point of view seems to him too much in accord with that set forth concerning modern art by the Nazis, the Fascist and today by the Communist officials of the Soviet. Nothing is more false than this suspicion! They wanted to suppress modern art. . . . The art of tomorrow . . . will very probably be produced in opposition and in reaction to modern art. . . . The day when painters understand the "futurist beauty" of Raphael will be the day when hope will be reborn in an artistic renaissance. . . ."

August 1950

A UNITED STATES BUREAU OF FINE ARTS, by George Biddle. The Art Digest, v.24, no. 19, p. 5, 30.
"We are, as far as I know, the only civilized nation in the world which lacks a bureau of Fine Arts. . . . I believe that the vitality of our art is, in the long run, dependent on the initiative of private organizations and individuals — not on Federal relief and Federal subsidy. But I believe that the Government can play a constructive role in stimulating the arts by co-ordinating and improving the cultural activities inevitably forced upon it. And it can help all the arts by exploring all the conditions which encourage the full and spontaneous expression of our creative citizens."

September 1950

THE ARTIST AND THE MUSEUM. The Report of the Third Woodstock Art Conference sponsored by Artists Equity Association and the Woodstock Artists Association, September 1 and 2, 1950. Edited by John D. Morse (American Artists Group, New York).
From the address by Lloyd Goodrich: "I believe that American art is the most free, varied and vital of any nation. I fear that public appreciation and support lag behind the creative achievement of our artists. Our business, as artists and museum people, is to awaken the public to the value and importance of what is going on in America today, and to the need for wider and more solid support. We can do this much more effectively together than separately, or at cross purposes. You artists and we museum workers must realize that, in spite of all our differences, we are partners in the same great enterprise, one of the greatest in the long history of art, that of making it possible for a great nation to fulfill its artistic potentialities."

EL grupo DAU AL SET se formó en septiembre de 1948, en Barcelona. Tiene sus poetas: Brossa y Cirlot. Sus pintores: Tapies, Ponc, Cuixart. Su aprendiz de filósofo: Puig. Y, por último, tiene a Tharrats, con sus actividades múltiples: pintor, escritor, impresor. La personalidad de todos ellos es diversa, pero coherente dentro del grupo, por tener como común denominador el cultivo de todas las conquistas plásticas y poéticas contemporaneas. Al principio, acaso haya tenido más puntos de contacto con el surrealismo que con otras tendencias. Como grupo, es el más definido y consecuente de los aparecidos en Cataluña en los diez años últimos.

Abans de fe
aprenia am

JOAN PONÇ

Jo no sé si en Ponç va aixecar la pel
de la terra o va destapar el forat d'a
gun volcà, quan des d'un temps enç
han començat a sorgir pertot arr
gues-reptils, d'u

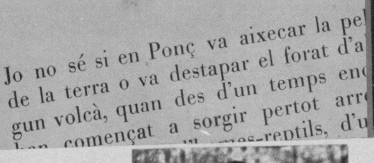

Heu truc
però us
l'hora s
onat un
ressa inc
sortir
ases del
onegut
e trasto
stris or
ortura
lles

Avui, en Cirlot, viu per tres obsessions: coleccio-
espases, pintures d'en Ponç, aquelles de di

Avui, en ple trio
pies ha posat el
solidificat les llà
flors presoneres,
ralls. Quan ha al
a les mans, les vi
gaven. Ha provo
temps els més ar
clarianes en les llò
quan ha trobat. a
cambra, en alçar-l
quet de carboncle

L'únic que no és bar
Tharrats. Va néixer, fa
a Girona. D'això n'està
per ell el número 7, c
Amb uns paisatges ta
poden fruir a la vora c
niel, no és gens estra
les ensopides classes d
tòria Natural de viu er
violetes en els corriol

i fòssils en les vessants de la muntanya de la
Torre de la O. L'anomenada li ve ja de molt petit,
en el col·legi. Quan els nois resaven la "Salve" en
lloc de dir "els desterrats fills d'Eva" deien, fent

da que us
sivelles és
zar, per e
per anar
sols es con
lògica, ja q
gunes faul
ses més at
cua de pe
ha encetat
món, un n
nostra, per
llargs hori
cartes de r
vis de tots
tots els dip
mes més
cietat. Ter
banda sem
els enigme
volta hem
cap a mar

MEAN OLD BEDBUG BLUES

VOICE:

Something was moaning in the corner
I tried my best to see.
It was the mother bedbug prayin' to the good Lord
For some more to eat.

ECHO:

Bedbug big as a jackass
Will bite you and stand and grim;
Will drink up all the chink poison
And come back and bit you again.

VOICE:

I had a quart of moonshine
Layin' on my dresser drawer,
Two big bedbugs came and drank it
And bit me 'cause there was'nt any more.

ECHO:

—Going to get myself a wishbone
Those bedbugs done got my goat.
—Going to wish that every bedbug
Goes off and cuts his throat.

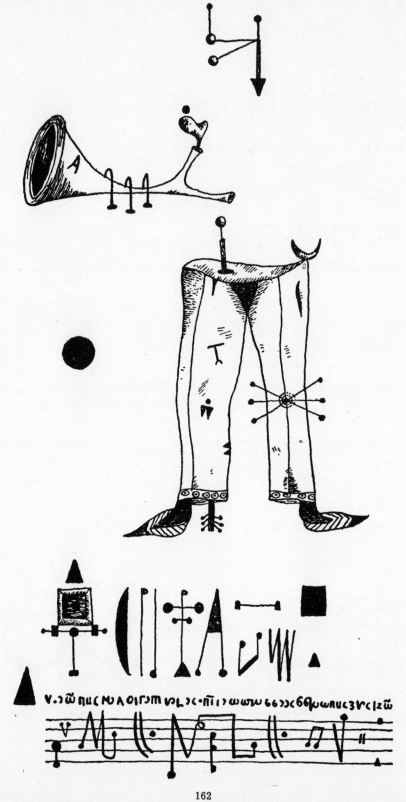

NOVA Y CURIOSA RELACIÓ,

Que succehí en lo any 1804, dels estragos que feu una fiera enomenat **ANIMAL SILVESTRE** en lo pais de Jerusalem, era format identich com se veu lo retrato en la estampa que tota la gent de aquell pais estaban etemorisats al veure ques perdia molta gent, y de tota mena de animals; y ultimament se descubrì, com lo demés que llegirá lo lector.

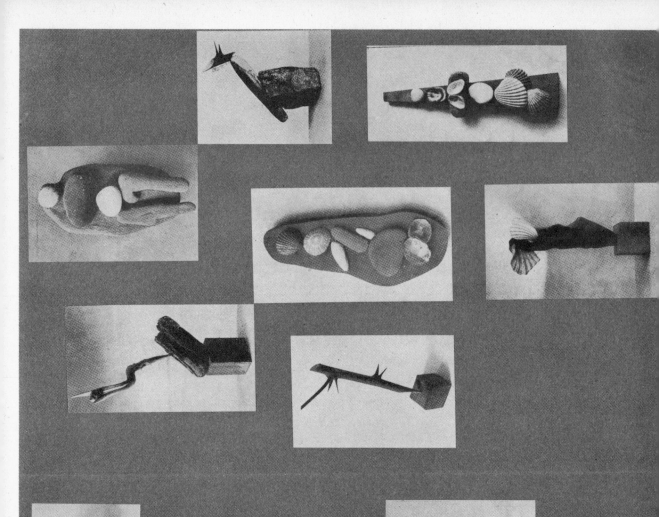

<u>A R T</u>

<u>PUBLICATIONS 1949 - 1950</u>

<u>AN INTERNATIONAL SELECTION</u>

WITH A PREFACE ON BIBLIOGRAPHY

BY BERNARD KARPEL

Librarian, Museum of Modern Art, N. Y.

OBJECTIVES IN BIBLIOGRAPHY

From the beginning, it had been the hope of the editors to provide in one place a yearly record of all printed materials on the subject of modern art. Logically, that place should be the Modern Art Annual, under which title this publication was first projected. While the documents of modern art are extensive, they are certainly not endless, and exceeded in many instances by the literature provided for other areas of study. The advantages of coordinating widely scattered, frequently unpublicized information seemed obvious, and equally obvious, the wisdom of undertaking this effort in compilation while the record was warm, the artist alive, and the ephemeral tangible. Unfortunately, the spiralling costs of printing even as compact a bibliography as this, costs which became prohibitive in 1950, made such an ambition impossible to realize. Plans for individual reviews likewise had to be abandoned. Of necessity, then, the following list represents a selective approach.

Covering many arts and many lands, the books, portfolios and pamphlets noted here reflect the panorama of activity in modern art, on an international basis, during 1949-1950. Although classified under broad subjects to suit the convenience of the general reader, the detailed index will readily locate specific authors and artists. Competent use of the general categories should satisfy the needs of all but the most intensive researchers. In any event, they will know, undoubtedly, that other bibliographical tools like the exhaustive international list of exhibitions published in Les Arts Plastiques (Brussels) round out the picture sketched in below, and that the yearly bibliographies edited by Helmut Hungerland for the Journal of Aesthetics and Art Criticism contain information which is detailed and far reaching. These must do until the advent of an inclusive, scholarly inventory.

Perhaps this is the moment to indicate the design for the next biennial record which will span as much material as circumstances permit. Certainly, there should be a section which will mention, however, briefly, where data on books and catalogs in the modern field regularly appear. For instance, monthly checklists printed by a number of New York libraries are probably not as well known as they deserve to be; again, the usefulness of particular domestic and European dealer catalogs needs pointing out. In this way, knowledge of specialized sources will be diffused. Secondly, a widening circle of bibliographers — modestly but energetically occupied in Italy, Switzerland and elsewhere — will be invited to participate in a national inventory of modern art. All can profit from such an intensive overview of the home scene. Finally, reviews of the critically important books of the year, assembled from numerous periodicals or freshly written for the audience of this biennial, will focus attention on titles and critiques that should not be overlooked, regardless of the emphasis in American journals and publicity-ridden magazines. As a case in point, one may mention the diverse evaluations of the imposing Skira histories of modern painting that have appeared in the domestic and foreign press, or to the fact that an extraordinary graphic serial, Dau Al Set, issued under the auspices of young, imaginative artists in Barcelona, has gone unnoticed in any art journal known to the editors.

For its "Second Series", this section of the biennial Modern Artists in America will publish the first of a group of bibliographic studies similar to those already compiled for the Documents of Modern Art (Wittenborn, Schultz, Inc., New York). Marcel Raymond's From Baudelaire to Surrealism (bibl. no. 488), and the forthcoming The Dada Painters and Poets, edited by Robert Motherwell, exhibit the method to be followed. Selection of themes will be determined by three criteria. First, does this investigation of sources deal with a concept rather than an artist, with styles rather than individuals, with movements in contrast to men? Second, does this bibliography survey all the relevant media of expression, poetry as well as art history, psychology as well as literature? In short, does it establish its framework in terms of the interrelationships of the arts of analysis and value? Lastly, does this documentation represent a fresh statement on the literature of modern art? Suitably illustrated by reproductions from little magazines, pages from rare catalogs and publications, reviews from the press of yesterday and, of course, plastic work of today, Bibliographic Studies No. 1 will be THE IDEA OF THE AVANT-GARDE IN AMERICA.

Both the annual listings and critical bibliographies which will appear on a systematic basis in the first and subsequent series of Modern Artists in America are planned to supplement a basic bibliography THE MODERN ARTS IN REVIEW. Scheduled for the immediate future, compiled by the writer, and issued under the same imprint of Wittenborn, Schultz, Inc., it will be the first extensive and independent bibliography on the whole of modern art to be published in any language. Including no titles issued after 1950, this evaluation of over a half-century of art publishing will be continually renewed by the contemporaneous record in Modern Artists in America which likewise is concerned with vital tendencies in visualization and form manifested in the plastic, tectonic and kinetic arts of our time. Despite the diversity of content, the bibliographic and the artistic problems are similar. Materials and methodology differ, happily enough, and the energies that actuate them vibrate along separate channels. Yet, even at this moment "wherein we tremble evenly between decay and evolution", as Louis Sullivan put it, the larger relationships are apparent. On the one hand, an attempt to order our culture towards humanistic ends, on the other, an effort to compress the data of experience into patterns of significance.

At the beginning of the 20th century, Thieme-Becker's Allgemeines Lexikon der bildenden Künstler (1907) began to list some of the newer writings. Although this vast directory remained a fragmentary effort as a modern bibliography for a generation, it did refer to such works as Charles Malpel's Notes sur l'Art d'Aujourd'hui et Peut-être de Demain (1911), described by Germain Bazin, outstanding French bibliographer, as the first book on the art of our day. Publicizing the artists who would be represented in the Palace of Fine Arts at the Panama-Pacific International Exposition, Robert B. Harshe, later director of the Chicago Art Institute, edited a small index which he called A Reader's Guide to Modern Art (1914). But a more substantial gesture was undertaken by the American collector Arthur J. Eddy who published his Cubists and Post-Impressionism in 1914 (written 1913, revised 1919). In a note more precise than the inventory itself, the author limited the periodical readings from 1908 on, and included a current list of English, French and German books and articles. While the intervening period was signalized by the appearance of Du Cubisme by Gleizes and Metzinger (1912), Les Peintres Cubistes by Apollinaire (1913), Neue französische Malerei by Neitzel and Arp (1913) and Der Weg zum Kubismus (1915, but published 1920), only occasional studies included bibliographical data, e.g. P. E. Küppers Der Kubismus (1920) and F. Landsberger's Impressionismus und Expressionismus (1921). In spite of its devotion to the more historical epochs, one must not overlook the issuance of the extraordinary study by Julius Schlosser Die Kunstliteratur: ein Handbuch zur Quellenkunde der neueren Kunstgeschichte (1924). However, by 1928, Franz Roh had published an essay Zur neueren kunstgeschichtlichen Literatur über des 19. und 20. Jahrhundert (Deutsche Vierteljahrschrift, Bd. VII). The following year, under the direction of Alfred H. Barr, Jr., the Museum of Modern Art (New York) began its distinctive series of exhibition catalogs which have continuously emphasized the value of bibliography and, in their entirety, contain an invaluable inventory of the literature of the contemporary arts. These catalogs have served as exemplary expositions of their type, and bibliographically speaking, have presented the available evidence with a thoroughness and precision slighted by European counterparts. In 1933, Hellmut Lehmann-Haupt prepared an annotated list of Fifty Books about Bookmaking for an exhibition at Columbia University. Now in its third, enlarged edition (100 Books, 1949), it is a remarkable instance of an arts literature completely comprehended, urbanely revealed. In marked contrast is the extensive but mechanical inventory submitted in 1934 by Eric R. McColvin as a thesis for the British Library Association Painting: a Guide to the best Books with special Reference to the

Requirements of Public Libraries. From 1933 through 1934, L'Amour de l'Art (Paris) issued a masterly series of biographical and bibliographical "notices" by Charles Sterling and Germain Bazin, which were finally assembled into a monumental Histoire de l'Art Contemporain: La Peinture (Alcan, 1934) edited by René Huyghe. That same year, for the Kunstmuseum exhibition at Lucerne titled Thèse, Antithèse, Synthèse Konrad Farner compiled a bibliography constructed on the following encyclopedic basis: "ideologische situation der gesellschaft, periodica, theorie, mathematik, psychologie-psychoanalyse, monografie". In spite of its inclusion of material not strictly "modern art", it constituted, at that point, a compact and intelligent statement of the latest literature, and demonstrated a defensible partiality for avant-garde manifestations.

Further effort at selective presentation of art books, fortunately accompanied by annotations, were begun in 1936 by the Pratt Library of Baltimore. Overwhelmingly an English record, its condensed and handy Art Booklists included several relating to aspects of modern art and design, were addressed to the widespread public of the American library system, and sponsored, necessarily, by a foundation, the Carnegie Corporation. Continuing this educational objective of the 'forties, Teachers College at Columbia issued an Art Bibliography (1941, revised 1949) edited by Arthur B. Young, which serves as a useful title-list in English for art teachers concerned with multiple problems of background, theory and practice. In 1942, the Museum of Modern Art printed for Claremont Colleges an exhaustive text of great technical interest Vincent Van Gogh: a Bibliography comprising a Catalogue of the Literature published, with an introductory Essay and Notes by Charles M. Brooks, Jr. Both the New York Public Library and William E. Rudge, publisher, joined hands in 1943 to issue a work of 244 pages Books and Printing: a selected List of Periodicals, 1800-1942. This collaboration by Carolyn F. Ulrich and Karl Küp possesses great value as an example of full documentation in a clearly defined subject, with functional categories and pithy annotations. About this time, the Journal of Aesthetics and Art Criticism (1945) began to print current bibliographies to keep its critical and historical minded clientele abreast of a voluminous literature. John Rewald's History of Impressionism (1946) made an ideal presentation of a specific movement. His deft annotations were based on intimate knowledge of the texts themselves and a keen understanding of what was reliable in reference to the subject, yet relevant in relation to the reader. In addition, Rewald's distinctive bibliography fruitfully enlarges the message of the work itself. The Hague Rijksbureau voor Kunsthistorische Documentatie continued its detailed inventory of journals, catalogs and texts in its Bibliography, with useful English annotations, which as an exhibition record

169

should be supplemented by the more up-to-date first pamphlet of Les Arts Plastiques Bibliographie Internationale des Catalogues d'Expositions (1948). Under the direction of Robert Motherwell, the Documents of Modern Art began, also in 1948, the publication of a series of monographic and subject bibliographies by the writer which eventually promise to encompass, on a scale not heretofore undertaken, the major movements and personalities of our era. In the 1949 revision of René Huyghe's La Peinture Francaise one finds a neatly classified "guide succinct" whose only disadvantage is the conscious restriction of material to the French language. The international art publisher, Albert Skira of Geneva, has completed an outstanding History of Modern Painting in a multi-lingual edition which contains a notable summary relating to its origin, evolution and present position of prestige, a panoramic bibliography credited to Hans Bolliger of Zurich.

Of course, there have been other efforts devoted to the totality of the arts rather than to one medium or area of study. As long ago as 1897, sponsored by the American Library Association, Russell Sturgis published an Annotated Bibliography on Fine Art. While from 1902-1920 Fröhlich, Jellinek, Beth, etc. edited the Internationale Bibliographie der Kunstwissenschaft in Berlin, the French began in 1910 the regular issue of the Répertoire d'Art et d'Archéologie, with separate indexes during the 1910-1924 period. The extensive Kunstgeschichte und Kunstwissenschaft compiled by Walter Timmling in 1923 was soon followed by a supplement Die Kunstliteratur der neusten Zeit (1928). The next year the Americans had begun The Art Index, the most efficient and current of the periodical indices. For the well-known book firm of Ulrico Hoepli of Milan, Giovanni Scheiwiller prepared a bibliographic guide Arte Italiana dall'Origine al Novecento (1933), while an Essai d'une Bibliographie Internationale d'Histoire, 1934-1935 was compiled by Giuseppe Delogu for the Comité International d'Histoire de l'Art (1936). That same year, E. Louise Lucas of the Fogg Museum brought to fruition a sizable Books on Art, a Foundation List begun long ago as a purchase guide under the initiative of the scholarly Art Bulletin. Among the numerous and worthwhile inventories of museum and library holdings, one can mention the excellent catalog of the Copenhagen Kommune-bibliothekar Litteratur om Kunst (1948). Most recently, T. Ballauf and G. Beyrodt have assembled, on an encyclopedic basis, a "Bibliographie 1944-1949" which constitutes the major portion of the Jahrbuch für Aesthetik und Allgemeine Kunstwissenschaft (1951).

Competent for their time, or adequate in terms of the immediate conditions responsible for their being, these bibliographic tools lack a sense of contemporaneous vitality. It is not so much the embodiment of fresh ideas in old forms, as the formulation of techniques equivalent to contemporary expressions. One is reminded of Sigfried Giedion's brilliant observation in Transition: "Methods are instruments for the creation of a new reality". Obviously the issue is the transformation of a routine operation, accessible equally to mechanical or selective process, into a conscious and fully articulate performance. In a single work, such as the collective Histoire de l'Art Contemporain: La Peinture (1934) edited by the distinguished historian and critic, René Huyghe, the reader is confronted by thousands of references, all related to the evolution of one art form during a few decades. To comprehend the full scope of the available documents, one must multiply such a collection by the substantial literature devoted to the other forms of plastic expression which have characterized our experimental century: contemporary sculpture and architecture, industrial and graphic design, the theatrical and photographic arts. As these recent years of a Pulitzer award for history (Larkin's Art and Life in America) and the expansive and chromatic Skira volumes (History of Modern Painting) bear witness, we are faced with an ever-increasing, almost frustrating flow of texts and pictures.* Is it accident, or coincidence, that such new titles contain the longest bibliographies to have appeared in works of this type for some time? Our problem, then, is not solely one of harvesting an abundance of mixed value, but to prune this growth so that it is not choked by its own profusion.

Both the novice and the skilled specialist find common ground in a joint concern for the central core of development. Casual collections without apparent method and sloppy scholarship without justification have cloaked themselves as contemporary bibliography. By taking one's cues from superior, but unfortunately limited examples of intelligent effort, it is possible to substitute evaluation for inventory, and impose upon the sensation of fact a pattern of significance. In this sense, a reasoned bibliography of the arts approaches the objective of the art museum itself, which, as defined by Lewis Mumford, seeks "to enlarge upon the circle of contemporary experience (by selective) intercourse with the past". It would also seem that this fruitful objective rejects the mechanistic reportage of each physical datum in favor of the emotional evaluation of meaningful relations. In short, the abandonment of realism and the acceptance of abstraction. By no means does this approach imply a perversion of reality, or a desertion of the fact. Instead, we recognize that an inventory of the facts, to simultaneously relevant and revelational, predicates a conviction of what is valid. Can it be amiss to say that, as in art itself, the act of choice is a moral one?

---

*Technological causes for this modern phenomenon, statistical descriptions of the rate of change, and potential mechanical solutions of controlling this supra-abundance — somewhat outside the present discussion — are the subject of addresses just published as Bibliography in an Age of Science (Urbana, University of Illinois Press, 1951).

OBJECTIVES IN BIBLIOGRAPHY

Not frequently realized but nevertheless attainable, the pursuit of bibliography in the arts involves the selection of fragments and their assemblage into an interrelated and expressive pattern. Technique may or may not be adequate to the experience at issue; fashions and prejudice exist in this field as in others. What cannot be submitted to indolence or whimsy, obscurity or falsification is the integrity of the material itself. The continuous challenge is how to condense and clarify the essential meaning of the research without suppression or distortion. Since the pertinent record is technically tangible, this process constitutes, from the practical point of view, the artistry of documentation. In another light, this is the conscience of bibliography haunted by the architectonic image of Mies van der Rohe: "the crystallization of its inner structure, the slow unfolding of its form."

ART PUBLICATIONS: 1949-1950

MODERN ART
Nos. 1 - 26
Surveys Dictionaries Movements: Fauvism Cubism Futurism

NATIONAL GROUPS
Nos. 27 - 33
General Australian British German Italian

EXHIBITIONS
Nos. 34 - 81
International Selection Austria Great Britain Germany Haiti
Hungary Italy Low Countries Scandinavia Switzerland

CRITICISM
Nos. 82 - 114
Esthetics & Essays Conferences & Education Periodicals

PAINTING & PAINTERS
Nos. 115 - 276
Surveys National Groups: Argentina Belgium France Germany
Italy Norway Spain Monographs & Catalogs: Alphabetical Record

AMERICAN ART
Nos. 277 - 316
Surveys Monographs & Catalogs Exhibitions The American
Scene in Photography

ARCHITECTURE & DESIGN
Nos. 317 - 360
History Reprints National Studies Essays Monographs & Catalogs
Exhibitions Construction & Design Design in Modern Life:
Exhibitions and Monographs

SCULPTURE
Nos. 361 - 391
General Works Collective Exhibitions Catalogs & Monographs
Techniques

GRAPHIC ARTS
Nos. 392 - 440
Surveys & Pictorial Works Monographs & Catalogs Book &
Advertising Arts

COLLECTIONS
Nos. 441 - 470
Public & Private Collections Sales Catalogs

GALLERIES & MUSEUMS
Nos. 471 - 482

LITERATURE & LETTERS
Nos. 483 - 514
Surveys Critiques Memoirs Bibliography Surrealism
Contemporary Anthologies Classic Editions Modern Editions

ADDENDA
Nos. 515 - 525

INDEX TO BIBLIOGRAPHY
Page 193 - 196

The past decade in America has been a period of great creative activity in painting. Only now has there been a concerted effort to abandon the tyranny of the object and the sickness of naturalism and to enter within consciousness.

We have had many fine artists who have been able to arrive at Abstraction through Cubism: Marin, Stuart Davis, D...th, among others. They have been the pioneers . revolt from the American tradition . Naturalism and of subservience to the obj... Thus has, in the main, been an objective art as differen- tiated from the new paint...

The Intrasubjec... sonal experien... world rathe... no attempt... ulate nos... deals, in... experien... painti... rev... sc...

tator's horizon.

painting (in its inception) ...ghts. As the per... Ta...'s "Death Cry" (so inti... ...very small when c... ...ing revulsion to fasc... "G..." ...on these w... the great urge to creativity, the ... intellectual elegance, and always the jealous adherence to individual statement.

Intrasubjectivism is a point of view in paint- ing, rather than an identical painting style. ...in the varied personalities here shown, ...cism of Pollock, the sensitive callig- ...phy.. Tobey and Graves, the poetry of ...quiet and understated, as opposed ...ism and fury of Hofmann), Mother- ...well's..images, Gottlieb's inventive recall of ...cient..and modern myth, de Kooning's love of..ese, and the others included, have a..on for ideas and for a subtler, ...sur... of expressing them.

The...exhibit have been among the fir.. to pr.. this new realm of ideas. ...th.. and understood, we sh.. side.. their ranks, until ..evo...ivism be- comes...to emerge in Americ..—James Nelson

---

The painter who sees something that inspires him will reproduce landscapes, nudes, apples, merchants, battles, angels, hunting dogs—on one condition: that this image put him in touch with space, glamor, solidity, whatever it is that arouses him beyond ... of course, subjective—or, in Leonardo's term, a mental thing. ... is a thing outside the painter's head that awakens the men- ... the spectator may recognize it in the painting. As the painted hills speak to him, he hears also the hills of "nature". This happy duet makes painting "intelligible".

The modern painter is not inspired by anything visible, but only by some- thing he hasn't seen yet. No super-lively kind of object in the world for him. Everything of that sort has to be put there. Things have abandoned him, including the things in other people's heads (odysseys, crucifixions). In short, he begins with nothingness. That is the only thing he copies. The rest he invents.

The nothing the painter begins with is known as Space. Space is very com- plex: it is merely the canvas before it has been painted. Space is very com- plex; it is nothing wrapped around every object in the world, soothing or strangling it. It is the growing darkness in a coil of trees or the trunk of an elephant held at eye level. It is the mental habit of a man with a ruler or a ball of string — or of one who expects to see something de- lightful crop up out of nowhere. Everyone knows it is the way things keep getting larger and smaller.

All this is space of nothingness, and that is what the modern painter begins by copying. Instead of m... copies, nudes, etc., it is his space that speaks to him, quiver... grey or yellow with bile, gives him a sense of sport, at sign lang... of the absolute.

When the spectator recognizes the nothingness copied by the modern painter, the latter's work becomes just as intelligible as the earlier painting.

Such recognition is not really very difficult. The spectator has the noth- ing in himself, too. Sometimes it gets out of hand. That busy man does not go to the psychiatrist for pleasure or to learn to cook. He wants his cavity filled and the herr doctor does it by stepping up his "func- tioning" and giving him a past all his own. At any rate, it was knowing the nothing that made him ring that fatal doorbell.

Naturally, under the circumstances there is no use looking for silos or madonnas. They have all melted into the void. But, as I said, the void itself, you have that, just as surely as your grandfather had a sun- speckled lawn.—Harold Rosenberg

The Intrasubjectivists: see bibl. 305.

MODERN ART

Surveys

1. ARCHITECTURE D'AUJOURD'HUI (periodical). Arts Plastiques. 138 p. illus. Boulogne, Éditions de l'Architecture d'Aujourd'hui, 1949.
   2nd special number (hors série). Partial contents: Artistes chez eux (Maywald). —— L'Atélier (F. Ponge). —— Hommage à Paul Klee (J. Cassou). —— Marseille, Pavillon suisse, O. N. U. (Le Corbusier). —— Art abstrait et architecture (C. Estienne). —— Manifeste du Corréalisme (F. J. Kiesler). —— Peintres instinctifs (P. Guéguen). —— L'Art brut (P. Guéguen).

2. L'Art Abstrait: Ses Origines, Ses Premiers Maîtres. 322 p. illus. Paris, Maeght, 1949.
   Edited by Michel Seuphor. Statements by the artists. Biographical and bibliographical sections.

3. FELS, FLORENT. L'Art Vivant de 1900 à Nos Jours. 260 p. illus. Genève, Pierre Cailler, 1950.
   Peintres at sculpteurs d'hier at d'aujourd'hui, no. 17. 550 illustrations, 16 color plates.

4. GAUNT, WILLIAM. The March of the Moderns. 319 p. illus. London, J. Cape, 1949.
   From the death of Cézanne to Dali.

5. GILBERT, DOROTHY B., Compiler. Guide to Art Films. Washington, D. C., American Federation of Arts, 1949-50.
   "Compiled . . . for the Magazine of Art, New York." First edition, 1949. Second edition, 1950, compiled by Dorothy B. Gilbert and Helen M. Franc.

6. GOMBRICH, E. H. The Story of Art. 462 p. New York, Phaidon, 1950.
   A history of art until today, lucidly written by a member of the Warburg Institute, London. Ch. 27 —— Experimental art: the twentieth century.

7. LEEPA, ALLEN. Challenge of Modern Art. 256 p. illus. New York, Beechhurst Press, 1949.
   Foreword by Herbert Read.

8. RAMSDEN, E. H. An Introduction to Modern Art. 2. ed. 48 p. illus. London, New York, Toronto, Oxford University Press, 1950.
   First edition, 1940.

9. READ, HERBERT. Art Now: an Introduction to the Theory of Modern Painting and Sculpture. 144 p. illus. New York, Pitman, 1949.
   Third enlarged edition, also published by Faber and Faber (London, 1948). 196 plates. Contains "Epilogue 1947" which includes "a representative selection of contemporary American artists."

10. SALVINI, ROBERTO. Guida all'Arte Moderna. 307 p. illus. Firenze, L'Arco, 1949.
    Bibliography.

11. SCHATZ, OLGA. Juval Sings into the Spirit of Art. 118 p. [Berkeley, Cal.?] Circle Edition, 1949.
    500 copies printed at Superior Press, Berkeley, Cal.

12. Three Lectures on Modern Art. By Katherine Dreier, James Johnson Sweeney, Naum Gabo. 91 p. illus. New York, Philosophical Library, 1949.

13. U. N. E. S. C. O. Films on Art: a Specialized Study, an International Catalog. 72 p. illus. 1950.
    "The text of this booklet appeared originally in

Architecture and Technology: **Ludwig Mies van der Rohe**

Director, Department of Architecture

Illinois Institute of Technology

Technology is rooted in the past.
It dominates the present and tends into the future.
It is a real historical movement —
one of the great movements which shape and
represent their epoch.
It can be compared only with the Classic
discovery of man as a person,
the Roman will to power,
and the religious movement of the Middle Ages.
Technology is far more than a method,
it is a world in itself.
As a method it is superior in almost every respect.
But only where it is left to itself as in
the construction of machinery, or as in the
gigantic structures of engineering, there
technology reveals its true nature.

There it is evident that it is not only a useful means,
that it is something, something in itself,
something that has a meaning and a powerful form —
so powerful in fact, that it is not easy to name it.
Is that still technology or is it architecture?
And that may be the reason why some people
are convinced that architecture will be outmoded
and replaced by technology.
Such a conviction is not based on clear thinking.
The opposite happens.
Wherever technology reaches its real fulfillment,
it transcends into architecture.
It is true that architecture depends on facts,
but its real field of activity is in the realm
of the significance.
I hope you will understand that architecture
has nothing to do with the inventions of forms.
It is not a playground for children, young or old.
Architecture is the real battleground of the spirit.
Architecture wrote the history of the epochs
and gave them their names.
Architecture depends on its time.
It is the crystallization of its inner structure,
the slow unfolding of its form.
That is the reason why technology and architecture
are so closely related.
Our real hope is that they grow together,
that someday the one be the expression of
the other.
Only then will we have an architecture worthy
of its name:
Architecture as a true symbol of our time.

See bibl. 328.

Mies van der Rohe

French as an issue of the Belgian art review "Les Arts Plastiques" . . . Copyright 1949 by Les Editions de la Connaissance, Brussels and Unesco, Paris." New titles added to directory issued no. 1-2 Janvier-Février 1949.

Dictionaries

14. BÉNÉZIT, E. Dictionnaire Critique et Documentaire des Peintres, Sculpteurs, Dessinateurs et Graveurs. Nouv. éd. illus. Paris, Gründ, 1949-50. Vol. 2: Bonnardel-C (1949). — 3: D-Forain (1950).

15. SCHWARZ, KARL. Jewish Artists of the 19th and 20th Centuries. 273 p. illus. New York, Philosophical Library, 1949.

16. Who's Who In Art. 5. ed. 552 p. London, Art Trade Press [1950].

Movements

17. CIRLOT, JUAN EDUARDO. Diccionario de los Ismos. 414 p. illus. Barcelona, Argos, 1949.

Fauvism

18. DUTHUIT, GEORGES. Les Fauves: Braque, Derain, Van Dongen, Dufy, Friesz, Manguin, Marquet, Matisse, Puy, Vlaminck. 254 p. illus. (col. plates) Genève, Trois Collines, 1949.
"Couverture originale d'Henri Matisse. Publiée sous la direction de Jean Descoullages et François Lachenal." Bibliography by Bernard Karpel.

19. DUTHUIT, GEORGES. The Fauvist Painters. 146 p. illus. (col. plates) New York, Wittenborn, Schultz, 1950.
Documents of Modern Art, no. 11, edited by Robert Motherwell. Translation by Ralph Manheim of French text issued by Lachenal (bibl. 18). Bibliography and list of exhibitions by Bernard Karpel, p. 102-124.

Cubism

20. APOLLINAIRE, GUILLAUME. The Cubist Painters: Aesthetic Meditations, 1913. 65 p. illus. New York, Wittenborn, Schultz, 1949.
Documents of Modern Art, no. 1, edited by Robert Motherwell. Translated by Lionel Abel. Bibliography by Bernard Karpel, p. 54-65.

21. APOLLINAIRE, GUILLAUME. Les Peintres Cubistes. 139 p. illus. Genève, Pierre Cailler, 1950.
Illustrations vary from original edition.

22. AZCOAGA, ENRIQUE. El Cubismo. 35 p. illus. Barcelona, Omega, 1949.

22a. CRASTRE, VICTOR. La Naissance du Cubisme, (Céret 1910). 61 p. illus. Genève, Pierre Cailler, [1950].
"Ophrys" printed on title-page.

23. KAHNWEILER, DANIEL HENRY. The Rise of Cubism. 35 p. illus. New York, Wittenborn, Schultz, 1949.
Documents of Modern Art, no. 9, edited by Robert Motherwell. Translation by Henry Aronson of "Der Weg zum Kubismus." Bibliography of "Writings by Daniel-Henry Kahnweiler," by Bernard Karpel.

24. KAHNWEILER, DANIEL HENRY. Les Années Héroiques du Cubisme. 15 p. illus. Paris, Braun, 1950.
"Les Maîtres," edited by George Besson.

Futurism

25. BENET, RAFAEL. El Futurismo Comparado, el Moviemento Dada. 77 p. illus. Barcelona, Omega, 1949.

Surrealism

26. WYSS, DIETER. Der Surrealismus: eine Einführung und Deutung Surrealistischer Literatur und Malerei. 88 p. illus. Heidelberg, Lambert Schneider, 1950.

NATIONAL GROUPS

Australian

27. SMITH, SYDNEY URE. Present Day Art in Australia. 64 p. illus. Sydney, S. U. Smith, 1949.
Revised edition of 1943 and 1945 work.

British

28. JOHNSTONE, WILLIAM. Creative Arts in Britain from the Earliest Times to the Present. 318 p. illus. New York, Macmillan, 1950.
Edition previously published in England.

German

29. RAVE, PAUL ORTWIN. Kunstdiktatur im Dritten Reich. 95 p. illus. Hamburg, Gebr. Mann, 1949.

Italian

30. CAHIERS D'ART (Paris). Un Demi-Siècle d'Art Italien. 276 p. illus. 1950.
Special number 1, 25e année, 1950, edited by Christian Zervos. Bibliography.

31. CARRIERI, RAFFAELE. Pittura, Scultura d'Avantguardia (1890-1950) in Italia. 345 p. illus. Milano, Conchiglia, 1950.
Bibliography.

32. NEW YORK. MUSEUM OF MODERN ART. Twentieth-Century Italian Art. 144 p. illus. New York, Museum of Modern Art, 1949.
Text by James T. Soby and Alfred H. Barr, Jr. for catalog issued on the occasion of the exhibition held June 29-Sept. 18, 1949. Bibliography by Bernard Karpel.

33. Panorama dell'Arte Italiana. Eds.: Marco Valsecchi, Umbro Apollonio. 419 p. illus. Torino, Lattes, 1950.
Modern and older arts; articles and biographical notices; list of exhibitions and publications, etc.

EXHIBITIONS

International Selection

34. AMSTERDAM. STEDELIJK MUSEUM. Expressionisme: Van Gogh tit Picasso. 22 p. illus. 1949?

35. BERNE. KUNSTHALLE. Les Fauves . . . und die Zeitgenossen. 12 p. illus. 1950.
Fauves: Derain, Dufy, Friesz, Braque [etc.].—— Contemporaries: Amiet, Giacometti.

36. BERNE. KUNSTHALLE. Moderne Primitive Maler. 20 p. illus. 1949.
Exhibit held July 28-Aug. 28, including Rousseau, Bauchant, Bertheau, Bombois, Dietrich, Metelli, Peyronnet, Seraphine, Trillhaase, Rosina Viva, Vivin. Foreword by A. Rüdlinger. Bibliography.

37. CAMBRIDGE, MASS. MASSACHUSETTS INSTITUTE OF TECHNOLOGY. The Painter and the City. 4 p. illus. 1950.
Exhibition held May 8-June 15, with introduction by S. Giedion.

38. LONDON. INSTITUTE OF CONTEMPORARY ARTS. 40,000 Years of Modern Art. 54 p. illus. 1949.
Texts by W. G. Archer, Melville, Read.

39. MEMPHIS, TENN. BROOKS MEMORIAL ART GALLERY. Paintings from France. 30 p. illus. 1949.
"French taste today and tomorrow . . . American premiere." Foreword in French and English by Jean Cassou. Biographical notes.

40. NEW YORK. CENTURY ASSOCIATION. Trends in European Painting, 1880-1930. 41 p. illus. 1949.
Loan exhibition held Feb. 2-Mar. 31.

41. NEW YORK. MUSEUM OF MODERN ART. Modern Art Old and New. 4 p. plus 40 plates (boxed), 1950.
Teaching Portfolio no. 3, based on an exhibit titled "Timeless Aspects of Modern Art," organized by René d'Harnoncourt, who contributes an introduction.

42. NEW YORK. PAUL ROSENBERG GALLERY. Loan exhibition: The 19th Century Heritage . . . 51 p. illus. 1950.
Exhibit held Mar. 7-Apr. 1, Catalog no. 69, with extensive essay by Alexandre P. Rosenberg.

43. OSTENDE. PALAIS DES THERMES. Gloires de la Peinture Moderne, 61 p. illus. Bruxelles, La Connaissance, 1949.
"Hommage à James Ensor. Textes de En. Langui." Biographical notes: Braque, Chagall, De Chirico, Dali, Ernst, Matisse, Picasso, Klee. Collotype plates.

44. PARIS. COMPAGNIE DE L'ART BRUT. L'Art Brut Préféré aux Arts Culturels. 52 p. illus. 1949.
Text by Jean Dubuffet for October exhibit at the Drouin Gallery.

45. PARIS. MUSÉE PEDAGOGIQUE. De Van Gogh et Seurat aux Dessins d'Enfants. 152 p. illus. 1949.
Text by Dr. F. Minkowska, for exhibit "à la recherche du mondes des formes (Rorschach)" held Apr. 20-May 14.

46. RHODE ISLAND SCHOOL OF DESIGN. MUSEUM OF ART. Isms in Art since 1800. 92 leaves (mimeographed). Providence, 1949.
For an exhibit held Feb. 3-Mar. 9, with commentary by Gordon Washburn.

47. SAN FRANCISCO. CALIFORNIA **PALACE OF**

THE LEGION OF HONOR. Illusionism & Trompe l'Oeil. 78 p. illus. 1949.
Articles by Douglas MacAgy, Jermayne MacAgy and Alfred Frankenstein. Exhibit held May 3-June 12.

48. SAO PAULO. MUSEU DE ARTE MODERNA. Do Figurativismo ao Abstracionismo. 71 p. illus. 1949.
Text in Portuguese, French, English.

49. SPRINGFIELD, MASS. MUSEUM OF FINE ARTS. In Freedom's Search. 11 p. illus. 1950.
Preface by F. B. Robinson. Paintings exhibited Jan. 15-Feb. 19.

50. TOULON. PALAIS DE LA BOURSE. Exposition Comparative de l'Art Figuratif à l'Art Spatial. 8 p. 1950.
Prefatory letter by A. Herbin.

51. VENICE. BIENNALE. Catalogo . . . XXV Biennale. 474 p. illus. Venezia, Alfieri, 1950.
Includes special sections on E. De Fiori, The Fauves, Cubist Masters, Futurists, M. Rosso, C. Carra, G. Seurat, J. Villon, Rousseau, Kandinsky, as well as the usual international representatives. The American contingent consisted of Marin, Bloom, Gatch, Lebrun, Gorky, Pollock, de Kooning. Notes by D. Phillips, A. M. Frankfurter, A. H. Barr, Jr. See also special Biennale number of Ulisse (Roma) June 1950, with extensive commentary.

52. VERVIERS, SOCIÉTÉ ROYALE DES BEAUX-ARTS. La Peinture Sous le Signe d'Apollinaire. 39 p. illus. [Bruxelles, Les Arts Plastiques] 1950.
Catalog of 75 works shown Oct. 22-Nov. 5, and at Brussels in December.

53. ZURICH. KUNSTHAUS. Futurismo & Pittura Metafisica. 34 p. illus. 1950.
Exhibit held Nov.-Dec.

Austria

54. ART CLUB. AUSTRIAN SECTION. Internationale Ausstellung. 14 p. illus. Wien, Wiener Secession, 1950.
"Internationaler imabhängiger Künstler verband Osterreich." Exhibited Oct. 7-Nov. 12.

Great Britain

55. AMSTERDAM. STEDELIJK MUSEUM. 12 Britse Schilders. 3 p. plus plates. 1949.
February exhibit of Graham Sutherland, Robert MacBryde and others, with introduction by Herbert Read.

56. GREAT BRITAIN. ARTS COUNCIL. Some Twentieth Century English Paintings and Drawings. 32 p. illus. 1950.
W. R. Sickert, P. W. Steer, Duncan Grant, Mark Gertler, Stanley Spencer, with introduction by David Bell.

Germany

57. BAD NAUHEIM. INFORMATION CENTER BRANCH. FINE ARTS SECTION. Berliner Künstler: Malerei, Grafik, Plastik. 48 p. illus. Bad Nauheim, 1950.
Introduction by Will Grohmann.

58. Berliner Neue Gruppe 1950. 70 p. illus. Berlin, Brüder Hartmann, 1950.
Exhibit of 186 paintings and sculptures, with texts by M. Kaus, A. Camus, W. Grohmann.

59. BERNE. KUNSTHALLE. Lehmbruck, Macke, Marc. 21 p. illus. 1949.
Statements by the artists. Bibliography.

60. GREAT BRITAIN. ARTS COUNCIL. Modern German Prints and Drawings. 15 p. illus. London, Arts Council and Institute of Contemporary Arts, 1949.
Texts by P. James and C. G. Heise.

61. MUNICH. CENTRAL ART COLLECTING POINT. Kunstschaffen in Deutschland. 44 p. illus. 1949.
Exhibited June-July. "First comprehensive showing of German contemporary art," edited by Stefan P. Munsing, O. M. G. B. Foreword by Alfred Hentzen.

62. MUNICH. HAUS DER KUNST. Der Blaue Reiter: München und die Kunst des 20. Jahrhunderts, 1908-1914. 45 p. illus. München-Pasing, Filser, 1949.
Text by Ludvig Grote for exhibit held Sept.-Oct. Extracts from writings of Klee, Kandinsky, Marc. Also exhibited at the Basel Kunsthalle (1950).

63. MUNICH. HAUS DER KUNST. Die Maler am Bauhaus. 65 p. illus. München, Prestel, 1950.
Text by L. Grote for exhibit held May-June.

64. ZURICH. KUNSTHAUS. Kunst in Deutschland, 1930-49. 36 p. 1949.
Texts by W. Wartmann, Alfred Hentzen.

Haiti

65. AMSTERDAM. STEDELIJK MUSEUM. 19 Schilders uit Haiti. 8 p. illus. 1950.

Hungary

66. PARIS. MUSÉE NATIONAL D'ART MODERNE. Exposition d'Art Hongrois Contemporain. 24 p. illus. 1949.
Exhibit held Mar. 25-Apr. 24. Introduction by J. Cassou.

Italy

67. AMSTERDAM. STEDELIJK. Figuren uit de Italiaanse Kunst na 1910. 12 p. illus. 1950.

68. FLORENCE. Italienische Kunst der Gegenwart, Ausstellung 1950-1951. [72] p. illus. München, Prestel, 1950.
Organized under the patronage of the Italian government, and exhibited at Florence. Catalog lists 339 works, with forewords by Werner Haftmann and Bernard Degenhart. Biographical notes.

69. GREAT BRITAIN. ARTS COUNCIL. Modern Italian Art. 16 p. illus. London, 1950.
Text by Paolo d'Ancona. Exhibited under auspices of the Amici di Brera and Italian Institute.

70. VENICE. PROMOSSA DAL PREMIO "LA COLOMBA." Rassegna di Pittura Italiana Contemporanea. illus. 1949.
Exhibit held Oct. 1-31. Introduction by Nicola Ciarletta in Italian, French, English. Biographical notes.

The Low Countries

71. THE HAGUE. GEMEENTEMUSEUM. Facetten van Hedendaagse Schilderkunst: België. Luxemburg, Nederland. 88 p. illus. 's-Gravenhage, Dienst voor Schone Kunsten, 1949.
Exhibit held June 25-Aug. 8.

71a. KOUWENAAR, GERRIT & NIEUWENHUYS, CONSTANT. Goede Morgan Haan. 14 p. illus. Amsterdam, Experimentele Groep in Holland, 1949.

72. LUXEMBOURG. MUSÉES DE L'ÉTAT. Artistes Wallons Contemporains. 42 p. illus. Bruxelles, 1949.
Exhibited Nov. 12-Dec. 4. Includes Delvaux, Magritte and others.

73. STOCKHOLM. NATIONALMUSEUM. Nutida Holländsk Expressionism. 69 p. illus. 1949.
Utställningskatalog, nr. 158.

74. VAN DIEMEN-LILIENFELD GALLERIES, NEW YORK. Modern Belgian Art in Private American Collections. 32 p. illus. 1950.
Exhibit held May 13-26 under the auspices of the Belgian Government Information Center.

Scandinavia

75. BRUSSELS. PALAIS DES BEAUX-ARTS. Exposition d'Art Finlandais. 28 p. illus. 1949.
Preface by Onni Okkonen. Exhibited Oct. 6-30. Also shown at the Hague Gemeentemuseum, "Finse Kunst," Nov. 5-22.

76. COPENHAGEN. DEN FRIE UDSTILLING. Katalog, redigeret of Elof Risebye. 91 p. illus. København, Det Berlingske Bogtrykkeri, 1950.

77. THE HAGUE. GEMEENTEMUSEUM. Hondred Jaar Noorse Schilderkunst. 51 p. illus. 's-Gravenhage, 1950.
Introduction by Sigurd Willoch.

78. SPIRALEN, KUNSTNER SAMMENSLUTNINGEN. Katalog, 1949-1950. [20] p. illus. Charlottenborg, 1949.
Exhibit held Dec. 30. 1949-Jan. 15, 1950. Edited by R. Dahlmann Olsen. Previous exhibition catalog dated Dec. 29, 1948-Jan. 14, 1949.

79. STOCKHOLM. NATIONALMUSEUM. Nutida Schweizisk Konst. 54 p. illus. 1950.
Exhibition held Feb.-May 1950. Utställningskatalog, nr. 167.

Switzerland

80. AMSTERDAM. STEDELIJK MUSEUM. 6 Zwitserse Kunstnaars. 40 p. illus. 1950.
Schilders: Hans Berger, Ernst Morgenthaler, Coghut. —Grafici: Fritz Pauli, Hans Fischer. —Beeldhouwer: Walter Linck. Catalog 72.

81. BERN. KUNSTHALLE. Vier Winterthurer Künstler. 8 p. illus. 1949.
Exhibit, held Sept. 23-Oct. 23, included: Hans Schöllhorn, Robert Wehrlin, Rudolf Zender (painters); Robert Lienhard (sculptor).

CRITICISM

Esthetics & Essays

82. BERKMAN, AARON. Art and Space. 175 p. illus. New York, Social Sciences, 1949.

83. BOAS, GEORGE. Wingless Pegasus, A Handbook for Critics. 244 p. Baltimore, Johns Hopkins, 1950.

84. BURCHARTZ, MAX. Gleichnis der Harmonie, Gesetz und Gesfaltung der Bildenden Kunste. 214 p. illus. Munchen, Prestel, 1949.

85. FEIBLEMAN, JAMES K. Aesthetics: A Study of the Fine Arts in Theory and Practice. 463 p. New York, Duell, Sloan and Pearce, 1949.

86. GOERITZ, MATHIAS. Sobre la Libertad de Creación. 12 p. illus. Guadalajara, Jal., Galeria Camurauz, 1950.

87. GUGGENHEIMER, RICHARD. Creative Vision in Artist and Audience. 173 p. New York, Harper, 1950.

88. HARAP, LOUIS. Social Roots of the Arts. 192 p. New York, International, 1949.

89. HILDEBRAND, A. Il Problema della Forma. Messina-Firenze, Casa Edit. D'Anna, 1949.
Translation of a classic text, with introduction and notes, by S. Samek Lodovici.

90. HUBER-WIESENTHAL, RUDOLF. Sonderbares um Moderne Kunst. 184 p. illus. Affolfern a A., Aehren, 1949.

91. JOHNSON, MARTIN. Art and Scientific Thought. 200 p. New York, Columbia University Press, 1949.

92. MALRAUX, ANDRÉ. Psychologie de l'Art. 3 vols. illus. Geneve, Albert Skira, 1947-50.
Vol. 1: Le Musée Imaginaire (1947). — II: La Création Artistique (1948). — La Monnaie de l'Absolue (1950).

93. MALRAUX, ANDRÉ. The Psychology of Art. 3 vols. illus. New York, Pantheon, 1949-50.
The Bollingen Series, originally published in French by A. Skira. Translated by Stuart Gilbert. Vol. 1: Museum without Walls. — 2: The Creative Act. — 3: Twilight of the Absolute.

94. MASSON, ANDRÉ. Le Plaisir de Peindre. 202 p. illus. [Macon], La Diane Francaise, 1950.

95. MELLQUIST, JEROME, Compiler. "What They Said" — Postscript to Art Criticism. 24 p. illus. New York, Durand-Ruel Galleries, 1949.
Extracts illustrating the adverse criticism encountered by painters before their plastic achievement was accepted on its own terms.

96. MUNRO, THOMAS. The Arts and Their Interrelationships. 559 p. illus. New York, Liberal Arts, 1949.

97. NEWTON, ERIC. In My View. 258 p. London, Longmans, Green, 1950.
Reprints of critical articles, 1944-1949.

98. PEPPER, STEPHEN C. Principles of Art Appreciation. 326 p. illus. New York, Harcourt, Brace, 1949.

99. POPE, ARTHUR. The Language of Drawing and Painting. 162 p. illus. Cambridge, Mass., Harvard University Press, 1950.

100. Primera Semana de Arte en Santillana del Mar. 260 p. illus. Madrid, Léon Sánchez Guesta, 1950.
Contributions on contemporary art by S. Gasch, A. Sartoris, E. Westerdahl and others.

101. READ, HERBERT. The Grass Roots of Art. 92 p. illus. New York, Wittenborn, Schultz, 1949.
"Problems of Contemporary Art, v. 2."

102. READ, HERBERT. Education Through Art. 320 p. illus. New York, Pantheon, 1949.

103. READ, HERBERT. The Meaning of Art. Rev. ed. 191 p. illus. Bungay, Suffolk (England), Penguin Books in Association with Faber and Faber, 1949.

104. REINER, IMRE. Creative Desire. 79 p. illus. St. Gall, Zollikofer, 1949.

105. SAN FRANCISCO ART ASSOCIATION. The Western Round Table on Modern Art. 70 leaves (mimeographed) San Francisco, The Association, 1949.
"Abstract of proceedings, edited by Douglas MacAgy." Partly published in this biennial.

106. SCHNEIDER, DANIEL E. The Psychoanalyst and the Artist. 320 p. illus. N.Y., Farrar, Straus, 1950.

107. TAUBES, FREDERIC. Paintings and Essays on Art. 176 p. illus. New York, Dodd, Mead, 1950.

108. VITALI, LAMBERTO. Preferenze. 182 p. Milano, Domus, 1950.
Essays published 1930-1950.

109. WEITZ, MORRIS. Philosophy of the Arts. 239 p. Cambridge, Harvard University Press, 1950.

110. WINKLER, WALTER. Psychologie der Modernen Kunst. 303 p. illus. Tübingen, Alma Mater, 1949.

110a. ZAHAR, MARCEL. Le Désordre dans l'Art Contemporain. 62 p. Paris, La Vie Réelle, 1950.

Periodicals

111. Art d'Aujourd'hui, Revue Mensuelle d'Art Contemporain. Directeur, André Bloc, el al. Boulogne, Editions de l'Architecture d'Aujourd'hui, 1949-current.
Emphasis on European manifestations, with good international coverage. Excellent special numbers on movements, including one on contemporary American art by Michel Scuphor.

112. Dau Al Set. Barcelona, 1949-current.
Handsomely designed monthly brochures issued by an avant-garde group. Individual numbers represent work of J. E. Cirlot, Angel Ferrant, Joan Ponç, M. Cuixart, Brossa, A. Tàpies, etc. Special numbers include: Hommage à Paul Klee by Joan-Joseph Tharrats and others. See also no. 132, 160.

113. Eidos, a Journal of Painting, Sculpture and Design. London, Newman Wolsey Ltd., 1950-1951.
Editorial Advisors: W. P. Gibson, B. Ashmole, L. Ashton, J. Rothenstein, Nos. 1, 2, 3 issued in 1950. Includes modern and older arts, exhibition and book reviews. Ceased publication.

114. Trans/formation: Arts, Communication, Environment — A World Review. Editor, Harry Holtzman; Associate, Martin James. No. 1. New York, Wittenborn, Schultz, 1950-current.
Partial contents are: Modern Art and 20th Century Man (S. I. Hayakawa). — Museum Landscape (A. Reinhardt). — Home-Street-City (P. Mondrain). — Surrealist Intentions (N. Calas). Scheduled for no. 2 (1951): Cezanne and the Philosophy of his Time (P. M. Laporte). — The Renaissance and Order (W. de Kooning). — Artist-Symbol-Society (K. Seligmann). — The Art of This Time (S. W. Hayter).

BIBLIOGRAPHY

PAINTING & PAINTERS
Surveys

115. ARLAND, MARCEL. Chronique de la Peinture Moderne. 214 p. Paris, Corrêa, 1949.

116. ARP, HANS. Onze Peintres Vues par Arp. 37 p. illus. Zurich, Girsberger, 1949.
Text in French and German. Includes Taeuber, Kandinsky, Leuppi, Vordemberge, Arp, Delaunay, Schwitters, Kiesler, Morris, Magnelli, Ernst.

117. BETHERS, RAY. Composition in Pictures. 255 p. illus. New York, Pitman, 1949.

118. BLANSHARD, FRANCES BRADSHAW. Retreat from Likeness in the Theory of Painting. 178 p. illus. New York, Columbia University Press, 1949 (c 1945).

119. BRILL, REGINALD. Modern Painting, and its Roots in European Tradition. 32 p. illus. London, Avalon Press & Central Institute of Art, 1949.

120. The Faber Gallery. London, Faber & Faber, 1949-current.
Albums on painters past and present, with introductions and comment on color plates. Already issued: Cézanne, Klee, Renoir, Matisse, Van Gogh, Chagall, Gauguin, Seurat, etc. Released in New York under Pitman imprint.

121. History of Modern Painting. With texts by Maurice Raynal and others. 3 vols. illus. col. plates Geneva, Albert Skira, 1949-50.
Vol. 1: From Baudelaire to Bonnard: The Birth of a New Vision (1949). — 2: Matisse, Munch, Rouault: Fauvism, Expressionism (1950). — 3: From Picasso to Surrealism (1950). Text and documentation by Maurice Raynal, Arnold Rudlinger, Jacques Lassaigne, Werner Schmalenbach and others. Translated from the French edition. Bibliographical and biographical notices by Hans Bolliger. Vol. 2 also issued in German, with supplementary bibliography on Expressionism.

122. LHOTE, ANDRÉ. La Peinture, Le Coeur et L'Esprit, suivi de Parlons Peinture, Essais. 459 p. Paris, Denoël, 1950.

123. LHOTE, ANDRÉ. Treatise on Landscape Painting. 50 p. illus. London, A. Zwemmer, 1950.
Translation of French text.

124. LOEB, PIERRE. Regards sur la Peinture. 42 p. Paris, La Hune, 1950.
Also copies with etching by Alberto Giacometti.

125. MARCHIORI, GIUSEPPE. Pittura Moderna in Europa (da Manet à Pignon). 176 p. illus. Venezia, Neri Pozza, 1950.

126. MILIONE, EDIZIONI DEL. [Serie: Sei Tavole a Colori]. Milano, 1950.
Small folders with mounted color plates. So far issued: Picasso, Modigliani, Carra, Borra, De Chirico, Sironi. In process: Klee, Asnago, etc.

127. MUNDT, ERNEST. A Primer of Visual Art. 41 p. illus. Minneapolis, Minn., Burgess, 1950.

128. MYERS, BERNARD S. Modern Art in the Making. 457 p. illus. New York, McGraw-Hill, 1950.
Painting in the 19th and 20th centuries.

129. Orpheus, a Symposium of the Arts, Vol. 2. Edited by John Lehmann. 190 p. illus. London, J. Lehmann, 1949.

130. PORTER, BERNARD H. Contemporary Paintings. 12 p. illus. Los Angeles, W. McNaughton, 1949.

131. RATHBUN, MARY CHALMERS & HAYES, BARTLETT, H. JR. Layman's Guide to Modern Art: Painting for a Scientific Age. 108 p. illus. New York, Oxford, 1949.
Based on an exhibition at the Addison Gallery entitled "Seeing the Unseeable" (1947).

132. THARRATS, JOAN-JOSEP. Guia Elemental de la Pintura Moderna (1900-1950). 47 p. illus. Barcelona, Dau Al Set, 1950.

133. U. N. E. S. C. O. Catalogue de Reproductions en Couleurs de la Peinture de 1860 a 1949. 191 p. illus. Paris, United Nations Educational, Scientific and Cultural Organization, 1949.
Vol. 2 of its tri-lingual catalogs.

134. ZUCKER, PAUL. Styles in Painting, a Comparative Study. 338 p. illus. New York, Viking, 1950.

Argentina

135. Pintores Argentinos: Hector Basaldua, Horacio Butler, Raquel Forner, Paul Soldi. 18 p. col. plates. Buenos Aires, Pampa, 1950.

Belgium

136. Monographies de l'Art Belge. Anvers, De Sikkel, 1949-50.
Issued for the Ministry of Education. "Troisième Série" documents academic artists mainly.

France

137. ASSAILLY, GISELE D'. Avec les Peintres de la Réalité Poétique. 234 p. illus. Paris, Juillard, 1949.

138. BERNHEIM DE VILLERS, GASTON. Little Tales of Great Artists. 106 p. illus. Paris, Quatre Chemins; New York, E. Weyhe, 1949.
Translated and edited by Denys Sutton.

139. Bibliotheque Aldine des Arts. Paris, Fernand Hazen, 1949-50.
A series of booklets with introductions and two dozen color plates, edited by René Ben Sussan.

140. Collection Artistes de Ce Temps. Eds.: Pierre Descargues, Denys Chevalier. Paris, P L F, 1950.
Illustrated booklets with texts by the individual editors. So far issued: No. 1: Vieiva da Silva. — 2: Buffet. — 3: Minaux. — 4: Volte. — 5: Carzou. — 6: Y. Alde. — 7: Hajdu. — 8: Lorjou. — 9: Rivière. — 10: Viani. — 11: Piaubert. In process: Clavé, Franchina, Bertholle, etc.

141. COGNIAT, RAYMOND. French Painting at the Time of the Impressionists. Rev. ed. 163 p. col. plates New York, Hyperion, 1950.

142. COGNIAT, RAYMOND, ed. Orientations de la Peinture Française, de David à Picasso. 201 p. illus. Nice, La Diane Française, 1950.

143. GAUSS, CHARLES EDWARD. The Aesthetic Theories of French Artists, 1855 to the Present. 111 p. Baltimore, Johns Hopkins Press, 1949.
Statements by and views on French painters.

144. GAUTHEIR, MAXIMILIEN. Six Maîtres de l'Art Contemporain Français. 288 p. illus. Paris, Les Gémeaux, 1949.
Miniature monographs in boxed set: Friesz, Vlaminck, Despiau, Segonzac, Dufy, R. Subes.

145. HUYGHE, RENÉ. La Peinture Française: Les Contemporains. 122 p. 164 plates. Paris, Tisné, 1949.
Revision of publication issued 1939. Notes by Germain Bazin, including bibliography.

146. LE POINT (Periodical). L'Art Officiel de Jules Grevy à Albert Lebrun. 48 p. illus. Souillac (Lot), Mulhouse, 1949.
Number 38, April 1949, edited by F. Jourdain.

147. REWALD, JOHN. Storia dell'Impressionismo. 316 p. illus. Firenze, Sansoni, 1949.
Italian translation of edition originally published by the Museum of Modern Art, New York.

148. SAN LAZZARO, G. Di. Painting in France, 1895-1949. 132 p. New York, Philosophical Library, 1949.
Translation of Danesi edition (Rome, 1945).

149. UHDE, WILHELM. Five Primitive Masters. 98 p. illus. New York, Quadrangle, 1949.
Rousseau, Vivin, Bauchant, Bombois and de Senlis. Originally Atlantis Verlag (Zurich, 1947).

150. VENTURI, LIONELLO. Impressionists and Symbolists. 244 p. illus. New York-London, Scribner, 1950.

151. WILENSKI, REGINALD HOWARD. Modern French Painters. 455 p. illus. New York, Harcourt, Brace, 1949.

Germany

152. HAFTMANN, WERNER. Deutsche Maler. 7 p. 10 col. plates. Steinheim am Main, Forum, 1950?
Reproductions in folio: Baumeister, Gilles, Kirchner, Klee, Macke, Marc, Mataré, Meistermann, Nay, Schlemmer.

Italy

153. APOLLONIO, UMBRO. Pittura Italiana Moderna. 160 p. illus. Venezia, Neri Pozza, 1950.

153a. APOLLONIO, UMBRO. La Pittura Metafisica. Venezia, Ed. del Cavallino, 1950.

154. GRADA, RAFFAELE DE. 12 Opere de R. Birolli, B. Cassinari, E. Morlotti, E. Trecanni. 17 p. plus 12 col. plates. Milano, Edizione del Milione, 1950.

155. Il Lavoro Nella Pittura Italiana d'Oggi. 463 p. illus. Milano, Verocchi, 1950.
Sponsored by the Guiseppe Verzocchi brickmaking concern. Includes statements by each artist.

156. MONTU, ERNESTO. Masterpieces of Modern Italian Art [11] p. plus color plates. Milan, Radio Giornale, 1950.
Includes Carra, de Chirico, Morandi, Sironi. Italian text, English translation by Anthony Barcroft.

157. ORENGO, V. & TURATI, A., Ed. Pittura Moderna Italiana. 180 p. illus. Turino, Orengo-Turati, 1949.
Introduction by G. Ghirnighelli.

158. UNGARETTI, GUISEPPE. Pittori Italian Contemporanei. 39 p. plus 66 plates (some col.) Bologna, Licino Cappelli, 1950.
With English translation of introduction.

Norway

159. OSTBY, LEIF. Modern Norwegian Painting. 262 p. illus. col. plates. Oslo, Mittet, 1949.

Spain

160. GAYA NUÑO, J. A. Medio Siglo de Movimientos Vanguardistas en Nuestra Pintura. [22] p. illus. Barcelona, Dau al Set, 1950.

Monographs & Catalogs

161. BORGESE, LEONARDO. Discorso sull'Oggettivismo a Proposito di ALOI. 19 p. illus. Milano, Enrico Gualdoni, 1950.

162. MONTGOMERIE, WILLIAM. A Modern Scottish Painter, Donald BAIN. 79 p. illus. Glasgow, William MacLellan, 1950.
Includes French translation.

163. BUCHER, JEAN, GALERIE (Paris). Exposition Willi BAUMEISTER. novembre-décembre. Stuttgart, Stuttgarter Verlag, 1949.

164. REIFENBERG, BENNO & HAUSENSTEIN, WM. Max BECKMANN. 82 p. illus. Munchen, Piper, 1949.

165. BELLMAR, HANS. Les Jeux de la Poupée. 82 p. illus. Paris, Éditions Premières, 1949.
Photographs. "Textes par Paul Eluard."

166. HASTINGS, BAIRD. Christian BERARD. 60 p. illus. Boston, Institute of Contemporary Art, 1950.

167. PARIS. MUSEE NATIONAL D'ART MODERNE. Christian BÉRARD. 34 p. illus. Paris, Éditions des Musées Nationaux, 1950.
Exhibit held Feb. 23-Apr. 23.

168. BÉRARD, HONORÉ MAURIUS. L'Art Non-Figuratif. 118 p. illus. Paris, 1950.

169. BUENOS AIRES. INSTITUTO DE ARTE MODERNO. H. M. BÉRARD. 23 p. illus. 1950.
Essays by Jean Cassou and Raymond Parker.

170. BERNHEIM-JEUNE & CIE (Paris). Exposition Rétrospective: BONNARD. 24 p. illus. Paris, 1950.
Exhibit held May-July. Preface by Ch. Terrasse.

171. ZURICH. KUNSTHAUS. Pierre BONNARD: Verzeichnis mit Einführung. . . . 38 p. illus. 1949.
Texts by W. Wartmann and J. Leymasse.

172. LÉJARD, ANDRÉ. BRAQUE. 15 p. illus. Paris, Fernand Hazan, 1949 (Bibliothèque Aldine des Arts).

173. NEW YORK. MUSEUM OF MODERN ART. Georges BRAQUE, by Henry R. Hope. 170 p. illus. New York, Museum of Modern Art, 1949.
"In collaboration with the Cleveland Museum." Note by J. Cassou. Bibliography by H. B. Muller.

174. CREMONA, ITALO. Felice CASORATI. 11 p. illus. Torino, Accame, 1949.

175. GUERRY, LILIANE. CEZANNE et L'Expression de L'Espace. 211 p. illus. Paris, Flammarion, 1950.

176. FALDI, ITALO. Il Primo de CHIRICO. 94 p. illus. Venice, Alfieri, 1949.

177. HANNOVER. LANDESMUSEUM. Lovis CORINTH. 22 p. illus. 1950.
"Gedächtnisausstellung." Preface by Stuttmann.

178. DALÍ, ANA MARIA. Salvador DALÍ visto por su Hermana. 142 p. illus. Barcelona, Juventad, 1949.

178a. GAYA NUÑO, JUAN ANTONIO. Salvador DALÍ. 49 p. illus. Barcelona, Ediciones Omega, 1950.

179. BOREL, PIERRE. Les Sculptures Inédites de DEGAS. 12 p. plus plates. Geneva, Cailler, 1949.

180. LEMOISNE, P. A. DEGAS et Son Oeuvre. 4 vols. illus. Paris, Paul Brame & C. M. Hauke, 1948-1949.

181. LANGUI, EMILE. Paul DELVAUX. 20 p. illus. Venezia, Alfieri, 1949.

182. ROTTERDAM. MUSEUM BOYMANS. Tentoonstelling Kees van DONGEN. 20 p. illus. 1949.
   Texts by A. Maurois and J. C. Ebbbinge Wubben.

183. ROGER-MARX, CLAUDE. Raoul DUFY, 15 p. illus. London-Paris, Zwemmer-Hazan, 1950.

184. BOSQUET, JOE & TAPIÉ, MICHEL. Max ERNST. 62 p. illus. Paris, René Drouin, 1950.
   11 drawings. List of works dated 1923-1950. Fifty copies issued with two signed lithographs.

185. BOSTON. INSTITUTE OF CONTEMPORARY ART. Jacques Villon, Lyonel FEININGER. 46 p. illus. New York, Chanticleer, 1950.

186. GAUGUIN, PAUL. Letters to His Wife and Friends. 255 p. illus. Cleveland, World Publishing Co., 1949.
   Edited by Maurice Malingue. Translation of edition issued by Grasset (Paris, 1946).

187. BASEL. KUNSTMUSEUM. Ausstellung Paul GAUGUIN. zum 100. Geburtsjahr. 64 p. illus. 1950.
   Catalog by George Schmidt.

188. PARIS. MUSÉE DE L'ORANGERIE. GAUGUIN, Exposition du Centenaire. 103 p. Paris, Éditions des Musées Nationaux, 1949.

189. WESTERDAHL, EDUARDO. Mathias GOERITZ. 58 p. illus. Barcelona, Cobalto, 1949.

190. GOGH, VINCENT VAN. Lettres de Van Gogh à Van Rappard. 251 p. illus. Paris, Grasset, 1950.

191. JAMES, PHILIP. Van GOGH. 56 p. illus. Forest Hills, L. I., Transatlantic Arts, 1949.
   Also issued by Faber and Faber (London).

192. NEW YORK. METROPOLITAN MUSEUM OF ART. Van GOGH. Paintings and Drawings. 96 p. 1949.
   Introduction by D. C. Rich. Loan exhibition.

193. SCHAPIRO, MEYER. Vincent van GOGH. 130 p. illus. New York, Harry N. Abrams, 1950.
   A major American monograph in a series of superior color reproductions.

194. WEISBACH, WERNER. Vincent van GOGH. Kunst und Schichsal. 28 p. illus. Basel, Amerbach, 1949.

194a. GROMAIRE, FRANÇOIS. Marcel GROMAIRE. 12 p. illus. Paris, Braun, 1949. (16 drawings).

195. HODIN, J. P. Isaac GRUNEWALD. 354 p. illus. Stockholm, Ljus, 1949.

196. ROUSSEAU, MADELEINE. Hans HARTUNG. 61 p. illus. Stuttgart, Domnick, 1949.
   Texts by M. Rousseau, J. J. Sweeney, O. Domnick.

197. FREIBURG. KUNSTVEREIN. Bilder, Drucke, 1911-1949: Erick HECKEL. 26 p. illus. 1950.
   Text by Walter Passarge.

198. HERBIN, AUGUSTE. L'Art Non-Figuratif, Non-Objectif. 131 p. illus. Paris, Lydia Conti, 1949.

199. NEW YORK. WHITNEY MUSEUM OF AMERICAN ART. Edward HOPPER retrospective. 60 p. illus. 1950.
   Text by Lloyd Goodrich.

200. IRONSIDE, ROBIN. David JONES. 17 p. illus. Harmondsworth, England, Penguin Books, 1949.

201. BILL, MAX. Wassily KANDINSKY. 10 p. 10 col. plates. Basel, Holbein, 1949.

202. DROUIN, RENÉ, GALERIE (Paris). KANDINSKY, Époque Parisienne, 1933-44. 12 p. illus. 1949.

203. ESTIENNE, CHARLES. KANDINSKY. 15 p. illus. Paris, de Beaune, 1950. "Collection Signe."

204. Omaggio a W. KANDINSKY. 49 p. illus. Roma, Age d'Or, 1950.
   "Forma 2, n. 1, maggio 1950." Bibliography.

205. ARMITAGE, MERLE, Ed. Five Essays on Paul KLEE. 121 p. illus. New York, Duell, Sloan and Pearce, 1950.
   16 unpublished drawings; articles by C. Greenberg, H. Devree, N. W. Ross, J. J. Sweeney.

206. BERNE. KLEE GESELLSCHAFT. Paul KLEE, 1. Teil: Dokumente und Bilder aus den Jahren 1896-1930. 13 p. plus 13 plates. Bern, Benteli, 1949.

207. BUCHHEIM-MILITON, GALERIE. Paul KLEE: Gëmalde, Aquarelle, Zeichnungen, Graphik. 16 p. illus. Frankfurt-Main, 1950.

208. COOPER, DOUGLAS. Paul KLEE. 16 p. illus. Harmondsworth, England, Penguin Books, 1949.

209. HAFTMANN, WERNER. Paul KLEE. 175 p. illus. München, Prestel, 1950.

210. NEW YORK. MUSEUM OF MODERN ART. Paintings, Drawings and Prints by Paul KLEE from the Klee Foundation. 60 p. illus. 1949.
   Introduction by J. T. Soby. Catalog of 202 works.

211. KOLBE, GEORG. Auf Wegen der Kunst: Schriften, Skizzen, Plastiken. 37 p. illus. Berlin-Zehlendorf, Konrad Lemmer, 1949.

212. MUNICH. HAUS DER DEUTSCHEN KUNST. Oskar KOKOSCHKA: aus seinem Schaffen, 1907-1950. 58 p. illus. München, Prestel, 1950.

213. NEW YORK. MUSEUM OF MODERN ART. Oskar KOKOSCHKA. 87 p. New York, Chanticleer, 1949.
   Introduction by James S. Plaut. Issued on the occasion of an exhibition held at the Boston Institute of Contemporary Art and in New York.

214. THURSTON, DORIS. Notes on Oskar KOKOSCHKA. 27 p. Chappaqua, N. Y. [The Author], 1950.

215. BUENOS AIRES. INSTITUTO DE ARTE MODERNO. LABISSE. 24 p. illus. 1950.
   Texts by Desnos, Dotremont, Deharme, Eluard, Prévert. Lettered on title: "No. 6, Labisse."

216. LA FRESNAYE, ROGER DE. Oeuvre complète de Roger de La Fresnaye. Vol. 1. 45 p. plates. Paris, Rivarol, 1950 (c 1949).
   Essays by R. Cogniat and W. George. Bibliography.

217. PARIS. MUSÉE NATIONAL D'ART MODERNE. Roger de LA FRESNAYE. 47 p. illus. Paris, Éditions des Musées Nationaux, 1950.

218. COOPER, DOUGLAS. Fernand LÉGER at le Nouvel Espace. 194 p. illus. Geneva, Éditions de Trois Collines, 1949.
    Translated by F. Lachenal.

219. PARIS. MUSEE NATIONAL D'ART MODERNE. Fernand LÉGER. Exposition Retrospective, 1905-1949. 39 p. illus. Paris, 1949.
    Texts by J. Cassou, G. Apollinaire, B. Cendrars.

220. MILLNER, SIMON L. Isaac LICHTENSTEIN. [32] p. illus. New York, Machmadin Art Editions, 1949.

221. CAMO, PIERRE. MAILLOL, Mon Ami. 87 p. illus. Lausanne, Henri Kaiser, 1950.
    Illustrated by 55 unpublished drawings, 8 in color.

222. MARC, FRANZ. 6 Aquarelle, 1 leaf plus 6 col. plates. Munich, Munchner Verlag, 1949.

223. BUNEMANN, HERMANN. Franz MARC: Zeichnungen-Aquarelle. 44 p. illus. 13 col. plates. Munich, Münchner Verlag, 1949.

224. EHRHART, GEORG. Franz MARC, oder die Abstrakte Kunst. 24 p. illus. Stuttgart, Reclam-Verlag, 1949.

225. LANKHEIT, KLAUS. Franz MARC. 78 p. illus. Berlin, Konrad Lemmer, 1950.

226. SCHONE, WOLFGANG. Gerhard MARCKS. 11 p. illus. Krefeld, Scherpe, 1949.

227. MULHOUSE. MUSÉE DES BEAUX ARTS. Albert MARQUET, Jean PUY. 23 p. plates in folio 1950.
    De luxe catalog. Texts by Besson, Sembat, Gay, etc.

228. LUCERNE. MUSEE DES BEAUX ARTS. Henri MATISSE. 51 p. illus. 1949.
    Texts by J. Cassou, H. Landolt. Cover by Matisse.

229. MALINGUE, MAURICE. MATISSE Dessins. Préface de Maurice Malingue. 16 p. 96 illus. Paris, Deux Mondes, 1949.

230. PARIS. MUSÉE NATIONAL D'ART MODERNE. Henri MATISSE, Oeuvres récentes, 1947-48. 37 p. illus. 1949.

231. CIRICI-PELLICER, ALEXANDER, MIRÓ y la Imaginación. 41 p. illus. Barcelona, Omega, 1949.

232. CIRLOT, JUAN EDUARDO. Joan MIRÓ. 52 p. illus. Barcelona, Cobalto, 1949.

233. COCTEAU, JEAN. MODIGLIANI. 13 p. plus 24 col. plates. Paris, Fernand Hazan, 1950.

234. SCHEIWILLER, GIOVANNI. Amedeo MODIGLIANI. 5 ed. illus. Milano, Hoepli, 1950.

235. MOHOLY-NAGY, LASZLO. The New Vision, and Abstract Of An Artist. 92 p. illus. New York, Wittenborn, Schultz, 1949.
    Documents of Modern Art, 3.

236. FOGG ART MUSEUM. Works of Art by MOHOLY-NAGY. 27 leaves. illus. Cambridge, Mass., 1950.
    Memorial show held Feb. 6-27.

237. MOHOLY-NAGY, SIBYL. MOHOLY-NAGY: Experiment in Totality. 253 p. illus. N.Y., Harper, 1950.
    Introduction by Walter Gropius. Biography of an international figure in the arts whose influence in America, until his recent death, was aptly expressed in the "Chicago Bauhaus," the School of Design, and in a series of imaginative publications.

238. ARCANGELI, FRANCESCO. 12 Paintings by Giorgio MORANDI. col. plates Milan, Il Milione, 1950.

239. MORISOT, BERTHE. Correspondance de Berthe Morisot avec Sa Famille et Ses Amis: Manet, Puvis de Chavannes, Degas, Monet, Renoir et Mallarmé. 185 p. illus. Paris, Quatre-Chemins, 1950.
    "Documents réunis . . . par Denis Rouart."

240. MUCHE, GEORG. George Muche: Bilder, Fresken, Zeichnungen. 48 p. illus. Tübingen, Wasmuth, 1950.

241. TROEGER, EBERHARD. Otto MUELLER. 28 p. illus., col. plates Freiburg im Breisgau, Crone, 1949.

242. MUNCH, EDVARD. Edvard Munchs Brev; Familien. Et Utvalg ved Inger Munch. 307 p. Oslo, Johan Grundt Tanum, 1949.
    Munch-museets skrifter, 1.

243. GREAT BRITAIN. ARTS COUNCIL. Edvard MUNCH, 1863-1944: Etchings, woodcuts and Lithographs. 16 p. illus. 1950.

244. NEW YORK. MUSEUM OF MODERN ART. Edvard MUNCH, by Frederick Deknatel. 120 p. illus. New York, Museum of Modern Art in collaboration with the Institute of Contemporary Art, Boston, 1950.
    Bibliography by H. B. Muller.

245. NASH, PAUL. Outline: an Autobiography and Other Writings. 271 p. illus. London, Faber and Faber, 1949.

246. LEMMER, KONRAD. Max PECHSTEIN und der Beginn des Expressionismus. 50 p. illus. Berlin, Konrad Lemmer, 1949.

247. SAMOS GALERIA (Buenos Aires). Emilio PETTORUTI. 47 p. illus. 1949.
    Text by C. Iturburu for exhibit held June 6-21.

248. SANTIAGO DE CHILE. MUSEO NACIONAL DE BELLAS ARTES. Exposicion Retrospectiva . . . Emilio PETTORUTI. 15 p. illus. (August) 1950.

249. DESCARGUES, PIERRE. PIAUBERT. 20 p. illus. Paris, PLF, 1950.
    Also 20 copies with original lithograph.

250. CAHIERS D'ART (Paris). PICASSO: 32 Peintures Recentes . . . 40 p. illus. Paris, 1949.
    From exhibit at the Maison de la Pensée Française.

251. CIRICI-PELLICER, ALEXANDER. PICASSO avant Picasso. 209. p. 282 illus. Gèneve, Pierre Cailler, 1950.
    Translation of Picasso Antes de Picasso (Barcelona, Iberia-Joaquin, 1949). Bibliography.

252. LASSAIGNE, JACQUES. PICASSO. 13 p. 97 plates. Paris, Aimery Somogny, 1949.

253. MARCHIORI, GUISEPPE. L'Ultimo PICASSO. 90 p. illus. Venezia, Alfieri, 1949.

254. TAURINES-MÉRY, BLANCHE-JEAN. Des Influences Subies par PICASSO. 13 p. illus. Paris, Triquet-Robert, 1950.

255. ZERVOS, CHRISTIAN. Pablo PICASSO: Oeuvres. vol. 3. 1917-1919. 16 p. 465 illus. Paris, Cahiers d'Art, 1949.

256. HAUSEN, EDMUND. Der Maler Hans PURRMANN, 99 p. illus. Berlin, Konrad Lemmer, 1950.

257. BAUDOT, JEANNE. RENOIR, Ses Amis, Ses Modèles. 137 p. illus. Paris, Éditions Littéraires de France, 1949.

258. GUAL, ENRIQUE. 50 Years of the Works of Diego RIVERA: Oils, Water Colors, 1900-1950.14 col. plates in folio Mexico, Ediciones de Arte, 1950.

259. SAO PAULO. MUSEU DE ARTE. Massa Guassú . . . por Roberto SAMBONET. Introducao de P. M. Bardi. 12 p. illus. 1949.

260. HILDEBRANDT, HANS. Oskar SCHLEMMER. 31 plates Stuttgart, Verlag KG, 1949.
A prospectus with illustrated cover.

261. NEW YORK. MUSEUM OF MODERN ART. SOUTINE by Monroe Wheeler. 116 p. illus. 1950.
Bibliography by H. B. Muller.

262. DUTHUIT, GEORGES. Nicolas de STAËL. 24 p. illus. Paris, Transition Press, 1950.

263. MELVILLE, ROBERT. Graham SUTHERLAND. 116 p. illus. London, Ambassador, 1950.
Bibliography by Henry Aronson.

264. MEXICO. MUSEO NACIONAL DE ARTES PLÁSTICAS. TAMAYO: 20 Anos de su Labor Pictorica. 22 p. illus. 1949.

265. THARRATS, JOAN-JOSEPS. Antoni TÀPIES. 24 p. illus. Barcelona, Dau al Set, 1950.

266. BUENOS AIRES. INSTITUTO DE ARTE MODERNO. Pavel TCHELITCHEW, Pinturas y Dibujos. 1925-1948. 25 p. illus. 1949.
Text by Lincoln Kirstein for August exhibit.

267. TENNANT, MADGE. Autobiography of an Unarrived Artist. 180 p. illus. New York, "Distributed by Brentano's," 1949 (c 1939).

268. MACK, GERSTLE. TOULOUSE-LAUTREC. 379 p. illus. New York, Alfred Knopf, 1949 (c 1938).

269. VERSIEN, GEORGES. Georges Versien: Zwölf Farbige Bildtafeln. 4 p. 12 col. plates. Reutlingen, Schuler [1949?].

270. LASSAIGNE, JACQUES. Jacques VILLON. 16 p. illus. Paris, de Beaune, 1950. "Collection Signe."

271. BOSTON. INSTITUTE OF CONTEMPORARY ART. Jacques VILLON, Lyonel Feininger. 46 p. illus. New York, Chanticleer, 1950.

272. AMSTERDAM. STEDELIJK MUSEUM. Jean van der VLUGT. 31 p. illus. 1949.
French and Dutch text by R. P. Maydieu.

273. ARP. JEAN. VORDEMBERGE-GILDEWART, Époque Néerlandaise. 34 p. illus. Amsterdam, Duwaer, 1949.
Text in German, French, English.

274. Notre Ami Charles WALCH. 61 p. illus. Saint-Jeoire en Faucigny (Haute-Savoie), L'Art en Village, 1949.
Testimonials by Besson, Dorval, Rouault, etc.

275. PARIS. MUSÉE NATIONAL D'ART MODERNE. Ch. WALCH. 1928-1948. 8 p. col. front. 1949.
Exhibit held Nov. 30, 1949-Jan. 10, 1950.

276. VORDEMBERGE-GILDEWART, F. & DE VRIES, H. WERKMAN. 8 p. 24 illus. Arnheim, Holland; S. Gouda Quint, D. Brouwer & Son, 1949.
Netherlands Informative Art Editions.

AMERICAN ART
Surveys

277. COMMAGER, HENRY STEELE. The American Mind, an Interpretation of American Thought and Character Since the 1880's. 476 p. New Haven, Yale University Press, 1950.
Ch. XIX: Architecture and Society. Bibliographies.

278. COOPER UNION FOR THE ADVANCEMENT OF SCIENCE AND ART. ART SCHOOL. Art Professions in the United States. Ed. & comp. by Elizabeth McCausland, Royal Bailey Farnum and Dana P. Vaughan. 111 p. New York, Cooper Union, 1950.

279. LARKIN, OLIVER W. Art and Life in America. 547 p. illus. New York, Rinehart, 1949.
Bibliographies. Pulitzer prize work.

279a. LIPMAN, JEAN & WINCHESTER, ALICE. Primitive Painting in America. 1750-1950. 182 p. illus. New York, Dodd, Mead, 1950.

280. PEARSON, RALPH. The Modern Renaissance in the U.S.A. n. p. S. Nyack, N. Y., Design Workshop, 1950. (Critical Appreciation Course, no. 2.)
A series of pamphlets on contemporary artists.

281. SUTTON, DENYS. American Painting. 31 p. illus. New York, Transatlantic Arts, 1949.
Also published by Avalon Press (London).

282. A Symposium: The State of American Art. illus. New York, Magazine of Art, 1949.
A series of articles published in the "Magazine of Art," v. 42, p. 82-102 March 1949.

283. WIGHT, FREDERICK S. Milestones of American Painting in our Century. 134 p. illus. Boston, Institute of Contemporary Art; New York, Chanticleer, 1949.
An exhibition of 50 outstanding painters. Introduction by L. Goodrich. Bibliography.

Monographs & Catalogs

284. NEW YORK. MUSEUM OF MODERN ART. Charles DEMUTH by Andrew Carnduff Ritchie. 96 p. illus. New York, 1950.
Bibliography by Anne Bollmann.

285. LOMBARDO, JOSEF VINCENT. Chaim GROSS, Sculptor. 247 p. illus. New York, Dalton House, 1949.

286. GOODRICH, LLOYD. Edward HOPPER, 15 p. illus. Harmondsworth, Middlesex, England, 1949.

287. HURD, PETER. Portfolio of Landscapes and Portraits. 8 col. plates (in folio) Albuquerque, N. M., University of New Mexico, 1950.

288. MARIN, JOHN. Selected Writings of John MARIN. 241 p. illus. N. Y., Pellegrini & Cudahy, 1949.
Edited, with an introduction, by Dorothy Norman.

289. MARIN, JOHN. John MARIN—Drawings and Water Colors. [9] p. plus 34 plates (some col.), New York, Twin Editions, 1950.
Introduction by artist reproduced in mss. Printed in 300 copies; 125 copies contain etching.

290. MINNEAPOLIS. WALKER ART CENTER. A. H. MAURER, 1868-1932, by Elizabeth McCausland. 43 p. illus. Minneapolis, 1949.
Also shown at the Whitney Museum.

291. NEW YORK. MUSEUM OF MODERN ART. Franklin C. WATKINS, by Andrew C. Ritchie. 48 p. illus. 1950.
Bibliography by Anne Bollmann.

292. NEW YORK. WHITNEY MUSEUM OF AMERI-
CAN ART. Max WEBER, Retrospective Exhibition.
58 p. illus. 1949.
    Text by Lloyd Goodrich; research by Rosalind Ir-
    vine. Also shown at Walker Art Center.

293. PORTER, BERNARD H. Sciart: A School of
Painting. 45 p. illus. Sausalito, Cal., 1949.
    Another Sciart manifesto "The Union of Science &
    Art" (4 p.) was issued in 1949(?).

Exhibitions

294. ALBERTINA, VIENNA. Amerikanische Meister
des Aquarells; Ausstellung, Herbst. 1949. 20 p. Wien,
Anton Schroll, 1949.
    Texts by O. Benesch, L. Goodrich. Exhibition shown
    1950 at the Syracuse Museum, N. Y.

295. AMSTERDAM. STEDELIJK MUSEUM. Amerika
Schildert. 40 p. illus. 1950.
    Foreword by Bartlett H. Hayes and others.

296. CALIFORNIA. STATE FAIR. 1949 Arts Exhibition, California State Fair. 52 p. illus. 1949.
    Foreword by the director, T. P. Tupman.

297. CHICAGO. BORDELON GALLERY. Momentum
Nineteen-Fifty: A Portfolio of Reproductions of Creative Work Originating in the Chicago Area. 31 sheets
(issued loose in oblong folio) Chicago, 1950.
    Brochure inserted: "A forum: 9 viewpoints."

298. CINCINNATI. ART MUSEUM. Artists of Cincinnati and Vicinity, 1950. [20] p. illus. 1950.

299. COLORADO SPRINGS. FINE ARTS CENTER.
New Accessions USA. 24 p. incl. illus. Colorado, 1950.
    "The third biennial exhibition of contemporary
    American paintings acquired by 31 major art mu-
    seums." Introduction by Aline B. Louchheim.

300. LONDON. INSTITUTE OF CONTEMPORARY
ARTS. Symbolic Realism in American Painting, 1940-
50. 12 p. illus. 1950.
    Preface by Lincoln Kirstein. Biographical notes.

301. MINNEAPOLIS. WALKER ART CENTER. Second Biennial Exhibition of Paintings and Prints. [24]
p. illus. 1949.
    "Selected from works of artists in Iowa, Minne-
    sota, Nebraska, North Dakota, South Dakota, Wis-
    consin." Foreword by D. S. Defenbacher.

302. MINNEAPOLIS. WALKER ART CENTER. Contemporary American Painting. [16] p. illus. 1950.
    5th biennial. Foreword by H. H. Arnason.

303. NEW YORK. DOWNTOWN GALLERY. The Artist
Speaks in Paint, Stone And Words. [5] p. (April) 1949.

304. NEW YORK. KNOEDLER GALLERY. To Honor
Henry McBride: an Exhibition of Paintings, Drawings
and Watercolors. 27 p. plus plates. 1949.
    Testimonial exhibit; essay by Lincoln Kirstein.

305. NEW YORK. KOOTZ GALLERY. The Intrasubjectivists. 4 p. illus. 1949.
    Catalog of Sept. 14-Oct. 3 exhibition, issued as
    folded sheet with colored sketches by Baziotes,
    Gottlieb and Hofmann. Statements by Harold Rosen-
    berg and Samuel M. Kootz.

306. NEW YORK. METROPOLITAN MUSEUM OF
ART. 100 American Painters of the 20th Century:
Works selected from the collections of the Metropol-
'tan Museum of Art. 23 p. plus 111 plates 1950.

Introduction by Robert Beverly Hale.

307. RICHMOND. VIRGINIA MUSEUM OF FINE ARTS.
American Painting 1950. Exhibition Directed by James
Johnson Sweeney. 21 p. illus. 1950.
    Foreword by J. J. Sweeney. Exhibited Apr. 22-
    June 4. An excellent review of contemporary cur-
    rents severely criticized by the local press.

308. SAN FRANCISCO. CALIFORNIA PALACE OF
THE LEGION OF HONOR; 3rd Annual Exhibition of
Painting. illus. 47 p. illus. [1948-1949].
    Foreword by Jermayne MacAgy.

309. SAN FRANCISCO. CALIFORNIA PALACE OF
THE LEGION OF HONOR. 4th Annual Exhibition of
Contemporary American Painting. 70 p. illus. 1950.
    Exhibited Nov. 25, 1950-Jan. 1, 1951. Texts by
    T. C. Howe, Jr., J. MacAgy, F. S. Bartlett.

310. URBANA, ILL. UNIVERSITY OF ILLINOIS.
Contemporary American Painting. 217 p. illus. 1950.
    Shown at the College of Fine and Applied Arts,
    Feb. 25-Apr. 2. Introduction by R. Newcomb.
    Essay by Allen S. Weller: "Subject Matter in Con-
    temporary Painting." Biographical notes, p. 154-
    217, include statements by the artists.

311. WASHINGTON, D. C. CORCORAN GALLERY OF
ART. De Gustibus: an Exhibition of American Paintings Illustrating a Century of Taste and Criticism.
59 p. illus. 1949.

THE AMERICAN SCENE IN PHOTOGRAPHY

312. STRAND, PAUL & NEWHALL, NANCY. Time in
New England. Photographs by Paul Strand; text se-
lected and edited by Nancy Newhall. 248 p. illus. New
York, Oxford, 1950.

313. GILPIN, LAURA. The Rio Grande, River of
Destiny: an Interpretation of the River, the Land, and
the People. 243 p. illus. New York, Duell, Sloan and
Pearce, 1949.

314. ADAMS, ANSEL. My Camera in the National
Parks. 30 Photographs with Interpretative Text . . .
97 p. including plates Boston, Houghton Mifflin; Yosemite National Park, Virginia Adams, 1950.
    With "A Personal Statement." The photographer
    had issued in 1949 a similar publication titled:
    "My Camera in Yosemite Valley: 24 Photographs
    and an Essay on Mountain Photography."

315. WESTON, BRETT. White Sands. Carmel, Cal.,
Brett Weston, 1949.
    Ten original photos of the New Mexico desert,
    with introduction by Nancy Newhall.

316. WESTON, EDWARD. My Camera on Point Lobos.
30 Photographs and Excerpts from E. W'S Daybook.
[82] p. illus. Boston, Houghton Mifflin; Yosemite
National Park, Virginia Adams, 1950.

ARCHITECTURE & DESIGN
History

317. WHITTICK. ARNOLD. European Architecture in
the Twentieth Century, Vol. 1. 249 p. illus. London,
Crosby Lockwood, 1950.
    Vol. 1 will cover "until 1924," vol. 2 the years
    1924-33, vol. 3 from 1933-50. Bibliography.

318. ZEVI, BRUNO. Saper Vedere l'Architettura:
Saggio sull'Interpretazione Spaziale dell'Architettura.
193 p. illus. Torino, G. Einaudi, 1949.

BIBLIOGRAPHY

318a. ZEVI, BRUNO. Storia dell'Architettura moderna. 786 p. illus. Torino, G. Einaudi, 1950.

319. ZEVI, BRUNO. Towards an Organic Architecture. 180 p. illus. London, Faber and Faber, 1950.

320. GIEDION, SIEGFRIED. A Decade Of New Architecture, Dix Ans d'Architecture Contemporaine. Zurich, Girsberger, 1950 (1951?).

Reprints

321. GIEDION, SIEGFRIED. Space, Time and Architecture. 645 p. 361 illus. Cambridge, Harvard University Press, 1949 (c 1941).

322. SARTORIS, ALBERTO. Introduzione alla Architettura Moderna. 3rd rev. and enl. ed. 575 p. 190 illus. Milano, Ulrico Hoepli, 1949 (c 1944).

323. SULLIVAN, LOUIS H. The Autobiography of an Idea. (3. ed.) 330 p. New York, Peter Smith, 1949.

National Studies

324. HIORT, ESBJORN. Nyere Dansk Bygningskunst; Contemporary Danish Architecture. 108 p. illus. Kobenhavn, Jul. Gjellerups Forlag, 1949.

325. SMITH, G. E. KIDDER. Switzerland Builds: Its Native and Modern Architecture. 234 p. illus. New York & Stockholm, Albert Bonnier, 1950.

Essays

326. CREIGHTON, THOMAS H., Ed. Building for Modern Man: a Symposium. 219 p. Princeton, N. J., Princeton University Press, 1949.
   Neutra, Kepes, Giedion, Gropius, Wright, others.

327. HUDNUT, JOSEPH. Architecture and the Spirit of Man. 301 p. Cambridge, Harvard University, 1949.

328. ILLINOIS INSTITUTE OF TECHNOLOGY (CHICAGO). Three addresses at the Blackstone Hotel . . . by Ludvig Mies van der Rohe, Serge Chermayeff, Walter Gropius. 13 p. Chicago, 1950. (See p. 175.)
   The Institute of Design is added to Illinois Tech.

Monographs & Catalogs

Aalto

329. PARIS. ÉCOLE NATIONALE DES BEAUX ARTS. Exposition des Oeuvres d'Aino et Alvar Aalto. 35 p. illus. 1950.
   Text by S. Giedion for April exhibition.

Ain

330. NEW YORK. MUSEUM OF MODERN ART. The Museum of Modern Art-Woman's Home Companion Exhibition House: Gregory Ain, architect; Joseph Johnson & Alfred Day, Collaborating. 19 p. illus. 1950.

Gaudi

331. CIRLOT, JUAN EDUARDO. El Arte de Gaudi. 110 p. illus. Barcelona, Ediciones Omega, 1950.

Gropius

332. ARCHITECTURE D'AUJOURD'HUI. Walter Gropius et Son École. 116 p. illus. Paris, 1950.
   Special number 28, Feb. 1950, with text in English. Also issued as The Spread of an Idea.

Le Corbusier

333. LE CORBUSIER [CHARLES-ÉDOUARD JEANNERET - GRIS], Oeuvre Complète. 1938-46. Publié par Willy Boesiger. 2 ed. 207 p. illus. Zurich, Girsberger, 1950.

334. LE CORBUSIER [CHARLES-ÉDOUARD JEANNERET-GRIS]. L'Unité d'Habitation de Marseille. 58 p. illus. Souillac (Lot), Le Point, 1950.
   No. 38 of Le Point, Nov. 1950. Bibliography.

Maillart

335. BILL, MAX. Robert Maillart. 180 p. illus. Zurich, Girsberger, 1949.

Niemeyer

336. PAPADAKI, STAMO. The Work of Oscar Niemeyer. 220 p. illus. New York, Reinhold Publishing Corp., 1950.

Neutra

337. SAO PAULO. MUSEU DE ARTE. Neutra: residencias. 1950.

Sullivan

338. WRIGHT, FRANK LLOYD. Genius and the Mobocracy. 112 p. illus. New York, Duell, Sloan and Pearce, 1949.
   On Louis H. Sullivan and architecture.

Exhibitions

339. NEW YORK. KOOTZ GALLERY. The Muralist and the Modern Architect. [11] p. illus. 1950.
   Exhibition of Oct. 3-23, including W. Baziotes & P. Johnson, A. Gottlieb & M. Breuer, D. Hare & F. Kiesler, H. Hofmann & J. Sert-P. Wiener, R. Motherwell & Architects Collaborative.

340. PARIS. MUSÉE NATIONAL D'ART MODERNE. L'Architecture Contemporaine Danoise. Exposition au Musée Municipal d'Art Moderne. 55 p. illus. Paris, 1949.

341. SAN FRANCISCO. MUSEUM OF ART. Domestic Architecture of the San Francisco Bay Region. 28 p. illus. 1949.
   Texts by Lewis Mumford, R. B. Freeman, W. W. Wurster and others.

Construction & Design

342. ECKBO, HARRETT. Landscape For Living. 262 p. illus. New York, Architectural Book; Duell, Sloan and Pearce, 1950.

343. KEIM, JEAN A. La Tour Eiffel. 51 p. illus. Paris, Éditions "Tel," 1950.
   An unusual pictorial study.

344. LE CORBUSIER [CHARLES-ÉDOUARD JEANNERET-GRIS]. Le Modulor: Essai Sur Une Mesure Harmonique à l'Echelle Humaine. . . . 239 p. illus. Boulogne, L'Architecture d'Aujord'hui, 1950.

345. MICHAELS, LEONARD. Contemporary Structure in Architecture. 229 p. illus. New York, Reinhold, 1950.

346. MOCK, ELIZABETH B. The Architecture of Bridges. 128 p. 170 illus. New York, Museum of Modern Art, 1949.

Design in Modern Life

347. ART TODAY. An Introduction to the Fine and Functional Arts. Revised edition. By Ray Faulkner, Edwin Ziegfield, Gerald Hill. 519 p. illus. New York, Henry Holt, 1949.

348. KAUFMANN, EDGAR, JR. What is Modern Design? 32 p. illus. New York, Museum of Modern Art, 1950. Bibliography.

349. KNOLL ASSOCIATES, INC. Knoll Index of Designs. 80 p. illus. New York, 1950.
Edited by Hockaday associates; designed by Herbert Matter.

350. PEVSNER, NIKOLAUS. Pioneers of Modern Design from William Morris to Walter Gropius. 151 p. illus. New York, Museum of Modern Art, 1949.
Substantial revision, supervised by Dr. Herwin Schaefer, of text issued 1936 as Pioneers of the Modern Movement (Faber and Faber).

351. SOCIETY OF INDUSTRIAL DESIGNERS (New York). U. S. Industrial Design, 1949-50. 176 p. illus. New York, Studio Publications, 1949.

352. TEAGUE, WALTER DORWIN. Design This Day. Rev. ed. 302 p. illus. New York, Harcourt, Brace, 1949 (c 1940).

Exhibitions

353. DETROIT. INSTITUTE OF ARTS. An Exhibition For Modern Living. 101 p. illus. 1949.
Edited by A. H. Girard; texts by John Kouwenhoven, Edgar Kaufmann, Jr., E. P. Richardson.

354. NEW YORK. MUSEUM OF MODERN ART. Modern Art in Your Life, by Robert Goldwater in collaboration with René d'Harnoncourt. 47 p. illus. 1949.
Vol. XVII, No. 1, 1949 of the Museum Bulletin.

355. NEW YORK. MUSEUM OF MODERN ART. Prize Designs for Modern Furniture from the International Competition for Low-Cost Furniture Design. 77 p. illus. 1950.
Text by Edgar Kaufmann, Jr.

356. ZURICH. KUNSTGEWERBEMUSEUM. Die Gute Form. 24 p. illus. 1950.
"Wanderausstellung des Schweizerischen Werkbundes." Texts by Johannes Itten and Max Bill.

357. ZURICH. KUNSTGEWERBEMUSEUM. SWB Ausstellung der Ortsgruppe Zürich des Schweizerischen Werkbundes. 50 p. illus. 1950.

Monographs

358. KATZENBACH AND WARREN, INC. Mural Scrolls, no. 1: Calder, Matisse, Matta, Miro. 8 p. 4 col. plates New York, Katzenbach & Warren, 1949.
Introduction by James T. Soby. Folio, with examples of contemporary designs in silk-screen, produced in limited editions for a wallpaper firm.

359. KAUFMANN, EDGAR, Jr. Prestini's Art in Wood. 7 p. 24 plates Lake Forest, Pocahantas; New York, Pantheon (distributor), 1950.
Photographs by Barbara Morgan.

360. RAMIÉ, SUZANNE & RAMIÉ, GEORGES. Ceramics by Picasso. 18 p. 18 col. plates Geneva, Paris, Albert Skira; New York, Transbook, 1950.
Forword translated from French edition (1948).

SCULPTURE

361. FIERENS, PAUL. Trois Sculpteurs Belges: Carles Leplae, Georges Grard, Pierre Caille. 62 p. illus. Bruxelles, La Connaissance, 1949.
"Notes par Albert Dasnoy."

362. MARTINIE, A.-H. Sculpture en France. XXᵉ Siècle. 12 p. 60 illus. Paris, Braun; London, Soho Gallery; New York, E. R. Herrmann [1949?].

363. NEW YORK. MUSEUM OF MODERN ART. Modern Sculpture. 4 leaves plus 40 plates (boxed) New York, 1949 (Teaching Portfolio no. 1).
Text by Elodie Courter Osborn. Bibliography.

364. SAPORI, FRANCESCO. Scultura Italiana Moderna. 501 p. Roma, Libreria dello Stato, 1949.

365. SEYMOUR, CHARLES. Tradition and Experiment in Modern Sculpture. 86 p. illus. Washington, D. C., American University Press, 1949.
Based on exhibition at the Watkins Gallery.

366. RAMSDEN, E. H. Twentieth Century Sculpture. 42 p. 63 plates London, Pleiades, 1949.

Collective Exhibitions

367. AMSTERDAM. STEDELIJK MUSEUM. 13 Beeldhouwers uit Paris. 48 p. illus. 1949.

368. ANTWERP. PARC MIDDELHEIM. Exposition Internationale en Plein Air de Sculpture, 1900-1950. 38 p. illus. Anvers, Nederlandsche Bockhandel, 1950.

369. THE HAGUE. GEMEENTEMUSEUM. Franse Beeldhouw Kunst: Rodin, Bourdelle, Maillol, Despiau. 32 p. illus. 1950.

370. NEW HAVEN. YALE UNIVERSITY ART GALLERY. Sculpture Since Rodin: Catalogue of Exhibition. 20 p. illus. 1949.
Bulletin of the Associates in Fine Arts, Jan. 1949.

371. VENICE. GIARDINO DEL PALAZZO VENIER DEI LEONE. Mostra di Scultura Contemporanea, Presentata da Peggy Guggenheim. 34 p. illus. 1949.
Preface by G. Marchiori.

372. ZURICH. KUNSTHAUS. Antoine Pevsner, Georges Vantongerloo, Max Bill. 30 p. illus. 1949.
Texts by the artists. Preface by W. Wartmann.

Catalogs & Monographs

373. American Sculptors Series, edited by John Cunningham. illus. Athens, Ga., Univ. of Georgia, 1950.
New issues include: Jose de Creeft. — Cecil Howard. — C. Paul Jennewin. — A. A. Weinman.

374. CINGRIA, CHARLES ALBERT. Otto Charles BÄNNINGER. 23 p. illus. Zürich, Graphis, 1949.
Text in German and French.

375. ROH, FRANZ. Otto BAUM. 36 p. illus. Tübingen, Otto Reichl, 1950.
Text in German, French, English.

376. BARDI, P. M. Ernesto de FIORI. 23 p. illus. Milano, Hoepli, 1950.

377. LOMBARDO, JOSEF VINCENT. Chaim GROSS. 247 p. illus. New York, Dalton House, 1949.

378. DUSSELDORF. KUNSTSAMMLUNGEN DER STADT. Wilhelm LEHMBRUCK. 47 p. illus. 1949.
Preface by W. Passarge.

379. CARLI, ENZO. Marino MARINI. 27 p. illus. Milano, Hoepli, 1950.

380. READ, HERBERT. Henry MOORE, Sculpture and Drawings. 3 rev. & enl. ed. 350 p. illus. New York, Curt Valentin, 1949 (c 1944).
Bibliography by H. B. Muller.

381. BERNE. KUNSTHALLE. Henry MOORE. 12 p. illus. 1950.
Texts by the artist and Herbert Read.

382. KAHNWEILER. DANIEL-HENRY. Les Sculptures de PICASSO. 13 p. plus 216 plates London, Rodney Phillips, 1949.
Photos by Brassai. French edition by Du Chêne.

383. VERDET, ANDRÉ. L'Homme au Mouton de Pablo PICASSO. 24 p. illus. Paris, Falaize, 1950.

384. JANNASCH, ADOLF. Renée SINTENIS. 16 p. illus. Potsdam, Edvard Stichnote, 1949.

385. VILLA, EMILIO. Sculpture e Disegni di TOT. 43 p. illus. Roma, La Palma, 1950.

386. CHEVALIER, DENYS. ZADKINE, Sculptures. 4 p. plus plates Paris, Guy Le Prat, 1949.

387. ROTTERDAM. MUSEUM BOYMANS. ZADKINE. Text by A. H. Hammacher. 14 p. illus. 1949.

388. NEW YORK. ART STUDENTS LEAGUE. William ZORACH. Retrospective Exhibition. 20 p. illus. 1950.

TECHNIQUE

389. PUTNAM, BRENDA. The Sculptor's Way. rev. ed. 380 p. illus. New York, Watson Guptill, 1949.

390. ROOD, JOHN. Sculpture in Wood. 179 p. illus. Minneapolis, University of Minnesota Press, 1950.

391. SLOBODKIN, LOUIS. Sculpture, Principles and Practice. 255 p. illus. Cleveland & New York, World Publishing Co., 1949.

GRAPHIC ARTS

General

392. BERGER, KLAUS. French Master Drawings of the Nineteenth Century. Selected and Edited by Klaus Berger. 90 p. illus. New York, Harper, 1950.
Also published in French and German.

393. Graphisme 50. No. 1, 2. Antwerp, Le Lion Assis, 1950-current.
No. 1: Bois et Linos. — 2: Tekeningen, Dessins.

394. HAYTER, STANLEY WILLIAM. New Ways of Gravure. 275 p. illus. New York, Pantheon, 1949.
The first modern work on technique.

395. REESE, ALBERT. American Prize Prints of the 20th Century. 257 p. illus. New York, American Artists Group, 1949.

396. REYNOLDS. GRAHAM. Nineteenth Century Drawings, 1850-1900. 52 p. plus 72 plates London, Pleiades Books, 1949.

397. TALLER DE GRÁFICA POPULAR (México). Album T G P, México: 50 Graphic Artists. 450 illus. México, La Estampa Mexicana, 1949.

Exhibitions

398. BROOKLYN MUSEUM. American Woodcuts, 1670-1950: a Survey of Woodcuts and Wood-Engravings in the United States by Una E. Johnson. 55 p. illus. Brooklyn, N. Y., 1950.

399. CINCINNATI. ART MUSEUM. First International Biennial of Contemporary Color Lithography. 25 p. illus. col. plates 1950.

400. COPENHAGEN. STATENS MUSEUM FOR KUNST. Moderne Fransk Grafik. 27 p. illus. 1949.
Text by Jean Valery Radot.

401. MADRID. GALÉRIA PALMA. Los Nuevos Prehistóricos: Dibujos de Artistas Nuevos. 15 leaves illus. 1949.
Foreword by Carlos Edmundo de Ory.

402. MINNEAPOLIS. WALKER ART CENTER. A New Direction in Intaglio: the Work of Mauricio Lasansky and his Students. 40 p. illus. 1949.
Exhibited also at Colorado Springs.

403. NEW YORK. LAUREL GALLERY. Atelier 17. 31 p. illus. New York, Wittenborn, Schultz, 1949.
The influence of S. W. Hayter and his school. Color plates.

404. PARIS. PETIT PALAIS DES BEAUX ARTS. Exposition Internationale de la Gravure Contemporaine. 61 p. illus. Paris, L. P. A., 1949.

Monographs & Catalogs

405. Drawings: Dixon, Diebenkorn, Hultberg, Kuhlman, Lobdell, Stillman. 16 mtd. plates Mill Valley, Cal., Eric T. Ledin [1950?].

406. ARP, HANS (JEAN). Elemente: Holzschnitte, Entwurfe aus dem Jahre 1920. 2. Stubendrude. Zurich, Werkstatt Karl Schmid, 1949.
230 copies in folio, signed and numbered.

407. BUCHHEIM-MILITON, COLLECTION. Georges BRAQUE, das Graphische Werk: Sammlung Buchheim-Militon. 16 p. illus. Feldafing, 1950.

408. LAUDE, J. Le [Scaphandrier] des Reves: Douze Collages par Max BUCAILLE. 6 p. 12 plates, loose in folder Paris, G L M, 1950.

409. GOERITZ, MATHIAS. El Circo, Once Dibujos y Una Vineta. Guadalajara, Jal., Camarauz, 1950.
Contains prefaces from other editions.

410. CASSOU, JEAN. Maruja MALLO: Arquitecturas. 5 p. plus plates Madrid, Clan, 1949.

411. MARCKS, GERHARD. Vierundzwanzig Zeichnungen. 11 p. 24 illus. Krefeld, Scherpe, 1949.
Introduction by W. Schoene.

412. WILLOCH, SIGURD. Edvard MUNCH etchings. Oslo, Johan Grundt Tanum, 1950.
Large folio of boxed prints and brochure. "City of Oslo Art Collections. Munch-Museum Series."

413. GREAT BRITAIN. ARTS COUNCIL. Edvard MUNCH. 1863-1944: Etchings, Woodcuts and Lithographs. 16 p. illus. London, 1950.
Texts by P. James, H. Langaard, J. P. Hodin.

414. KIRSTEIN, LINCOLN. Elie NADELMAN Drawings. 53 p. illus. New York, H. Bittner, 1949.

415. PEAKE, MERVYN. Drawings. 11 p. 62 illus. 8 col. plates London, Grey Walls, 1950.

416. BOURET, JEAN. PICASSO: Dessins. 96 p. illus. Paris, Deux Mondes, 1950.

417. MOURLOT, FERNAND. PICASSO Lithographe. 2 vols. illus. Monte-Carlo, André Sauret, 1949-50.
Cover and frontispiece are original lithographs. Introduction for vol. 1 by Jaime Sabartés.

418. ZERVOS, CHRISTIAN. Dessins de Pablo PICASSO, 1892-1948. 33 p. 153 plates Paris, Cahiers d'Art, 1949.

419. MISTRAL, GABRIELA. Poemas de las Madres. Illustrations by André RACZ. Santiago de Chile, Cuadernos del Pacifico, 1950.

420. BESSON, GEORGE. SIGNAC—Dessins. 11 p. illus. Paris, Braun, 1950.

421. GUAL, ENRIQUE F. Dibujos de TAMAYO. 9 p. 43 plates Mexico, D. F., Ediciones Mexicanas, 1950.

422. TANNING, DOROTHEA. Les 7 Périls Spectraux. Paris, Les Pas Perdus, 1950.
Album of color lithographs. 50 signed portfolios, with preface by A. Peyre de Mandiargues.

423. JULIEN, ÉDOUARD. Les Affiches de TOULOUSE-LAUTREC. 101 p. incl. plates Monte-Carlo, André Sauret, 1950.
Excellent color reproductions. Includes "Décomposition de couleurs de la première affiche."

424. AUBERTY, J. & PERUSSAUX. C. Jacques VILLON: Catalogue de son Oeuvre Gravé. 50 p. 544 illus. Paris, Paul Proute, 1950.
Frontispiece is original etching.

425. VUILLARD, E. Cahier de Dessins. 12 p. 50 plates. Paris, Quatre Chemins, 1950.
Sketchbook. Texts by J. Salomon, A. Vaillant.

Book and Advertising Arts

Booklists

426. CRAMER, GÉRALD (Geneva). Oeuvres originales de peintres, 1867-1950: Livres Illustrés, Estampes, Sculptures, Divers, 56 p. illus. 1950.

427. GUTEKUNST & KLIPSTEIN (BERNE). Editions Vollard. 13 p. illus. 1949.
Sale catalog of complete collection.

428. LEHMANN-HAUPT, HELLMUT. One Hundred Books about Bookmaking: a Guide to the Study and Appreciation of Printing. 3 ed. 83 p. New York, Columbia University Press, 1949.

Book Design

429. BEGG, JOHN. Form and Format: Abstract Design and its Relation to Book Format. 30 p. illus. New York, George McKibbin, 1949.

430. DIJON. MUSÉE DE DIJON. Le Livre Illustré Contemporain. 21 p. 1949.
Texts by P. Quarré and J. Guignard.

431. Graphic Forms: the Arts as Related to the Book. 128 p. illus. Cambridge, Mass., Harvard University Press, 1949.
Essays by Kepes, Rand, Armitage & others.

432. MORNAND, PIERRE & THOME, J. R. Vingt Artistes du Livre. 312 p. 324 illus. Paris, Le Courrier Graphique, 1950.
Introduction by R. Cogniat. Bibliographies.

433. ART DIRECTORS CLUB OF CHICAGO. Integration, an Exhibition by Will Burtin. 8 p. illus. 1949.
Excellent installation.

434. ART DIRECTORS CLUB, NEW YORK. 28. Annual of Advertising and Editorial Art. Reproductions from the exhibition held . . . at the Museum of Modern Art, March 15 to Apr. 17, 1949. 312 p. illus. New York, Pitman (for the Association), 1949.
The Museum also published a checklist "Guide."

435. ART DIRECTORS CLUB, NEW YORK. 29. Annual of Advertising and Editorial Art. 388 p. illus. New York, Pitman (for the Club), 1950.

436. Graphic Arts Production Yearbook. 728 p. illus. New York, Colten, 1950.
Lead article is "Eleven painters influencing the graphic arts" by T. B. Hess.

437. International Poster Annual, 1949. 180 p. illus. New York, Pitman, 1949.
Text in English, French and German.

438. Modern Publicity, 1950-51. Editors: F. A. Mercer & C. Rosner. 128 p. illus. London & N.Y., Studio, 1950.

439. Portfolio, a Magazine for the Graphic Arts. Cincinnati, Ohio, Zebra Press, 1950.
No. 1 Winter; no. 2 Summer 1950. Folio format.

440. Publicité et Arts Graphiques. Revue de la Publicité et des Arts Graphiques en Suisse. Genève, Maurice Collet, 1950.
Lavishly illustrated. French and English texts.

COLLECTIONS

441. ABERDEEN. ART GALLERY. Catalogue: Oil Paintings, Watercolors, Drawings, Modern Sculpture. 3. ed. 84 p. 1950.

442. ANN ARBOR. UNIVERSITY OF MICHIGAN. MUSEUM OF ART. Accessions to the Collection, 1949. [15] p. front. 1950.

443. BALTIMORE, MUSEUM OF ART. Cone Bequest: Catalogue. 29 p. illus. 1949.
October number of the Museum News, v. 13, no. 1.

444. BOSTON. MUSEUM OF FINE ARTS. French Painters in the Museum of Fine Arts: Corot to Utrillo. 98 p. illus. 1949.
Text by G. H. Edgell.

445. BRUSSELS. PALAIS DES BEAUX ARTS. Le Palais des Beaux-Arts de Bruxelles. 32 p. illus. 1949.

446. BUFFALO. FINE ARTS ACADEMY. ALBRIGHT ART GALLERY. Catalogue of the Paintings and Sculpture in the Permanent Collection. Edited by Andrew C. Ritchie. 213 p. illus. 1949.
With its companion volume, noted below, these were the finest catalogs of this type issued by any American museum during the year.

447. BUFFALO. FINE ARTS ACADEMY. ALBRIGHT ART GALLERY. Catalogue of Contemporary Paintings and Sculpture. Edited by Andrew C. Ritchie. 212 p. illus. 1949.

448. CHICAGO. ART INSTITUTE. 20th Century Art, from the Louise and Walter Arensberg Collection. 103 p. illus. 1949.
Introductions by Katherine Kuh and Daniel C. Rich.

449. COLOGNE. WALLARD-RICHARTZ MUSEUM. Moderne Abteilung-Sammlung Haubrich. 36 p. illus. Koln, 1949.

450. DETROIT. INSTITUTE OF ARTS. Exhibition of Fifty Drawings from the Collection of John S. Newberry, Jr. 32 p. illus. 1949.

451. FLORENCE. LA STROZZINA. La Collezione Guggenheim. 42 p. illus. Firenze, 1949.
Exhibited at the Strozzi Palace and at the Palazzo Realle, Milan. Preface by F. Flora.

452. HANNOVER. LANDESMUSEUM. Verzeichnis der Kunstwerke nach 1800. 89 p. illus. 1950.

453. LIÈGE. MUSÉE DES BEAUX-ARTS. Catalogue des Peintures Françaises. 24 p. illus. Bruxelles, La Connaissance, 1950.
Foreword by Jules Bosmant, Conservateur.

454. LONDON. TATE GALLERY. Modern Foreign Pictures in the Tate Gallery. 13 p. plus 100 plates. 1949.
Largely French paintings, 19th & 20th centuries.

455. NASHVILLE, TENN., FISK UNIVERSITY. Catalogue of the Alfred Stieglitz Collection for Fisk University. 48 p. illus. 1949.
Texts by Van Vechten, O'Keeffe, Zigrosser.

456. NEW HAVEN. YALE UNIVERSITY. ART GALLERY. Collection of the Société Anonyme. 247 p. 181 illus. New Haven, 1950.
An encyclopedia catalog of the Katherine Dreier-Marcel Duchamp collection, with detailed biographical and bibliographical records and statements by the artists. Catalog edited by G. H. Hamilton, Curator of the collection.

457. NEW YORK. METROPOLITAN MUSEUM OF ART. 100 American Painters of the 20th Century: Works Selected from the Collections of the Metropolitan Museum of Art. 23 p. plus 111 plates. 1950.
Introduction by Robert Beverly Hale.

458. NEW YORK. MUSEUM OF MODERN ART. The Museum of Modern Art, New York: Paintings and Sculpture Collection, by Alfred H. Barr, Jr. 62 p. illus. Paris, Braun, 1950.
Brief text in French, German, English.

459. NEWARK, N. J. NEWARK MUSEUM. [Catalog issue of "The Museum"] 40 p. 1950.
Vol. 2, no. 3-4 of their Bulletin.

460. PARKE-BERNET GALLERIES (New York). Modern Paintings . . . from the Collection of Walter P. CHRYSLER, Jr. Second Part. 63 p. illus. New York. 1950.

461. PARKE-BERNET GALLERIES (New York). Modern French Prints, Drawings, Illustrated Books . . . from the Collection of Carleton LAKE. Part II. 91 p. illus. New York, 1950.

462. PARKE-BERNET GALLERIES (New York). Lithographs, Etchings and Drawings [from the] Collection of Col. Daniel SICKLES, acquired mainly from the Estate of the late Ambroise Vollard. 52 p. illus. 1950.

463. PARKE-BERNET GALLERIES (New York). Modern Paintings and Drawings . . . Sculptures [from the] Collection of Josef von STERNBERG. 60 p. illus. 1949.

464. OSLO. NASJONALGALLERIET. Katalog over Norsk Malerkunst. 365 p. illus. Oslo, 1950.

465. OTTERLO. RIJKSMUSEUM KRÖLLER-MÜLLER. Catalogus van 264 Werken van Vincent van Gogh behorende tot de Verzameling van het Rijksmuseum Kröller-Müller. 147 p. illus. 1949.

466. STOCKHOLM. NATIONALMUSEUM. Modern Konst ur Ester Londhals Samlung. 39 p. illus. 1950.

467. STOCKHOLM. NATIONALMUSEUM. Nationalmusei Samling av Moderna Målningar och Skulpturer. 175 p. illus. 1950.

468. WASHINGTON, D. C. NATIONAL GALLERY OF ART. Rosenwald Collection, an Exhibition of Recent Acquisitions. Compiled by Elizabeth Mongan. 40 p. illus. 1950.

469. WINTERTHUR. KUNSTMUSEUM. Hauptwerke des Kunstmuseums Winterthur. 177 p. illus. 1949.

470. —— KUNSTMUSEUM. Winterthurer Privatbesitz II: Werke des 20. Jahrhunderts. 39 p. illus. 1949.

GALLERIES & MUSEUMS

Galleries

471. BUCHHOLZ GALLERY, CURT VALENTIN, NEW YORK. 1949-1950, Catalogues: Sculpture, Beckmann, Masson, Calder, Gris, Marini, Callery, Feininger, Klee. 9 parts in 1 vol. illus. New York, 1950.

472. FERNANDEZ, JUSTINO. Catalogos de la Exposiciones de Arte. Mexico, Instituto de Investigaciones Esteticas, 1949-50.
Supplement to no. 17 of the Anales covers 1947-1948, completing 10 years of publication. Supplement for no. 18 covers 1949 (published 1950).

473. GRANOFF, KATIA. Histoire d'un Galerie. 68 p. illus. Paris, Chez l'Auteur, 1949.

474. KESTNER-GESELLSCHAFT, HANNOVER. [Exhibition Catalogues] 2 v. 1949-50.
v. 1, 1948-49.——v. 2, 1949-50.

475. REISNER, ROBERT GEORGE, Compiler. Fakes and Forgeries in the Fine Arts, a Bibliography. 58 p. New York, Special Libraries Association, 1950.

476. WORLD COLLECTORS ANNUARY. Edited by Fred A. Van Braam. Vol. 1, 1946-49. 705 p. Delft, Brouwer [1950?].
An international record of auction prices.

Museums

477. THE WORLD OF LEARNING 1950. 3. ed. 881 p. London, Europa Publications [1950].
An international directory of educational institutions of all types, including museums.

478. ANNUAIRE DES MUSÉES DE FRANCE 1950. 2. ed. 306 p. Paris, Direction des Musées de France, Palais du Louvre, [1950] (c 1946).
Includes section "Les Musées de France à 1949."

479. WITTLIN, ALMA S. The Museum: its History and its Tasks in Education. 297 p. illus. London, Routledge & Kegan Paul, 1949.

480. MUSEUMS IN MODERN LIFE. 108 p. illus. London, Royal Society of Arts, 1949.
Reprinted from their Journal, vol. XCVIII.

481. BOSTON. INSTITUTE OF CONTEMPORARY ART. A Statement on Modern Art, by the Institute of Contemporary Art, Boston; the Museum of Modern Art, New York; Whitney Museum of American Art, New York. [4] p. 1950.
Joint manifesto issued to clarify their position in relation to current controversial issues.

482. BLACK, MISHA, Ed. Exhibition Design. 186 p. illus. London, Architectural Press, 1950.

LITERATURE & LETTERS

Surveys, Critiques & Memoirs

483. MICHIGAN STATE COLLEGE. DEPARTMENT OF LITERATURE AND FINE ARTS. An Introduction to Literature & the Fine Arts. 418 p. illus. East Lansing, Michigan State College Press, 1950.
Chapter VII, "Contemporary Art." Bibliography.

484. BOWRA, C. M. The Creative Experiment. 255 p. London, Macmillan, 1949.
An analysis of selected European poets.

485. COHN, ROBERT GREER. Mallarmé's Un Coup de Dés: an Exegesis. 139 p. New Haven [The Author] 1949 (Yale French Studies).

486. JOLAS, EUGENE, ed. Transition Workshop. 413 p. New York, Vanguard, 1949.
Major articles on art and literature which appeared in "Transition" magazine.

487. RAFOLS, J. F. Modernismo y Modernistas. 450 p. illus. Barcelona, Destino, 1949.
The arts in Spain at the turn of the century.

488. RAYMOND, MARCEL. From Baudelaire to Surrealism. 480 p. illus. N.Y., Wittenborn, Schultz, 1949.
Documents of Modern Art. Director: Robert Motherwell. Bibliography by Bernard Karpel.

489. SACHS. MAURICE. La Décade de l'Illusion. 6. ed. 252 p. Paris, Gallimard, 1950.
"Paris (1922-1932)." Text written 1932.

490. STEIN, LEO. Journey into the Self, Being the Letters, Papers and Journals of Leo Stein, ed. by Edmund Fuller. 345 p. illus. New York, Crown, 1950.

Bibliography

491. MODERN LANGUAGE ASSOCIATION OF AMERICA. BIBLIOGRAPHY COMMITTEE OF FRENCH CONTEMPORARY LITERATURE. Bibliography of Critical and Biographical References for the Study of Contemporary French Literature. 2 vols. New York, Stechert-Hafner, 1949-1950.
Vol. 1: 1940 to 1948.——Vol. 2: 1949 supplement. Compiled by Douglas W. Alden and others.

492. MATARASSO, LIBRAIRIE (Paris). Surréalisme: Poésie et Art Contemporain. 108 p. illus. Paris, Matarasso, 1949.
Extensive bibliography issued as priced catalog.

493. BERGGRUEN, HEINZ, Compiler. Bibliographie des Oeuvres de Tristan Tzara, 1916-1950. 13 p. illus. Paris, Berggruen & Cie, 1950.

Surrealism

494. BOSQUET, ALAIN. Surrealismus. 1924-49: Texte und Kritik. 192 p. Berlin, Henssel, 1950.

495. FOWLIE, WALLACE. Age of Surrealism. 203 p. [New York] Swallow & Morrow, 1950.

496. LA NEF (Paris). Almanach Surréaliste de Demi-Siècle. 228 p. illus. 1950.
No. 63/64, Mar.-Apr., Ed. by André Breton.

497. LA NEF (Paris). Order et Désordre de la France (1939-49). 272 p. 1950.
No. 60/61, Dec. 1949-Jan. 1950.

Contemporary Anthologies

498. À la Gloire de la Main. illus. Paris, Aux Dépens d'un Amateur, 1949.
Preface by A. Flocon "pour le groupe GRAPHIES." Edition of 164 boxed copies.

499. Poésie de Mots Inconnus. 29 leaves, in folio Paris, Le Degre 41 [1949].
"Livre fait par Iliazd." 157 copies in vellum.

Classic Editions

500. D'ORLÉANS, CHARLES. Poèmes, Manuscrits et Illustrés par Henri Matisse. 104 p. illus. Paris, Tériade, 1950.
Entirely lithographed in color. 1200 copies.

501. GOETHE, JOHANN WOLFGANG. Prométhée. Traduction par André Gide. Lithographs de Henry Moore. Paris, H. Jonquières, P. A. Nicaise, 1950.
Decorated cover. 183 copies, issued boxed.

502. NOVALIS [FRIEDRICH VON HARDENBERG]. The Novices of Sais. 144 p. illus. New York, Curt Valentin, 1949.
60 drawings by Paul Klee; frontispiece by André Masson; preface by Stephen Spender.

Modern Editions

503. ARP, JEAN. Souffle. 8 p. Paris, Benoit, 1950.
"Poème . . . pour saluer la naissance de 1950 à 50 exemplaires. Bois de Jean Arp gravé en 1918."

504. BRAQUE, GEORGES. Cahier de Georges Braque 1917-1947. Paris, Maeght, 1949.
Loose leaves in folio. Also English edition in reduced format, no. 505.

505. BRAQUE, GEORGES. Notebook 1917-1947. 96 p. illus. New York, Curt Valentin, 1949.
92 drawings, with mss. by the artist. Translation by Bernard Frechtman inserted.

506. ELUARD, PAUL. Le Dur Désir de Durer. Illustrations by Chagall. 92 p. Philadelphia, Grey Falcon; London, Trianon, 1950.
Translation by Stephen Spender, F. Cornford.

507. LÉGER, FERNAND. Cirque, Lithographies Originales. Paris, Tériade, Editions Verve, 1950.
Text, manuscript and illustrations by the artist.

508. MILLER, HENRY & SCHATZ, BEZALEL. Into the Night Life. illus. [Los Angeles, 1949].
Silk-screen designs by Schatz with facsimile of Miller manuscript. Exhibited at the San Francisco Museum, Aug. 16-Sept. 11, 1949.

509. PÉRET, BENJAMIN & ERNST, MAX. La Brebis Galante. 119 p. illus. Paris, Éditions Premières, 1949.
"Illustré de trois eaux-fortes et de dessins coloriés au pochoir de Max Ernst." Collection GBMZ, 1.

BIBLIOGRAPHY

510. RIMBAUD, ARTHUR. Les Illuminations. Lithographies Originales de Fernand Léger. Lausanne, Louis Grosclaude, Editions des Gaules, 1949.
Preface by Henry Miller. 395 copies.

511. SAWYER, KENNETH & LOBDELL, FRANK. Poems & drawings. Sausalito, Cal., Bern Porter, 1949.
Edition of 500 copies; issued loose in folio.

512. TZARA, TRISTAN. L'Antitête . . . Illustrés par Max Ernst, Yves Tanguy, Joan Mirò. 3 vol. Paris, Bordas, 1949.
1: Monsieur Aa l'Antiphilosophe; 8 Eaux-fortes par Ernst.—2: Minuits pour Géants; 7 Eaux-fortes par Tanguy.—3: Le Désespéranto; 8 Eaux-fortes par Mirò.

513. TZARA, TRISTAN. De Mémoire d'Homme; Poème. Lithographies de Pablo Picasso, 116 p. Paris, Bordas, 1950.

514. TZARA, TRISTAN. Parler Seul: Poème. Lithographies de Joan Mirò. Paris, Maeght, 1948-1950.
"Copyright 1948 by Pierre à Feu," issued 1950.

ADDENDA

515. BALLAUFF, THEODORE & BEYRODT, GERHARD. Bibliographie 1944-1949. p. 255-383 In Jahrbuch für Aesthetik und Allegemaine Kunstwissenschaft. Hrsg. von Heinrich Lützeler. Stuttgart, F. Enke, 1951.
Includes History and Esthetics, Architecture and Pictorial Art, Literature, Music, Dance, Film, Reference Works. Lutzeler had previously published a Selective German Bibliography for the Year 1949 in the Journal of Aesthetics and Art Criticism, v. 9, no. 1, p. 74-79 Sept. 1950.

516. HUNGERLAND, HELMUT, Compiler. Selective Current Bibliography for Aesthetics and Related Fields [1949-1950]. Journal of Aesthetics and Art Criticism June 1950 & June 1951.
Jan. 1-Dec. 31, 1949 covered in v. 8, no. 4, p. 278-297, June 1950; Jan. 1-Dec. 31, 1950 covered in v. 9, no. 4, p. 349-362, June 1951. Also issued in reprints.

517. U. N. E. S. C. O. Répertoire Internationale des Archives Photographiques d'Oeuvres d'Art. 667 p. Paris, Dunod, 1950.
Text also in English.

518. CAHIERS D'ART. Vol. 25, No. 2 1950 (Paris).
Articles on the young Picasso, the collection of the Museum of Modern Western Art, Moscow, Antoine Pevsner, Nicolas de Staël, etc. A standard series, profusely illustrated, edited by Christian Zervos.

519. BUCHANAN, DONALD W. The Growth of Canadian Painting. 112 p. illus. London & Toronto, Collins, 1950.
20th century painting, by an editor of the magazine "Canadian Art."

520. EVERS, HANS GERHARD, Ed. Darmstädter Gespräch: Das Menschenbild in unserer Zeit. Hrsg. im Auftrag des Magistrats der Stadt Darmstadt und des Komitees Darmstädter Gespräch 1950 von Hans Gerhard Evers. 247 p. illus. Darmstadt, Neue Darmstädter Verlagstalt G.M.B.H. [1950?].
Contributions by Johannes Itten, Hans Sedlmayer, Willi Baumeister, Gotthard Jedlicka, and others.

521. FERNANDEZ, JUSTINO. Obras de Orozco en la Coleccion Carrillo-Gil, Mexico. Catalogo y notas de Justino Fernandez. 59 p. plus 132 illus. (col. plates) Mexico, Los Talleres de la Imprenta Nuevo Mundo [printed for] Dr. Alvar Carillo-Gil, 1949.
Also edition of 100 numbered copies.

522. GIANI, GIAMPIERO. Il Futurismo, 1910-1916. [8] p. 12 plates (col. cover) Venezia, Cavallino, 1950.
In same Cavallino series: I "Fauves" by Garibaldo Marussi, Umberto Boccioni by Marco Valsecchi.

523. LURÇAT, JEAN. Designing Tapestry; fifty-three examples both antique and modern chosen by the author. 61 p. illus. London, Rockcliff, 1950.
Translation of "Tapisserie Française" (Paris, Bordas, 1947).

524. PARIS. MUSÉE NATIONAL D'ART MODERNE. Exposition d'Art moderne Italien. [30] p. 16 illus. 1950.
Exhibited May-June; texts by J. Cassou, P. d'Ancona. Catalog by G. Vienne.

525. SMITH, JANET K. A Manual of Design. 193 p. illus. New York, Reinhold, 1950.
Bibliography, p. 172-185.

INDEX TO BIBLIOGRAPHY

Numbers refer to numbered items in the bibliography, not to text pages. Underlined items indicate titles.

INDEX TO BIBLIOGRAPHY

INDEX TO TEXT

Underlined items indicate illustrations.

Participants in the conference (p. 8-37) are noted only at the point where they first enter into the discussion, e.g., Lippold 10 ff; Duchamp 27 ff.

INDEX TO TEXT

Other Publications by Wittenborn, Schultz, Inc.

Write for announcements to: 38 East 57th Street, New York 22, N. Y.

American Abstract Artists, Essays by J. Albers, A. E. Gallatin, K. Knaths, F. Leger, L. Moholy-Nagy, P. Mondrian, G. L. K. Morris, ill. 1946. 2.50.

Atelier 17, Contributions by H. Read, J. J. Sweeney, H. Mayor, C. Zigrosser, S. W. Hayter. ill. 1949. 1.00.

Braque (Georges), Still Life, 1913. color silk-screen repr., oval. 1943. 7.50.

Burliuk (David) by K. S. Dreier. ill. 1944. 4.75.

Calder (Alexander), The Big "I". etching, 1944. 20.00.

Degas (Edgar), Huits Sonnets. ill. 1946. 4.00.

The Documents of Modern Art: (Director: Robert Motherwell).

d.m.a. 1 *Apollinaire, The Cubist Painters.* 12 ill. 1.75.
d.m.a. 2 *Mondrian, Plastic Art.* 26 ill., 2 in color. 2.50.
d.m.a. 3 *Moholy-Nagy, The New Vision.* 84 ill. 2.50.
d.m.a. 4 *Sullivan, Kindergarten Chats.* 18 ill. 4.50.
d.m.a. 5 *Kandinsky, Concerning the Spiritual in Art.* 10 ill. 2.50.
d.m.a. 6 *Arp, On My Way.* 50 ill., 2 orig. woodcuts. 4.50.
d.m.a. 7 *Ernst, Beyond Painting.* 140 ill. 6.00.
d.m.a. 8 *The Dada Painters and Poets.* 440 pages, 180 ill. cloth. 15.00.
d.m.a. 9 *Kahnweiler, The Rise of Cubism.* 23 ill. 1.75.
d.m.a. 10 *Raymond, From Baudelaire to Surrealism.* 3.75.
           Same title, bound in cloth. 5.00.
d.m.a. 11 *Duthuit, The Fauvist Painters.* 35 ill., 16 in color. 6.50.

Duchamp's Glass by K. S. Dreier & Matta Echaurren. 1944. 1.75.

Focillon (Henri), The Life of Forms in Art. 20 ill. 1948. 2.50.

Fuller (Sue), Cock. color engraving, 1944. 30.00.

Masson (Andre), Mythology of Being. ill. 1942. 6.00.

Modern Artists in America: Vol. 1. Ed. by R. Motherwell, Ad Reinhardt, B. Karpel. 150 ill. 1951. 5.50.

Problems of Contemporary Art:

p.c.a. 1 *W. Paalen, Form and Sense.* ill. Out-of-print.
p.c.a. 2 *H. Read, The Grass Roots of Art.* ill. 1.75.
p.c.a. 3 *A. Dorner, The Way Beyond Art: The Work of Herbert Bayer.* ill., 7 in color. 6.00.
p.c.a. 4 *Possibilities,* Vol. I. An occasional Review, ed. by John Cage (Music), Pierre Chareau (Architecture), Robert Motherwell (Art), Harold Rosenberg (Writing). ill. 1.50.
p.c.a. 5 *G. Vantongerloo, Paintings, Sculptures, Reflections.* ill. 3.00.

Rand (Paul), Thoughts on Design. 94 ill., 8 in color. 7.50.

Rilke (Rainer Maria), The Sonnets of Orpheus. With nine engravings by *Kurt Roesch.* 1944. 90.00.

Rodin (Auguste), A la Venus de Milo. ill. 1946. 4.00.

Schanker (Louis), Line, Form, Color. Five color prints. 75.00.

Seurat (Georges) by J. Rewald. 101 ill., 4 in color. 1946. 6.00.

trans/formation: arts, communication, environment. a world review. ed. by harry holtzman and martin james. subscription 3 issues 4.75, single 2.00.

Tschichold (Jan), Designing Books. ill. 1951. 5.00.

Vollard, A. Editeur, Catalogue by U. E. Johnson. ill. 1944. Out-of-print.